MARKET SOCIALISM

MARKET SOCIALISM

The Debate Among Socialists

Participants

DAVID SCHWEICKART

JAMES LAWLER

HILLEL TICKTIN

BERTELL OLLMAN

ROUTLEDGE
New York and London

Published in 1998 by
Routledge
29 West 35th Street
New York, NY 10001

Published in Great Britain in 1998 by
Routledge
11 New Fetter Lane
London EC4P 4EE

Printed in the United States of America on acid-free paper
Design and typography: Jack Donner

Library of Congress Cataloging-in-Publication Data

Market Socialism: the debate among Socialists / edited by Bertell Ollman;
    participants, David Schweickart, James Lawler, Hillel Ticktin,
    and Bertell Ollman
        p.   cm.
Includes bibliographical references and index.
ISBN 0–415–91966–5. — ISBN 0–415–91967–3 (pbk.)
1. Mixed economy.   2. Socialism.   3. Capitalism.
I. Ollman, Bertell.   II. Schweickart, David.
HB90.M365   1997
338.9—DC21   97–18313
                                                        CIP

Contents

Participants in the Debate

David Schweickart is a professor in the Department of Philosophy at Loyola University, Chicago. He holds Ph.D.s in mathematics (University of Kentucky) and philosophy (Ohio State University). He is the author of *Capitalism or Workers Control? An Ethical and Economic Appraisal* and *Against Capitalism*, and of numerous articles on Marxism, market socialism, and other topics related to socialist theory and practice.

James Lawler is a professor in the Department of Philosophy at the State University of New York at Buffalo and President of the Society for the Philosophical Study of Marxism. He received his Ph.D. from the University of Chicago. He is the author of *The Existentialist Marxism of Jean-Paul Sartre* and *I.O., Heredity, and Racism*, the editor of *How Much Truth Do We Tell the Children? The Politics of Children's Literature*, and has written numerous articles on the ideas of Marx, Hegel, and Sartre as well as on different aspects of educational theory.

Hillel Ticktin is a Reader in Russian and East European Studies and Chairman of the Center for the Study of Socialist Theory and Movements at the University of Glasgow. He is also Editor of *Critique: Journal of Socialist Theory*. His Ph.D. comes from the University of Moscow. He is the author of *Origin of the Crisis in the USSR: The Political Economy of Disintegration* and *Politics of Race Discrimination in South Africa*, and co-author of *The Ideas of Leon* Trotsky, and has written over eighty articles on various topics related to these titles.

Bertell Ollman is a professor in the Department of Politics at New York University. He received his doctorate from Oxford University. He is the author of *Alienation: Marx's Conception of Man in Capitalist Society, Social and Sexual Revolution*, and *Dialectical Investigations,* and co-editor of *Studies in Socialist Pedagogy, The Left Academy: Marxist Scholarship on American Campuses,* three volumes, and *The U.S. Constitution: 200 Years of Criticism.* He is also the creator of the *Class Struggle* board game.

Introduction

BERTELL OLLMAN

"Cheshire Puss [asked Alice]
Would you tell me please, which way I ought to go from here?"
"That depends a good deal on where you want to get to," said the
    Cat.
"I don't much care where," said Alice.
"Then it doesn't matter which way you go," said the Cat
                    —Lewis Carroll, *Alice's Adventures in Wonderland*

And so it is for all of us. Capitalism today occupies an increasingly narrow strip of land between the unnecessary and the impossible, with water from both sides washing over it in ever larger waves. But before the beleaguered population seeks the safety of higher ground, they have to be persuaded that the already colossal problems of capitalism are not only getting worse but that there is indeed a higher ground to which they can decamp. Margaret Thatcher's words, "There is no alternative," are now found on millions of lips the world over. People who believe this will put up with almost any degree of suffering. Why bother to struggle for a change that cannot be? The collapse of the Soviet Union seems to have reinforced this view, oddly enough, even among many on the Left who never considered the Soviet Union a model of anything. In this historical setting, those of us who believe that a qualitatively superior alternative is possible must give top priority to explaining and portraying what this is, so that people will have a good reason for choosing one path into the future rather than another. Developing our criticisms of capitalism is simply not enough, if it ever was. Now, more than ever, socialists must devote more of our attention to—socialism.

Many socialists in the United States and elsewhere have begun to respond to this crisis in belief by giving future possibilities an increasingly important place in their account of present troubles. One group of socialists who have done this more systematically, and more persistently, than perhaps anyone else are those who have come to be called "market socialists," with the result that market socialism is now one of the main topics of debate on the Left world-wide. The main questions addressed here include—What is market socialism? How would it work? Which of our current problems would it solve, which leave untouched? How would it come about? What is its relation to capitalism? How does it compare with more traditional visions of socialism? Did Marx take a position on it? What do other socialists find lacking in it, and what do they propose instead? In the present volume, four socialist scholars, who have been deeply involved in this debate—two for, two against—give their answers to these questions.

First, a proviso. The four of us are well aware that the oppressed of this world are not asking "How do we organize society to obtain a more efficient use of resources?" Likewise, for them, "Do we need more workers' coops or a rational economic plan?" is not a pressing question. Instead, they want to know how the content of their lives will be better under socialism. Will they have more interesting, safer, higher paid, and more secure jobs? Will they still be worried about not having enough money to buy the things they want? Will they get the education and medical help that their family needs? Will they still have bosses and landlords and crooks and—yes—cops who threaten their well being in so many ways and make them anxious and afraid? Most of the rest is "mechanics," important to be sure, but, in the eyes of most people, to be taken up only after these essentials are spoken to. Yet, every end comes with its appropriate means. Without ignoring any of these questions, the authors of this book have been mainly concerned with defining the structural reforms that could bring about these needed changes. The work of translating whatever is of value in our scholarly exchange into direct answers to what people are actually asking remains, of course, an ongoing challenge.

David Schweickart, James Lawler, Hillel Ticktin, and I participated in a debate on market socialism at the Socialist Scholars' Conference in New York City in April 1995. We have all been involved in similar debates with each other and with other scholars at various meetings both in the United States and abroad, and we have all written articles on this subject—in Schweickart's case, two books. In the present volume, we have tried to convey not only our views on market socialism but also something of the intellectual excitement that comes from being in a debate of this kind. So rather than simply stating our positions, each of us also criticizes one person from the other side, and then responds to criticisms made of him. The order of the book is as follows: Part I—essays by Schweickart and Lawler that defend market socialism; Part II—essays by Ticktin and me that oppose it (the greater length of my essay is due to the fact that half of it deals with the market in *capitalism,* thus offering one possible context in which to view the entire debate); Part III—shorter pieces in which Schweickart criticizes Ticktin, Ticktin criticizes Schweickart, Lawler criticizes me, and I criticize Lawler; and Part IV—again short pieces in which each of us responds to the criticisms made of him.

Whatever side the reader eventually comes down on, our hope is that he or she will be able to respond to Margaret Thatcher and her co-skeptics with fresh conviction that there is indeed an alternative. And, perhaps, knowing where we want to go, unlike Alice, we can at once set out in the right direction.

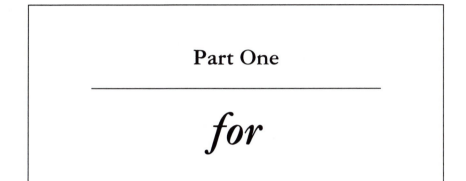

Part One

for

1.

Market Socialism: A Defense

DAVID SCHWEICKART

It is not *à la mode* these days to advocate socialism of any sort. The pundits have stopped repeating the mantra that socialism is dead and that liberal capitalism is the telos of history. This is no longer news. It is an accepted "fact." Socialism is dead.

The death certificate has been signed not only for classical command socialism but for all versions of market socialism as well, with or without worker self-management. Hungarian economist Janos Kornai, once an advocate of market socialism, now confidently asserts:

> Classical socialism is a coherent system. . . . Capitalism is a coherent system. . . . The attempt to realize market socialism, on the other hand, produces an incoherent system, in which there are elements that repel each other: the dominance of public ownership and the operation of the market are not compatible.[1]

As for self-management, "it is one of the dead-ends of the reform process."[2]

There are at least two good reasons, one theoretical, the other empirical, to dissent from Kornai's fashionable wisdom. First of all, there has developed over the last twenty years a large body of theoretical literature concerned with market alternatives to capitalism that reaches a different conclusion.[3] Secondly, the most dynamic economy in the world right now, encompassing some 1.2 billion people, is market socialist.

CHINA

If it is not fashionable to defend socialism these days, it is even less so to defend China. At least on the left there remain some stalwart defenders of socialism, but left, right, or center, no one likes China. In China there are executions, human rights violations, lack of democracy, workers working under exploitative conditions, misogyny, environmental degradation and political corruption. Moreover, China projects no compelling internationalist vision that might rally workers of the world or the wretched of the earth.

China is not inspirational now the way Russia was in the aftermath of the Bolshevik Revolution, or as China was for many on the Left in the 1960s or as Vietnam or Nicaragua or Cuba have been. One wishes that the defects of Chinese society were not so glaring.[4] There is a role for utopian imagery in a political project such as socialism. We need stirring visions. We need to be able to imagine what is, as yet, "nowhere." Yet there is also a need for realism in assessing the accomplishments and failures of actual historical experiments. Since there are few experiments more momentous than what is now transpiring in China, we need to think carefully about what can and cannot be deduced from the Chinese experience.

If by "socialism" we mean a modern economy without the major means of production in private hands, then China is clearly a socialist economy. Not only does China describe itself as "market socialist," but the self-description is empirically well-grounded. As of 1990, only 5.1 percent of China's GNP was generated by the "private" sector.[5] And despite considerable quantities of foreign capital flowing into the country (mostly from Hong Kong and Taiwan, mostly into joint ventures), that portion of Chinese investment in fixed assets utilizing funds from abroad is only thirteen percent (as of 1993), and employs barely four percent of the non-agricultural workforce, some five or six million workers. By way of contrast, there were, as of 1991, some 2.4 million cooperative firms in China, employing 36 million workers, and another 100 million workers employed in state-owned enterprises.

This "incoherent" market socialist economy has been strikingly successful, averaging an astonishing ten percent per year annual growth rate over the past fifteen years, during which time real per capita consumption has more than doubled, housing space has doubled, the infant mortality rate has been cut by more than fifty percent, the number of doctors has increased by fifty percent, and life expectancy has gone from sixty-seven to seventy. And on top of all this, inequality, as measured by the Gini coefficient, has actually *declined* substantially—due to the lowering of the income differential between town and country.[6] Even so skeptical an observer as Robert Weil, who taught at Jilin University of Technology in Changchun in 1993, concedes:

Changchun university students, who come even from poorer peasant backgrounds, speak of the transformation of their villages, with investments in modern farm implements and new consumer goods. For the working people in the city who until a year or so ago had to live through the winter on cabbage and root crops and buy what few other vegetables and fruits were available off the frozen sidewalks, the plethora of bananas, oranges, strawberries, greens and meats of all kinds that can now be purchased in indoor markets year round has changed their lives and their diet. Across the nation meat consumption per capita has increased some two and a half times since 1980. Millions of workers have gained new housing during "reforms," [the scare quotes are Weil's] built by their enterprises, so that the two or three families that used to share a single apartment now each have their own homes. Within the last few months, the work week in state owned firms has been lowered from forty-eight hours to forty-four, a major and widely welcomed improvement.[7]

The empirical evidence does not suggest that China is Utopia. It is far from that. Critics are not wrong to be concerned about human rights violations, the lack of genuine democracy, worker exploitation (evidenced by, among other things, a horrendous rate of industrial accidents), the markedly higher infant mortality rates for girls than for boys, environmental degradation and widespread corruption. Nevertheless, China's real accomplishments have been stunning. If socialism is an emancipatory project concerned with improving the real material conditions of real people, and not an all-or-nothing Utopianism, then socialists of good will (particularly those of us who have regular access to bananas, strawberries, greens, and meat) should not be too quick to dismiss these accomplishments.

Moreover, China's developmental trajectory remains unclear. It is possible that the contradictions of Chinese socialism will intensify to the point of social explosion. It is also possible that China will one day enter the ranks of capitalism. But those who maintain the inevitability of one *or* both of these eventualities are, it seems to me, reading tea leaves. We do not yet know how the Chinese experiment will come out. China may remain master of the productive energies it has unleashed, and may move to democratize itself and to address its other grave deficiencies. This too is possible.

In any event, to maintain in the face of such powerful evidence to the *contrary* that market socialism is *unworkable* is surely problematic. The Eastern European economists who so confidently made such assertions and who so wholeheartedly embraced the privatization and free-marketization of their own economies would do well to compare the wreckage induced by *their* reforms to what a market socialism has wrought.

WHAT IS MARKET SOCIALISM?

China demonstrates that a form of market socialism is compatible with a dynamic economy that spreads its material benefits broadly. But China is too complex a phenomenon, too much shaped by historical and cultural contingencies, too much in flux, for one to draw many firm conclusions. In order to go beyond the mere assertion of possibility it is more fruitful to engage the market socialism debate at a more theoretical level.

I wish to defend a two-part thesis: (a) market socialism, at least in some of its versions, is a viable economic system vastly superior, as measured by norms widely held by socialists and non-socialists alike, to capitalism, and (b) it is the *only* form of socialism that is, at the present stage of human development, both viable and desirable. Non-market forms of socialism are either economically non-viable or normatively undesirable, often both at once.

Let us be more precise about the meaning of "market socialism." Capitalism has three defining institutions. It is a market economy, featuring private ownership of the means of production and wage labor. That is to say, most of the economic transactions of society are governed by the invisible hand of supply and demand; most of the productive assets of society belong to private individuals either directly or by virtue of individual ownership of shares in private corporations; most people work for salaries or wages paid directly or indirectly by the owners of the enterprises for which they work. A market socialist economy eliminates or greatly restricts private ownership of the means of production, substituting for private ownership some form of state or worker ownership. It retains the market as the mechanism for coordinating most of the economy, although there are usually restrictions placed on the market in excess of what is typical under capitalism. It may or may not replace wage labor with workplace democracy, wherein workers get, not a contracted wage, but specified shares of an enterprise's net proceeds. If it does, the system is a "worker-self-managed" market socialism.

Various theoretical models of market socialism have been proposed in recent years, but all advocates of market socialism agree on four points.

1. The market should not be identified with capitalism.
2. Central planning is deeply flawed as an economic mechanism.
3. There exists no viable, desirable socialist alternative to market socialism; that is to say, the market is an essential (if imperfect) mechanism for organizing a viable economy under conditions of scarcity.
4. Some forms of market socialism are *economically* viable and vastly preferable to capitalism.

Let us examine each of these contentions.

THE "MARKET = CAPITALISM" IDENTIFICATION

The identification of capitalism with the market is a pernicious error of both conservative defenders of *laissez-faire* and most left opponents of market reforms. If one looks at the works of the major apologists for capitalism, Milton Friedman, for example, or F. A. Hayek, one finds the focus of the apology always on the virtues of the market and on the vices of central planning.[8] Rhetorically this is an effective strategy, for it is much easier to defend the market than to defend the other two defining institutions of capitalism. Proponents of capitalism know well that it is better to keep attention directed toward the market and away from wage labor or private ownership of the means of production.

The left critique of market socialism tends to be the mirror image of the conservative defense of capitalism. The focus remains on the market, but now on its evils and irrationalities. In point of fact, it is as easy to attack the abstract market as it is to defend it, for the market has both virtues and vices. Defenders of capitalism (identifying it as simply "a market economy") concentrate on the virtues of the market, and dismiss all criticisms by suggesting that the only alternative is central planning. Critics of market socialism concentrate on the vices and dismiss all defenses by suggesting that models of market socialism are really models of quasi-capitalism. Such strategies are convenient, since they obviate the need for looking closely at how the market might work when embedded in networks of property relationships different from capitalist relationships—convenient, but too facile.

THE CRITIQUE OF CENTRAL PLANNING

It must be said that conservative critics have been proven more right than wrong concerning what was until relatively recently *the* reigning paradigm of socialism: a non-market, centrally-planned economy. They have usually been dishonest in disregarding the positive accomplishments of the experiments in central planning, and in downplaying the negative consequences of the market, but they have not been wrong in identifying central weaknesses of a system of central planning, nor have they been wrong in arguing that "democratizing" the system would not in itself resolve these problems.

The critique of central planning is well-known, but a summary of the main points is worth repeating. A centrally-planned economy is one in which a central planning body decides what the economy should produce, then directs enterprises to produce these goods in specified quantities and qualities. Such an economy faces four distinct sets of problems: information problems, incentive problems, authoritarian tendencies, and entrepreneurial problems.[9]

As for the first: a modern industrial economy is simply too complicated to plan in detail. It is too difficult to determine, if we do not let consumers "vote with their dollars," what people want, how badly, and in what quantities and qualities. *Moreover,* even if planners were able to surmount the problem of deciding what to produce, they must then decide, *for* each item, how to produce it. Production involves inputs as well as outputs, and since the inputs into one enterprise are the outputs of many others, quantities and qualities of these inputs must also be planned. But since inputs cannot be determined until technologies are given, technologies too must be specified. To have a maximally coherent plan, all of these determinations must be made by the center, but such calculations, interdependent as they are, are far too complicated for even our most sophisticated computational technologies. Star Wars, by comparison, is child's play.

This critique is somewhat overstated. In fact planners *can* plan an entire economy. Planners in the Soviet Union, in Eastern Europe, in China and elsewhere did exactly that for decades. By concentrating the production of specific products into relatively few (often huge) enterprises and by issuing production targets in aggregate form, allowing enterprise managers flexibility in disaggregation, goods and services were produced, and in sufficient quantity to generate often impressive economic growth. It is absurd to say, as many commentators now do, that Ludwig von Mises and Friedrich Hayek have been proven right by events, that a centrally-planned socialism is "impossible." To cite only the Soviet Union: an economic order that endured for three-quarters of a century in the face of relentless international hostility and a German invasion, and that managed to industrialize a huge, quasi-feudal country, to feed, clothe, house and educate its citizenry, and to create a world-class scientific establishment should not be called "impossible."

However, the opposite of "impossible" is not "optimal." The Soviet economy and those economies modeled on Soviet economy always suffered from efficiency problems, and these became steadily worse as the economies developed. Information problems that were tractable when relatively few goods were being produced, and when quantity was more important than quality, became intractable when more and better goods were required. It is not without reason that *every* centrally planned economy has felt compelled to introduce market reforms once reaching a certain level of development.[10]

In theory a non-market socialism can surmount its information problems. In theory markets can be simulated. Planners can track the sale of goods, adjust prices *as if* supply and demand were dictating them, and convey this information to producers, instructing them to act *as if* they were in competition with each other to maximize profits. But market simulation and central planning generally founders on the second set of problems, those concerning *incentives*. There are many incentive problems inherent in central planning. Among the theoretically predicted and commonly observed:

- If output quotas are set by the planning board, enterprises have little incentive to expend resources or effort to determine and to provide what consumers really want.
- If both inputs and outputs are set by the planning board, enterprises will be inclined to understate their capabilities and overstate their needs, so as to make it easier to fulfill their part of the plan. They also have a large incentive to lobby the planning board for lower production quotas and for ample supplies of raw materials.
- If employment is guaranteed, but incomes are not tied to enterprise performance, workers have little incentive to work.
- If the planning board is responsible for the entire economy, it has little incentive to close inefficient units, since that will either contribute to unemployment or necessitate finding new jobs for the displaced workers.

There are also political problems associated with central planning. Planners have enormous power. Decisions as to production quotes (or prices) have major impact on enterprises, so the danger of corruption is large. A well-placed bribe that allows for a quota reduction or price rise can do a company far more immediate good than careful attention to product quality or the development of a new product line, or the introduction of a new production process.

Moreover, even if planners are scrupulously honest, they can be expected to centralize production into ever larger units, even when excessive size is inefficient, since it is easier to plan when there are fewer units with which to deal. They can also be expected to set up as many *barriers* as possible between themselves and workers or consumers. Planning a large economy is an enormously complex task, made infinitely more difficult when the plan is being constantly criticized, modified, or even rejected by an empowered citizenry. To be effective, planning must be coherent, so the modification of one part of the plan necessitates adjustments elsewhere. Adjustments that satisfy one group of angry constituents may impact adversely on other groups, causing them to clamor for change. Whatever public statements planners may make in support of participatory democracy, they cannot really be expected to like it. This problem, which is inherent in any democratic institution, is tractable when the number of options and variables are limited. But when everything in the economy is subject to political debate—every price, every product, every technology—the expected outcome is either anarchy, or, more likely, the subtle or not so subtle shutting down of democratic input.

Finally, there is the entrepreneurial problem. However much credit one wants to give to the accomplishments of centrally planned economies (and more credit should be given than is commonly given today), one cannot credit them with being highly innovative economically. Very few new products or new production techniques can be traced to these economies. Structural reasons are not difficult to locate. If enterprises do not compete, they have little need to innovate. They do not have to worry that if they do not keep abreast of the new technologies, their rivals will capture their markets, so the negative threat of failure is not there. Nor is there much in the way of positive incentive. An individual with an innovative idea cannot set up an enterprise, gambling that her great idea will pay off big. At best she can try to convince her superiors that a new product or a new technology will be worth the time, effort and risk involved. Not surprisingly, managers and planners in a centrally planned economy tend to be "conservative." Mistakes are more easily recognized, and hence career-threatening, than innovative successes. Risks are generally avoided—unless the high-risk ventures originate at the top, in which case one is reluctant to criticize even a bad idea, since one is absolved of responsibility if the project fails.

WHY NOT A NON-MARKET, DECENTRALIZED ECONOMY?

Many non-market socialists are inclined to object at this point in the argument that market socialists seem to think that the only alternative to the market is central planning. But why should that be the only alternative? Why not advocate and struggle for a non-market, democratic, *decentralized* economy?

The market socialists' reply is that such an economy, at the present state of economic development, is neither viable *nor* desirable. To be sure, if an economy were decentralized into small, semi-agrarian, autarchic communities, then, yes, a democratic, non-market economy might be possible. But given the complexities of modern technologies and given the range of goods that modern consumers (socialists included) may legitimately expect from their economy, the dream of small, self-sufficient communities is a dream without a constituency, a wholly Utopian fantasy.

If instead of decentralized autarchy, one wants decentralized, participatory bottom-up planning that results in a unified plan for a large industrial economy, it can't be done. I can think of no better proof than to invite the reader to look carefully at Michael Albert and Robin Hahnel's recent, detailed proposal for just such an economy, a participatory economy that utilizes personal computers, large data banks, and an array of neighborhood, regional and national councils. It is unworkable. Utterly. Moreover, even if it were workable, it would not be desirable. Too many hours on the computer. Too many meetings.[12]

MODELS OF MARKET SOCIALISM: JOHN ROEMER'S

Thus far my argument has been negative. I have argued that there cannot be a viable, desirable socialism without a market. It must be further demonstrated that market socialism *is* a viable, desirable option. There are in fact many different proposals for market socialism now under discussion. Let us consider two, John Roemer's and my own.[13]

In essence Roemer's market socialism looks much like contemporary capitalism, but with five fundamental differences:

1. All the stocks of all the corporations in the country have been redistributed, so as to give each citizen, initially, a per-capita share. Each citizen at birth receives a stock portfolio, and hence an entitlement to a share of the dividends generated by the companies whose stocks she holds. When she dies, the stocks return to the government. These stocks, once acquired, may be traded for other stocks, *but they may not be sold for cash.* (Hence it is impossible for the rich to buy out the poor and obtain controlling interest in the economy.)
2. All banks are nationalized. These banks collect funds from private savers and make loans to businesses, using substantially the same criteria as capitalist banks.
3. The management of a corporation is determined by the corporation's board of directors, which is comprised of delegates of the main commercial bank from which it gets its funding, representatives of the firms workers, and representatives of the stockholders.

4. The government undertakes significant investment planning, using differential interest rates to encourage or discourage certain kinds of specific investment.
5. Capitalist firms are permitted, if started by an entrepreneur, but a firm is nationalized (with compensation) when it reaches a certain size, or on the death of the founder, and shares of its stock redistributed to the general public.

Roemer argues cogently that this model is economically viable. The basic problems of the central-planning model have been alleviated. Firms in this economy compete with each other (and also with foreign firms) in a market setting, so the information and incentive problems disappear. There is no authoritarian tendency to this model, since firms are independent of the political process, and, since, moreover, there is no central planning agency on whose good will all firms depend. The entrepreneurial problem is addressed in two ways. Competition forces public firms to be alert to develop and implement new products and technologies. Secondly, there is a place in the economy for capitalist entrepreneurs, although not so large a place that they can come to dominate.

This model also addresses two of the most fundamental problems with capitalism: economic inequality and investment irrationality. Economic inequality is sharply curtailed (although not eliminated) by drastically reducing the basic source of capitalist income, the income arising from ownership of the means of production. All citizens have roughly equal shares of the collective assets of society, and so all benefit to a roughly equal degree from the surplus generated. What inequalities of asset ownership that do develop as citizens trade their shares are not allowed to persist beyond a person's lifetime, and so they do not accumulate and concentrate as they do under capitalism.[14]

Investment irrationalities are also addressed. Roemer's model recognizes explicitly what all economists know but do not much talk about in public. The market is *not* an efficient mechanism for making the investment decisions that determine the long-range health of an economy. The visible hand of the government must supplement Adam Smith's invisible hand. Virtually all the economies of the world today touted as miracles— Japan, Germany, South Korea, Taiwan have learned to guide the investment process. Experience suggests, however, that the visible hand should not be too heavy a hand—hence Roemer's reliance on interest-rate manipulation.

MODELS OF MARKET SOCIALISM: ECONOMIC DEMOCRACY

My own model of market socialism, designated Economic Democracy, is different from Roemer's, in that it puts worker self-management at the heart of the system, as opposed to egalitarian ownership of the means of production. As in Roemer's model, all enterprises compete. As in Roemer's model, funds for new investment come primarily from banks, which are public, not private, institutions.

In Economic Democracy there is no stock market, for there are no stocks. The capital assets of the country are thought of as collective property, but they are controlled by the workforces that utilize them. That is to say, each enterprise is run democratically, with workers legally empowered, one person, one vote, to elect the enterprise's management. The model for an enterprise under Economic Democracy is political community, not private property. An enterprise is not a *thing* that is *owned* by its workers; rather, it is an *association* that is *governed* by them. Ultimate authority resides with the workers of an enterprise, although, in all but small firms, workers will elect representatives to a worker council that will select and oversee the firm's management.

Worker self-management is the first defining feature of Economic Democracy. The second feature that sets it apart from capitalism (and from Roemer's model of socialism) is its mechanism for generating and dispensing funds for new investment. Both capitalism and Roemer's market socialism rely on private savings as the source of investment funding. Economic Democracy relies on taxation. Each enterprise must pay a tax on the capital assets under its control. (This tax may be thought of as rent paid society for access to the collective property of society.) Economically this tax functions as an interest rate on capital—and thus obviates the necessity of paying interest to private savers. Generating the investment fund by taxing enterprises rather than by "bribing" individuals to save not only shuts down a major source of capitalist inequality, namely interest payments to private individuals, but it frees an economy from its dependence on the "animal spirits" of savers and investors.

The proceeds of the capital-assets tax constitute society's investment fund, all of which are plowed back into the economy. The plow-back mechanism here is also different from what it is under capitalism. The market does *not* dictate investment flows. Under Economic Democracy investment funds are returned to communities on a *per capita* basis (as a *prima facia* entitlement). Thus capital flows to where the people are. People are not forced to follow the flow of capital. Once in communities, the investment funds are then "loaned" to the enterprises in the community, or to collectives wanting to set up new concerns, via a network of public banks, according to a double criteria: projected profitability and employment creation. Only at this stage are market criteria invoked, and even at this stage they are not the only criteria.[15]

In sum, Economic Democracy may be thought of as an economic system with three basic structures, worker self-management of enterprises, social control of investment, and a market for goods and services. These contrast with the defining elements of capitalism: wage labor, private ownership of the means of production, and a market for goods, services, capital, and labor.

I argue at length in *Against Capitalism* that this model is economically viable. The essential moves are these: At the enterprise level, the cooperative nature of the firm insures an efficient internal organization. (The empirical evidence is overwhelming that cooperative enterprises are almost always as efficient as comparable capitalist enterprises, often much more so.) At the level of enterprise interactions with each other and with consumers, the competitive nature of the economy insures that the informational and incentive problems associated with central planning do not arise. At the level of economic development over time, the investment mechanism allows for the kind of market-conforming planning that most economists agree is superior to unrestrained market forces. The entrepreneurial problem is addressed, much as it is in Mondragon, by having local banks set up an entrepreneurial division to seek out new investment opportunities, and to provide technical assistance and start-up capital to groups of individuals interested in developing a new enterprise. Competitive pressures compel existing firms to stay abreast of technical developments in their areas. The possibility of workers in an enterprise reaping either monetary gains, shorter working hours or better working conditions supplies a positive incentive to innovate.

I also argue at length in *Against Capitalism* that Economic Democracy is superior to capitalism over a whole range of issues. It is vastly more egalitarian, since it eliminates property income. It is vastly more democratic, since it extends democracy downward into the workplace, and upward into the determination of macro-economic developmental policies. It also confronts squarely what may be the single most destructive feature of contemporary capitalism: the hypermobility of capital. Given recent technological and political developments, capital now has a greater capability and a freer hand than ever before in history to move rapidly to whatever part of globe promises the highest return. The resulting job insecurities, destruction of communities, and mass migrations are now everywhere to be seen.

Economic Democracy radically alters this pattern. Worker-run enterprises do not vote to relocate to lower wage regions of the country or the world. Publicly generated capital does not cross borders in search of higher returns; the tax-generated investment fund is mandated by law to be returned to communities. Consequently, communities do not have to compete for capital (by offering lower wages, or fewer environmental restrictions). Moreover, they are assured a regular flow of new investment capital, and hence have far more control over their own economic destinies than do communities under capitalism.

BUT IS IT SOCIALISM?

Hillel Ticktin has written that "for an anti-Stalinist Marxist, socialism would be defined by the degree to which the society was planned."[16] By this definition neither Roemer's market socialism nor Economic Democracy is very socialist. Indeed, by this definition "market socialism" becomes a sort of oxymoron, since it is precisely the point of a market to remove a large part of a society's economic activity from the arena of conscious, society-wide planning.

But I (who am also an anti-Stalinist Marxist) would dissent from a definition that equates socialism to ever-more-extensive social planning. There is an important normative-conceptual issue that needs to be addressed here. It is certainly central to the socialist project that human beings be able to control, rather than be controlled by, economic forces. But control has both a positive and a negative sense. I control my dog when I train him to do tricks and obey my commands. I also control him when I teach him not to bite the neighbors or urinate on the carpet. In the first case, I am bending him to my will in a positive sense. In the second, I am trying to ward off unpleasant surprises.

I would contend that a socialist economy should aim more for negative control than positive control, particularly if a reasonably high level of development has been reached. We do not need an economy that will allow us to storm the heavens. There is a hubris in such a conception that has been given historical form in some of the worst excesses of Stalinism and Maoism. We need an economy that will allow us to get on with our lives without having to worry so much about economic matters. To be sure, at the workplace we may want to try to develop new products or new technologies, and in our communities we may want to try new ways of organizing our collective well-being. Occasionally we might want to give scope to a larger vision, a material project affecting the whole nation, but by and large the focus of our attention is more properly concerned with local matters. But this means *local* planning, at the workplace and community level, not *national* planning. Certainly there are problems that must be addressed at the national and international level, environmental damage, for example, or the terrifying poverty that exists in so many places. But to be able to focus on the large issues that require national and global attention, we need an economic environment where most of what goes on is relatively automatic. Indeed, even to concentrate on locally large issues, we need an environment where we, as citizens, need not think about most of what goes on in the economy.

The market has long been touted by apologists *for* capital as the automatic regulator that frees us from unnecessary complexity. Unfortunately, as we can now so clearly see, when the market extends beyond goods and services to capital and labor, it begins biting the neighbors, urinating on the carpet, and worse. And it does so automatically. The point of market socialism is to reign in these negative consequences without subjecting the economy to the massive discipline that maximal planning implies.

Is this really socialism? There is, after all, still competition, still inequality, still advertising, still potential unemployment. It is important here to invoke a Marxian distinction. Socialism is not to be identified with the highest form of communism. Socialism emerges from the womb of capitalism, and is marked by its origin. It is not a perfect society. It is a non-capitalist economic order that *preserves* the best that capitalism has attained, while overcoming its worst evils.

Advocates of market socialism often find themselves being urged by people without a Left background who finds the ideas persuasive not to call the position "socialist," since "socialism," it is said, has such negative connotations. I have never been tempted by that suggestion. The fact of the matter is, market socialism *is* socialism, and whether or not anti-market Leftists will call it that, every supporter of capitalism will, regardless of what label we give it. For market socialism is resolutely anti-capitalist, resting on the fundamental insight that the capitalist *qua* capitalist is, in the modern world, functionally obsolete. Capitalists are no longer needed to raise capital, manage industries, or create new products or technologies. There are other, better, ways of performing these functions.

Not only is market socialism resolutely anti-capitalist, but it also embodies the best ideals and values of the socialist tradition, and it is faithful to the vision of an economy controlled by, rather than controlling the producers. Market socialism is not a "utopian" socialism. It recognizes that at least at this stage of our development, none of our values will be perfectly realized, and there will indeed have to be tradeoffs. But this is simply good (Marxian) common sense.

NOTES

1. Janos Kornai, *The Socialist System: The Political Economy of Communism* (Princeton University Press, 1992), 500.

2. Kornai, p. 469. I cannot resist pointing out that Kornai's long, learned, sad book was underwritten, as he acknowledges in the preface, by the Sloan Foundation, the Ford Foundation, the McDonnell Foundation, and the Hungarian National Scientific Research Foundation. He composed much of the book at Harvard, where he taught regularly a course in political economy to, among others, "naive members of the 'New Left,' quite unaware of the grave absurdities of the socialist systems" (xxvi).

3. My own book, *Against Capitalism* (Cambridge University Press, 1993) draws heavily on this literature, and includes an extensive bibliography. See also, John Roemer, *A Future for Socialism* (Harvard University Press, 1994).

4. More appealing for many is the success of the Mondragon cooperative experiment, a network of some 100 cooperatives, employing 25,000 workers, in the Basque region of Spain. This network of worker-owned cooperatives is the leading economic actor in the Basque region, with sales in 1993 of 8 billion dollars. Its member enterprises are often capital intensive, and employ the most sophisticated technology available, some of it generated by its own internationally well-regarded research center. [For more details, see William Foote Whyte and Kathleen King White, *Making Mondragon: The Growth and Dynamics of the Worker Cooperative Complex* (Ithaca, NY: Cornell University Press, 1988) and Roy Morrison, *We Build the Road as We Travel* (Philadelphia: New Society Publishers, 1991).]

   My own model of market socialism draws heavily on the lessons of Mondragon, so I do not want to belittle its significance. Still and all, the Chinese experiment must be regarded as vastly more important.

5. This figure and subsequent data are drawn from Peter Nolan, "The China Puzzle," *Challenge* (January–February 1994) and from Robert Weil, "China at the Brink: Class Contradictions of 'Market Socialism'—Part 1," *Monthly Review* 4 (December 1994): 10–35.

6. See Nolan and also M. J. Gordon, "China's Path to Market Socialism," *Challenge* 35 (January–February 1992): 53–6.

7. Weil, 22–3.

8. Cf. Milton Friedman, *Capitalism and Freedom* (University of Chicago Press, 1962), Milton Friedman and Rose Friedman, *Free to Choose* (1980), F. A. Hayek, *The Road to Serfdom* (1942), F. A. Hayek, *The Constitution of Liberty* (1960)

9. This latter problem is essentially an incentive problem, but it is so important that it is worth treating separately.

10. Marxists should not find is surprising that at a certain point the productive forces of societies came into conflict with the relations of production, thus requiring a radical readjustment of the latter.

11. This is not to say that communities cannot become *more* self-sufficient, and hence more in control of their own destinies than they are now. Indeed, one of the structural consequences of the model of market socialism I advocate is that communities have considerably more economic autonomy than they do under capitalism.

12. See Michael Albert and Robin Hahnel, *The Political Economy of Participatory Economics* (Princeton University Press, 1991), and their less technical companion

volume, *Looking Forward: Participatory Economics the Twenty-First Century* (South End Press, 1991). I offer an extended critique of the Albert-Hahnel in *Against Capitalism,* 329–34.

13. For seven distinct models, see John Roemer and Pradham Bardan, eds., *Market Socialism: The Current Debate* (Oxford University Press, 1993). See also James Yunker, *Socialism Revised and Modernized: the Case for Pragmatized Market Socialism* (Praeger, 1992), and Leland Stauber, *A New Program for Democratic Socialism* (Four Willows Press, 1987).

    In what follows I will provide only an outline of one of Roemer's models and my own, so as to give the reader a sense of the range of structures that are compatible with a (socialist) market. What I am calling "the Roemer model" draws on his *A Future of Socialism.* For more details concerning my model, see *Against Capitalism.*

14. Frank Thompson, "Would Roemer's Socialism Equalize Income from Surplus?" prepared for the "A Future for Socialism Conference," University of Wisconsin, Madison, Wisconsin, 13–15 May 1994, has argued that substantial inequalities of a capitalist sort can still develop, since Roemer relies on private savings paid a market-determined rate of interest for his investment fund. This critique seems right to me. Roemer, however, could respond that this sort of inequality is relatively harmless, since it cannot be transformed into control over enterprises, and since a confiscatory inheritance tax can keep it from accumulating over generations.

15. At this stage differential tax rates can also be employed as in the Roemer model, to encourage or discourage certain types of production, thus giving society more direct control over its developmental trajectory.

16. Hillel Ticktin, "The Problem of Market Socialism," unpublished manuscript, 1993, p. 2.

2.

Marx as Market Socialist

JAMES LAWLER

A complex modern economy cannot be run effectively from a single command center. This has been the common economic criticism of the Soviet economic system. It was also the principal idea of the reformers in the former Soviet Union who launched the project of restructuring. The collapse of the socialist regimes of Eastern Europe and the Soviet Union appears to substantiate this criticism. A system of central planning of the economy that replaces market mechanisms of allocating resources with the decisions of central planning experts, so it is argued, conflicts with the requirements of a complex modern economy. Perhaps such economic centralism is workable under more primitive economic conditions, but an advanced economy requires a decentralized system of decision making, and such decentralization implies a market economy.

While there are those who take the truth of this conception to imply the triumph of liberal capitalist society as a world-historical "end of history," left-wing critics of capitalism have been divided in their response. Some argue that the collapse of socialist regimes can be explained primarily by technical imperfections in the planning system, together with pressures from the surrounding capitalist world, rather than by the system itself. Others explain the economic weakness of twentieth-century socialism by the absence of a genuine democracy, with democratic input, feedback and control in the planning mechanism. A growing number of socialists, on the other hand, have abandoned the notion of central planning altogether, arguing that socialism is compatible with the continuation of market relations. The centralized "state socialism" that characterized most of Soviet history—if this should really be called socialism—should, they argue, be distinguished from decentralized market socialism, linked to pluralist democratic institutions.

The thesis of this paper is that, contrary to most traditional interpretations, it is the latter concept that comes closest to the viewpoint of Marx and Engels on the nature of the newly emerging post-capitalist society. In fact, as Soviet reformers argued in the late eighties, Lenin too defended a form of market socialism that was established in the Soviet Union during the 1920s.[1] From this perspective, the idea that Marx's conception of socialism was essentially embodied in the centralized command system inaugurated by Stalin, beginning in 1929, is a retrospective reading of Marx's thought through the prism of the mainstream of socialist economies of the twentieth century.

COMMUNIST MANIFESTO: FIRST STEPS

There are certainly some striking passages in the *Communist Manifesto* that seem to foreshadow the Stalinist system. Marx and Engels argue that:[2]

> The proletariat will use its political supremacy to wrest, by degrees, all capital from the bourgeoisie, to centralise all instruments of production in the hands of the State, i.e., of the proletariat organised as the ruling class; and to increase the total productive forces as rapidly as possible.

At first glance this passage, announcing the centralization of the instruments of production in the hands of the state, seems altogether conclusive. On closer inspection, however, one notes that the process envisaged is a gradual one, to be effected "by degrees." This implies that for a certain period of time after the proletarian revolution there will be only imperfect centralization, and, by implication, a continuation of the market economy. This processual character of the post-revolutionary society is emphasized in the continuation of this passage:

> Of course, in the beginning, this cannot be effected except by means of despotic inroads on the rights of property, and on the conditions of bourgeois production; by means of measures, therefore, which appear economically insufficient and untenable, but which, in the course of the movement, outstrip themselves, necessitate further inroads upon the old social order, and are unavoidable as a means of entirely revolutionising the mode of production.

The Communist program that is proposed as generally applicable for "the most advanced countries" is only the beginning of a complex and perhaps lengthy process whose course should proceed in step-wise fashion. Several interconnected points stand out here: (1) despotic, i.e., state methods, of intervention will be necessary *only* "in the beginning," (2) the proposed Communist program will take place on the basis of bourgeois production, and (3) these starting points will turn out to be "economically insufficient."

Significantly, "despotic inroads on the right of property" as well as the continuation of "bourgeois conditions" are both regarded as characteristics of the post-revolutionary society. And both are said to be "economically insufficient." Thus the despotic methods that will be necessary in the beginning do not eliminate bourgeois production, but restrict it while introducing non-bourgeois, proletarian or communist conditions in ways that are enumerated in the revolutionary program. However the communist conditions that are first introduced using despotic inroads on bourgeois conditions do not entirely replace these, so that "bourgeois conditions" persist.

Political methods, necessary in the initial revolutionary period, are *economically* insufficient. The further course of development, then, should be decided on the basis of economic criteria. The post-revolutionary period will not focus primarily on political relations of force between the proletariat and the bourgeoisie, but on evolving socio-economic conditions. If *all* bourgeois property is not confiscated at the beginning, this is not because of Machiavellian political tactics, such as playing some bourgeois property owners against others until the proletarian state is strong enough to swallow up all of them. After an initial period in which despotic power is exercised, decisive political power is assumed to be in the hands of the proletariat. It is not a question of political power, but of socio-economic logic that should decide the step-by-step transformation (and not sweeping replacement) of the old social order. The primary criterion for the progressive centralization of property in the hands of the proletarian state is growing economic and social necessity.

A post-revolutionary program of the transformation of bourgeois society on the basis primarily of evolving economic conditions of a market society is therefore what is proposed. In some general sense, then, the Communist program inaugurates what many would recognize as a "market socialist" society, or at least a "mixed society" containing capitalist and socialist, or bourgeois and proletarian, components, with dynamic prominence given to the socialist dimension. Since state ownership is the main form of proletarian property, the economic system inaugurated by the communist revolution could be described as a "state market socialism."

No details about what further steps should be taken are given. An historical gap is therefore left open for socialist revolutionaries to fill in on the basis of developing socio-economic conditions, involving the continuation of market production. The *Manifesto* contains no recipes for the kitchens of the future. The program that is proposed is one that is based on the existing requirements for *some* capitalist countries, the "advanced" ones. What steps will be necessary after the implementation of the program cannot be anticipated in detail. However, general features of direction of this course of development, certain general *principles* can be stated in advance. The main thrust of this development will be the diminishment of bourgeois property and the increase of proletarian property. Progressive centralization of all instruments of production in the hands of the State simply means that there will be a growing number of proletarian state enterprises and a declining number of capitalist enterprises. It does not mean replacement of market production by "central planning." Recognition of this fact not only has led Stanley Moore to argue, correctly, that the *Manifesto* calls for a post-revolutionary market economy, but has even prompted him to believe, incorrectly as we will see, in its *indefinite* continuation.[3]

A necessary condition for this development is political: the proletariat must be raised to the position of ruling class; it must "win the battle of democracy." This is the "first step in the revolution."[4] But the following steps must be guided more by economic than by political considerations. Under the protective wing of the proletarian state a new economic order *begins,* with proletarian-state enterprises and bourgeois enterprises coexisting in a market context.

ROLE OF FORCE: DIRECT AND INDIRECT

After the enumeration of the chief planks of the proletarian platform for the post-revolutionary period, the *Manifesto* jumps over the intervening period of step-by-step development to envisage the outcome of this process.[5]

> When, in the course of development, class distinctions have disappeared, and all production has been concentrated in the hands of a vast association of the whole nation, the public power will lose its political character. Political power, properly so called, is merely the organised power of one class for oppressing another. If the proletariat during its contest with the bourgeoisie is compelled, by the force of circumstances, to organise itself as a class, if, by means of a revolution, it makes itself the ruling class, and,

as such, sweeps away by force the old conditions of production, then it will, along with these conditions, have swept away the conditions for the existence of class antagonisms and of classes generally, and will thereby have abolished its own supremacy as a class.

In place of the old bourgeois society, with its classes and class antagonisms, we shall have an association, in which the free development of each is the condition for the free development of all.

Here we have again the language of revolutionary negation of capitalism that can give support to post-Stalinist interpretations of Marxism. In this passage, the political method of "despotic inroads" on bourgeois property appears to be not only the first step or a necessary condition but the exclusive method of revolutionary change. Force now seems to be everything, and economic methods, hinted at earlier, fade completely from view. Little wonder that such an interpretation supports the notion that the state should be the master of the socialist economy. A contradiction therefore emerges between a careful reading of the passage, two pages earlier, in which "despotic inroads" are limited to the initial steps, and what seems to be a natural reading of the dramatic, nihilistic language of the concluding paragraph of the programmatic section two of the *Manifesto,* in which despotic, political methods are said to sweep away bourgeois conditions.

But such a reading clearly collapses an account of the initial steps of the post-revolutionary process and a statement of the final goal. Political power can be seen as occupying two levels. There is the initial period of direct intervention into the economy, which predominates in the period of revolutionary accession to power of the proletariat, and there is an *indirect* conditioning of further events by the proletarian state. In speaking of the forcible sweeping away of bourgeois conditions, the *Manifesto* elides direct and indirect use of force.

Certainly, the persistence of proletarian power is a necessary condition for the further development of the post-revolutionary society. There must be control of the state by the majority of society—through the instrumentation of the political parties of the proletariat. The Marxist Communist Party is said to be but one of those parties, the one that keeps most clearly in view the long-range perspective of communist transformation. But this political power, while necessary, is not sufficient to determine future evolution of the mixed bourgeois-proletarian economy. A logic of economic relations must be respected and followed, based on post-revolutionary experiences. It would not be possible to follow such a logic coherently were the bourgeoisie to have political power, and so in this sense the entire process, contradicting the will of the bourgeoisie, can rightly be described as a matter of force. But the force that is exercised in the subsequent period after some required despotic inroads into bourgeois property is indirect rather than direct force. It is the force that assures the stability of economic relationships, the unfolding logic of which is the decisive condition for the final elimination of bourgeois property.

PRINCIPLES OF COMMUNISM: DYNAMICS OF POST-REVOLUTIONARY SOCIETY

If the *Manifesto* describes the beginning and the end of the post-revolutionary process, perhaps more light needs to be shed on the intermediary period. Consider the following question. If at first only *some* capitalist property is to be placed under the control of the central government, using despotic methods, how should the proletarian state acquire the rest of the economy that still remains in private hands?

In a very illuminating work written a few months before the *Communist Manifesto*, "The Principles of Communism," Engels presents some of the above ideas in much greater detail. In a letter to Marx,[6] Engels says there was nothing in his "Principles" that conflicted with their views. However, instead of the "catechetical" form in which the "Principles" was written, Engels proposes the form of the manifesto as more appropriate to their purposes, especially for the presentation of their historical views. The "Principles" can therefore be regarded as a first, incomplete draft of the *Manifesto*. The *Communist Manifesto* is more detailed on the general historical foundations of the communist position of Marx and Engels. But "The Principles of Communism," as it turns out, is more detailed on the nature of the post-revolutionary society itself.

After outlining twelve chief measures of the proletarian program "already made necessary by existing conditions," Engels writes:[7]

> Of course, all these measures cannot be carried out at once. But one will always lead on to the other. Once the first radical onslaught upon private ownership has been made, the proletariat will see itself compelled to go always further, to concentrate all capital, all agriculture, all industry, all transport, and all exchange more and more in the hands of the State. All these measures work toward such results; and they will become realisable and will develop their centralising consequences in the same proportion in which the productive forces of the country will be multiplied by the labour of the proletariat. Finally, when all capital, all production, and all

exchange are concentrated in the hands of the nation, private ownership will already have ceased to exist, money will have become superfluous, and production will have so increased and men will be so much changed that the last forms of the old social relations will also be able to fall away.

Here we see many of the points later elaborated in the *Manifesto*. There is the "first radical onslaught" or despotic inroad at the beginning of the process. Then there is gradual evolution in which the instruments of production are concentrated in the hands of the state. This process of concentration of instruments of production is conjoined with growing economic productivity, i.e. with changing economic conditions. The end result is one in which "nation" noticeably replaces "state." Market relations continue, presumably, until the use of money becomes superfluous. Money is not abolished by decree, but, like the state, it gradually withers away. Crucial factors in this intervening process are the high development of productivity and the changed character of human beings, the direct producers, themselves.

Of particular interest are differences in the wording of some of the measures of the Communist program. The first point clearly opens with "limitation of private ownership," not "abolition of property," which the more militantly worded *Manifesto* describes as summarizing Communist theory.[8] The methods of limiting private property are "progressive taxation, high inheritance taxes, abolition of inheritance by collateral lines (brothers, nephews, etc.), compulsory loans and so forth."[9] The *Manifesto* is more draconian in proposing "Abolition of all right of inheritance."[10]

Clearly a lengthy period of time is indicated by these measures, with bourgeois property gradually being transferred to the proletarian state during the course perhaps of generations. But such measures do not by themselves lead to the elimination of bourgeois property.[11] Bill Gates did not inherit Microsoft. No doubt the sons and daughters of the bourgeoisie will continue to enjoy privileged conditions, if less so than before. By the measures of the Communist program, private property transference will have to become more meritocratic, less plutocratic. This is no more than making the bourgeoisie live up to their own ideals and myths of self-enrichment.

More significant as an answer to our question is the formulation of the second measure: "Gradual expropriation of landed proprietors, factory owners, railway and shipping magnates, partly through competition on the part of the state industry and partly directly through compensation in assignations."[12] Here another method of acquiring property is clearly spelled out. The proletarian state will buy out some capitalist enterprises.

The proletarian revolution is not to bring about a regime of forcible confiscation of bourgeois property. It will introduce a progressive tax system and eliminate "unearned" wealth through inheritance taxes. With such funds it will purchase enterprises as well as create them. A market context is accordingly presupposed. An economic logic, respectful of market production, is observed and perhaps even improved upon. Even more significant of the nature of the post-revolutionary society is the idea that the proletarian state will acquire property through competition with capitalist enterprises. This implies that socialist property will be more efficient than capitalist property and will win in a fairly structured market-place competition.

The only mention of unpaid forcible confiscation in this work occurs in the third plank: "Confiscation of the property of all emigrants and rebels against the majority of the people." This is also the only specific mention of how such despotic methods would be used in the *Manifesto*. "Despotic inroads on the right of property" and the "radical onslaught upon private ownership" are confined to the initial period of the revolution when some property owners will predictably engage in armed rebellion against the first government that represents the interests of the democratic majority of the society. To the confiscation of the property of such rebels is added that of emigrés. While certain passages of the *Manifesto* suggest sweeping confiscation of property, a closer reading, supplemented by the "Principles," discovers a more narrow conception, with strict delimitation of property rights. The program of nationalization of banks and transportation presumably falls under the heading of compensated acquisition of property.

The main point, for our purposes, is crystal clear. The proletarian revolution does not immediately do away with the market. The socialism that it initiates is a market socialism, albeit a "state market socialism." A certain amount of property must be acquired by the proletarian state. But state enterprises are to continue to operate on market principles, competing with non-state, privately owned enterprises.

USING THE MARKET AGAINST CAPITALISM

If the Communist program is more than a matter of limiting the property rights of the bourgeoisie in the creation of what might in the twentieth century be described as a program of social democracy, there should be some programmatic position indicating a qualitative break from capitalism. Such substantial modification is implied in the fourth measure of the "Principles":[13]

4. Organization of the labour or employment of the proletarians on national estates, in national factories and workshops, thereby putting an end to competition among the workers themselves and compelling the factory owners, as long as they still exist, to pay the same increased wages as the State.

Thus the immediate goal of the proletarian government is not the elimination of competition *per se.* It is the elimination of competition between workers over the price of their labor. It is this competition between workers, employed and unemployed, that Marx later described as riveting "the labourer to capital more firmly than the wedges of Vulcan did Prometheus to the rock."[14] So while market relations in the production of goods for sale is not ended, what is ended, or is in the process of ending, is the labor market, the market in human time, energy and skill. By becoming owners of their own means of production, workers no longer sell their ability to work as a commodity, subject to pressures of market forces—especially to the pressures arising from competition with other workers.

The method of achieving this goal consists in influencing and directing the market, not in doing away with it. By providing work for unemployed workers in national estates, factories and workshops, the proletarian state puts an end to unemployment and therefore to competition between workers for scarce jobs. Through their representation in the state, workers have become owners of nationalized production, and consequently, beginning in the state sector, they cease to be exploited for profit. They cease to produce surplus value. Their remuneration is raised to a level permitted by the value of their production—with deductions for reinvestment and various social programs, deductions that come back to them either through future economic gains or through the social programs from which they benefit. Given the virtual elimination of unemployment, this higher compensation for workers will force capitalist employers to pay a similar wage.

Consequently the kind of market initiated by the proletarian state is no longer strictly speaking a capitalist market. Thanks to conscious management by the proletarian state the market begins to work against the bourgeoisie and for the proletariat. It is no longer the blind elemental force in which the interaction of isolated producers takes place as if it were an external power of nature. The rational or conscious element—planning— transforms market production, rather than simply replacing it. Clearly there is a place for centralized state intervention in the economy. But this is not a matter of micro-managing the activities of enterprises. It is a matter primarily of creating and enforcing new rules of the game, rules that express the interests of workers rather than private owners. Hence a "socialist" market comes into existence, more or less rapidly changing the conditions in which workers sell their labor, so that for the first time there will really be "an honest day's work for an honest day's pay."

CONDITIONS FOR THE COMMON MANAGEMENT OF PRODUCTION

But why should property pass into the hands of the proletarian state, and not directly into the control of the workers of individual enterprises? Engels argues that it will take a significant length of time, perhaps several generations, before workers will develop the capacity to control their affairs themselves. He writes:[15]

> Just as in the last century the peasants and the manufactory workers changed their entire way of life, and themselves became quite different people when they were drawn into large-scale industry, so also will the common management of production by the whole of society and the resulting new development of production require and also produce quite different people. *The common management of production cannot be effected by people as they are today* [emphasis added, J.L.], each one being assigned to a single branch of production, shackled to it, exploited by it, each having developed only *one* of his abilities at the cost of all the others and knowing only *one* branch, or only a branch of a branch of the total production. *Even present-day industry finds less and less use for such people.* [Emphasis added, J.L.] Industry carried on in common and according to plan by the whole of society presupposes moreover people of all-round development, capable of surveying the entire system of production. [Emphasis added, J.L.] Thus the division of labour making one man a peasant, another a shoemaker, a third a factory worker, a fourth a stockjobber, *which has already been undermined by machines* [emphasis added, J.L.], will completely disappear. Education will enable young people quickly to go through the whole system of production, it will enable them to pass from one branch of industry to another according to the needs of society or their own inclinations. It will therefore free them from that one-sidedness which the present division of labour stamps on each one of them. Thus the communist organisation of society will give its members the chance of an all-round exercise of abilities that have received all-round development. . . .

This statement is remarkable for what it implies about our topic. After the proletarian revolution, Engels clearly says, "the common management of production" will not be possible! The reason is not that the proletarian state does not have power to wrest all property from the bourgeoisie, or that it does not have the technological cadre for the central planning of production. The reason is quite simply that the working people themselves, the direct producers, do not have the education and skills that would be required for this communist organization of society. There is no suggestion here that, in the meanwhile, this project could be managed by a technological elite, such as might be gathered together in a state central planning ministry. "Common management" means just that, management by the society as a whole, not by a particular body of experts engaged in "central planning."

Five points are made: (1) In the immediate aftermath of the proletarian revolution "common management" of production will not be possible. Hence, market production will persist while property relations change gradually. (2) Such market production is nevertheless increasingly conscious or planned, to the advantage of the working people. (3) When "industry carried on in common and according to plan" does become possible, thanks to the education of the population, it will be *common* management, not management by an elite central planning body of economic technocrats. (4) Capitalist production itself points in this direction, since the rigid division of labor and hierarchy of management characteristic of capitalist organization has already, thanks to machine production, become obsolete. (5) It is implied that the post-capitalist society must be divided into two stages. There is a first stage in which market relations involving capitalist enterprises continue to exist, while property passes gradually into the hands of the proletarian state primarily through economic means, with socialist enterprises successfully competing against capitalist ones. And there will be a second stage in which common management of the economy will be effected by the working people themselves. In Engels' conception, monetary-market relations will cease to play a significant economic function only with the later stage. Both the state and the market will wither away. But at no point will there be a system of central planning comparable to what existed in twentieth-century socialist societies.

CAPITAL AND THE FIRST CONSCIOUS REACTION OF SOCIETY TO THE UNFETTERED MARKET

This argument about the nature of the post-revolutionary society is supported by a reading of Marx's central work, *Capital*. The logic of Marx's *Capital* consists in a step by step investigation of the categories or structures of capitalism from the most general or abstract level to increasingly concrete levels. This analysis contains not only a structural investigation, but an investigation of the developmental dynamics of capitalism. In this investigation, the historical prominence of the initial, relatively abstract structures of capitalism corresponds to primitive stages of capitalist, and even precapitalist development. The passage to more complex, concrete categories tends to reflect more developed stages of capitalism. The analysis of capitalist development, furthermore, is more than what is sometimes understood by the "critique of political economy." I.e., it is more than a purely negative "refutation'" of capitalism as an intrinsically contradictory system. Marxism is not a form of "nihilistic socialism." It does not take a purely negative stance toward capitalism regarded as something wholly evil, to be destroyed or summarily replaced by a fundamentally different entity. In Marx's "dialectical socialism," the new society is seen as emerging in and through the old one.[16] *Capital* is a kind of theoretical ultra-sound for discerning the development, within the womb of capitalism, of the new society that will replace it.

Thus there is an evolution of the forms of organization of capitalism, both in respect to the way in which capitalists organize production within the factory, and in the corresponding way in which the relations between capitalist enterprises are organized. There is an evolution of the market itself, linked to changes in the way in which production is carried on. By examining the logic of the development of capitalist production and interconnected market relations, we can understand more concretely the way in which the capitalist market gives rise to the new relations of the future communist society.

First of all we should understand that the capitalist market system is only one stage in the history of market-related production. Capitalism is not identical with market production. It is market production of a particular kind. Before understanding complex capitalist commodity production, Marx argues, it is necessary to understand simple, non-capitalist commodity production. Market relations preexist capitalism, and so it is conceivable that they will continue in some form beyond capitalism. An understanding of the market relations of simple commodity production is necessary for understanding capitalism. But capitalism is a distinctive kind of market society. For the capitalist system of production and exchange to emerge a particular kind of commodity, and a particular kind of market, must appear on the scene. It is the commodification or marketization of the capacity of human beings to work that constitutes the essence of the capitalist system.

The early development of the industrial revolution in England coincided with the historical prominence of the tendency to extort surplus value in the simple, quantitative, absolute fashion. Resistance to the degradation of working conditions led to the rise of trade union struggles as well as to humanitarian protest against the dehumanization of workers. As a result, the Factory Acts fixed the length of the working day and limited the extent of child labor. Marx called the English factory legislation "that first conscious and methodical reaction of society against the spontaneously developed form of the process of production."[17]

The Factory Acts represented a conscious limitation of the operation of the labor market by society as a whole. Thanks to laws controlling and regulating the operation of the labor market, working people freed themselves from the tyranny of the primitive, completely unregulated or "free" market that forced them and their children to work long hours, pushing them to the limits of physiological endurance. At the same time this legislation was an intrinsic moment in the development of modern capitalism. It was "just as much the necessary product of modern industry as cotton yarn, self-actors and the electric telegraph.[18] This limitation of the unfettered operation of market production was at the same time a development of market production, involving an expansion of the productivity of society. Instead of pushing their workers to the limits of physical exhaustion, capitalist management increasingly turned to technological innovation as a means of increasing productivity. Thus capitalist development itself refutes the idea that the "free market" is the best stimulus for the economy.

This first step in the conscious regulation of the market has been followed by others in the history of capitalism, from anti-trust laws to the establishment of the welfare state. With the current globalization of the market, capitalism seems to be returning to early nineteenth-century conditions of unfettered market production, now on a global scale, overriding many of the national reforms of the nineteenth and twentieth centuries. National legislation that has regulated the sale of labor power needs to be reinforced by international laws. Such laws should protect the conditions of the sale of labor power in all countries, rich and poor. There is a heightened awareness, too, that ecological havoc caused by spontaneous market forces must be remedied by national and international legislation that takes into consideration what economists call the "externalities" of economic production, the hidden costs that do not (as yet?) appear in the "barometric fluxuation of the prices."

COOPERATIVE SOCIALISM

But there is a further stage in the evolution of the market suggested by all that has been said here, that distinguishes the liberal reformer of capitalism from the socialist revolutionary. This is the elimination of the market *in labor* altogether. Marx's *Capital* shows that this stage is not an arbitrary invention of utopians, but is itself a reality emerging within the development of the capitalist economy. In his study of the evolution of capitalism, Marx distinguished the early manufacturing system from the later factory system. The manufacturing system is one in which workers are specialized in one detail of the production process, using relatively simple hand-tools to perform their particular tasks. With the development of machine production properly speaking, Marx argued—following Engels' idea in the "Principles"—"the technical reason for the life-long annexation of the workman to a detail function is removed."[19] The technical basis for the reduction of the worker to a narrow specialty, and at the same time the technical need for elite supervisors of labor who specialize in the production process as a whole, are overcome with the development of the machine. As machines take over the work formerly performed by the combined labor of many detailed handicraft workers, the technical reason for the despotism of the capitalist management of labor is eliminated.

The possibility emerges for a different kind of organization within the factory, one that does away with despotic capitalist relations, one that allows workers to supervise their own work process, returning in some sense to the self-directing work styles of previous societies. The development of automation pushes in the direction of this possibility. What remains after the introduction of machinery of course is the non-technical reason for this hierarchical, despotic system of organisation of the workplace, the dominance of capital over the labor process with the objective of producing surplus value. Current forms of the "managerial revolution" that give greater initiatives to the direct producers are heightened expressions of this tendency. Such reforms continually run up against the barrier posed by the autocratic decision-making power of the top management.

In the third volume of *Capital,* where the possibilities of a new mode of production are most concretely studied on the basis of empirical developments, Marx identifies the outcome of this dialectic. Marx writes in an analysis of the credit system that

> The co-operative factories of the labourers themselves represent within the old form the first sprouts of the new, although they naturally repro-

duce, and must reproduce, everywhere in their actual organisation all the shortcomings of the prevailing system. But the antithesis between capital and labour is overcome within them, if at first only by way of making the associated labourers into their own capitalist, i.e., by enabling them to use the means of production for the employment of one's own labour. They show how a new mode of production naturally grows out of an old one, when the development of the material forces of production and of the corresponding forms of social production have reached a particular state. Without the factory system arising out of the capitalist mode of production there could have been no co-operative factories. Nor could these have developed without the credit system arising out of the same mode of production. The credit system is not only the principle basis for the gradual transformation of capitalist private enterprises into capitalist stock companies, but equally offers the means for the gradual extension of co-operative enterprises on a more or less national scale.[20]

Marx points to a strategy of socialist organization that takes advantage of trends that are promoted by the self-transforming logic of capitalist development itself. In his inaugural address to the Working Men's International Association in 1864, Marx strongly supported the multiplication of cooperative factories. He warned, however, against thinking that this trend would by itself arrest "the growth in geometrical progression of monopoly." Despite the economic superiority of cooperatives,[21] "the lords of the land and the lords of capital will always use their political privileges for the defense and perpetuation of their economical monopolies." The promotion of cooperatives must therefore be accompanied with a struggle for political power. "To save the industrious masses, cooperative labour ought to be developed to national dimensions, and, consequently, to be fostered by national means."[22]

Between 1848 and 1864 Marx and Engels modified their conception of the economic strategy of the proletarian state in this respect: Instead of calling for *state* property as the main form of transition from the old society to the new one, they saw the emergence of a cooperative movement as the most promising form of socialist property, as the starting point of the new society. The emergence of the factory system, the emphasis on the production of relative surplus value rather than absolute surplus value, and the corresponding regulation of the old unfettered market in labor power, together with the development of credit— enabling workers to buy their own factories—set the stage for the emergence of worker-owned cooperative industries.

Communism should not be regarded nihilistically as the negation of capitalism as an evil and its replacement by a radically different society. In their dialectical approach to understanding social reality, Marx and Engels once wrote, in the *German Ideology,* that: "Communism is for us not a state of affairs which is to be established, an ideal to which reality [will] have to adjust itself. We call Communism the real movement which abolishes the present state of things."[23] Hence Communism is a development already occurring within capitalism. Later, writing on the Paris Commune, Marx argues that the working people "have no ideals to realize, but to set free elements of the new society with which old collapsing bourgeois society itself is pregnant."[24]

The elements that needed to be set free, as Marx saw things in the 1860s, were the cooperative enterprises of the workers. These are "the first sprouts of the new" growing up within the old form of society. But the soil for this growth had to be prepared. General conditions subjecting the free or primitive market to conscious control in the form of new rules for production and exchange had prepared the way for the emergence of such sprouts of the new society. A proletarian state would free such developments to follow their inherent logic, to allow for the generalization of cooperatives to a national, and international, scale.

The main lines of their position of 1848 remains. The crucial first step, without which the cooperative movement is bound to be frustrated, is the establishment of a proletarian government. Under the political conditions of a proletarian government, "socialist" enterprises can more fully demonstrate their superiority to capitalist ones in marketplace competition. Such market socialism is transitional to the full development of a society in which workers will control their productive activity in common. But it is already the beginning of such a society, since with the progressive elimination of the market in creative human beings, what remains of the market no longer regulates production with the heartless brutality of a nature-imposed necessity. The market that remains for workers who work for themselves is a market that is increasingly subject to human consciousness. It is a market that is consciously used for human welfare.

MOORE VS. MARX

In *Marx. vs. Markets,*[25] Stanley Moore argues that Marx supported market socialism in the *Communist Manifesto,* but later, in *Capital* and the *Critique of the Gotha Program,* he abandoned this idea and proposed a non-market socialism. Moore is right, as we have seen, that the post-revolutionary order proposed by the *Manifesto* is one of "market socialism." So strong is the evidence of a post-revolutionary market society that Moore believes that the *Manifesto* effectively abandons the idea of a non-market outcome of this process. Having discarded the philosophical-moral principles of his earlier work, Marx can find no effective empirical arguments, in the spirit of historical materialism, to support his earlier conclusions that capitalism must give way to a society without any commodity exchange whatsoever. However, in later writings, such as *Capital* and the *Critique of the Gotha Program,* Marx reversed himself, according to Moore. Dogmatically reaffirming the anti-exchange conclusions of his youth without their moral premises, Marx jettisoned the market-socialist position of the *Manifesto* which allegedly contradicts such conclusions.

But in the perspective we have described, there is no inconsistency between the positions that are at least implicit in the *Manifesto* (read together with the "Principles") and those of the later writings. The long-range goal of the post-revolutionary society is a non-market communism. But this does not exclude a lengthy period of "market socialism" as an intermediate stage that is preliminary to the achievement of this final goal. It is true that Marx (and Engels) had little to say in that work in defense of the final goal of a society based on "the free development of each". But *Capital* and other later works that present more complex arguments about the end of commodity production continue to suppose the existence of an intermediary market-oriented socialist stage.

The passages cited on cooperatives presuppose just such a conception. Cooperative factories are described as the first sprouts of the new society. Clearly they have come into existence and operate in a market society. The first sprouts of the new society are enterprises producing for the market. What emerges within capitalism are what can be called "cooperative market socialist" enterprises. While noting the limitations of these enterprises, Marx nevertheless sees in them the beginnings of the new society. He does not reject them for their "bourgeois" imperfections. The proletarian revolution is needed to negate the negation that the capitalist state poses to these revolutionary developments, and to provide the political conditions that "foster" their full development. While the long-range perspective may be one in which market production ceases altogether, the immediate prospect for the post-revolutionary society is one in which market cooperatives are given a chance to flourish. Marx clearly does not display the negative attitude toward cooperatives as mere "huckstering" that was later deplored by Lenin in his essay "On Cooperatives."[26]

We have Engels' testimony that Marx in later life continued to support the idea of a postrevolutionary market socialist society. In his essay "The Peasant Question in France and Germany" (1894), Engels evokes the perspective of his "Principles":[27]

As soon as our Party is in possession of political power it has simply to expropriate the big landed proprietors just like the manufacturers in industry. Whether this expropriation is to be compensated for or not will to a great extent depend not upon us but the circumstances under which we obtain power, and particularly upon the attitude adopted by these gentry, the big landlords, themselves. We by no means consider compensation as impermissible in any event; Marx told me (and how many times!) that in his opinion we would get off cheapest if we could buy out the whole lot of them. But this does not concern us here. The big estates thus restored to the community are to be turned over by us to the rural workers who are already cultivating them and are to be organized into cooperatives. They are to be assigned to them for their use and benefit under the control of the community. Nothing can as yet be stated as to the terms of the tenure. At any rate the transformation of the capitalist enterprise into a social enterprise is here fully prepared for and can be carried into execution overnight, precisely as in Mr. Krupp's or Mr. von Stumm's factory. And the example of these agricultural cooperatives would convince also the last of the still resistant small-holding peasants, and surely also many big peasants, of the advantages of cooperative, large-scale production.

Although the long-range perspective may be one in which market production disappears, the immediate post-revolutionary society involves continuing market production. A mixed state-cooperative form of ownership is suggested here, as large estates are to be turned over to farm workers who will run them as cooperatives, while legal ownership of land is held by the community. The transformation of capitalist into "social" enterprises does not depend on the creation of a centralized system of planning, but simply on the transfer of legal ownership to the community and of direct control to the workers working in the enterprise.

A variety of forms of property is proposed for the post-revolutionary society. Although large-scale capitalist property will be eliminated, there will remain, together with cooperatives, small-scale capitalist firms, rich peasants with some employees, small-scale peasants and self-employed. The small peasantry should learn the advantage of voluntarily combining into cooperatives through economic necessity and example. Cooperatives will be able to produce more cheaply; cooperative workers will earn more, and work under better conditions. If example is insufficient, marketplace competition, we may surmise, will force individual peasants to form cooperatives, with the encouragement and help of the socialist state.

Engels attributes to Marx the notion of compensating the big capitalists and landowners. He has to make a special point of this in view of the fact that explicit mention of this idea was dropped in the *Manifesto,* perhaps because of the slim prospects, in 1848, for a peaceful proletarian revolution. But we know that this was his own proposal in the "Principles."

CRITIQUE OF THE GOTHA PROGRAM: PRODUCERS DO NOT EXCHANGE THEIR PRODUCTS

It seems highly improbable that Marx rejected the market socialist position of the *Manifesto* for a fundamentally different view of the post-revolutionary society. In the German preface to the *Manifesto* of 1872, Marx and Engels wrote that "the general principles laid down in this *Manifesto* are, on the whole, as correct as ever. Here and there some detail might be improved."[28] So momentous a difference as suggested by Moore between Marx's views of 1848 and those of later years would certainly fall under the heading of "general principles" rather than matters of detail. Marx and Engels do say that some of the practical measures of the Communist program had become outdated, and should be revised in connection with changed historical conditions—most notably, in light of the Paris Commune of the previous year. But this idea, they add, is one of the principles enunciated in the *Manifesto* itself.

The most persuasive basis for Stanley Moore's belief that Marx later rejected his early support of market socialism is found in Marx's *Critique of the Gotha Program.* This has become the classic text for Marx's thinking about communist society, although it consists of what Marx called "marginal notes" on the founding program of the German Social Democratic Party, was hurriedly written, and was not intended for publication.

Marx writes clearly and in a way that seems to allow of no doubt that there will be no commodity production, no market, in communist society:[29]

> Within the collective society based on common ownership of the means of production, the producers do not exchange their products; just as little does the labour employed on the products appear here *as the value* of these products, as a material quality possessed by them, since now, in contrast to capitalist society, individual labour no longer exists in an indirect fashion but directly as a component part of the total labour. The phrase 'proceeds of labour,' objectionable even today on account of its ambiguity, loses all meaning.

In the light of all that has been said so far, one is tempted to argue that the elimination of production for exchange does not apply to the immediate post-revolutionary society, but to the future goal of that society, when "common management" will be possible. If what has so far been argued reflects Marx's consistent opinion, this paragraph should apply to what I have called the second stage of the post-revolutionary society, not to the first. If so, it would be compatible with the existence of a prior "market socialist" stage. This interpretation seems to be suggested by the final sentence, in which Marx contrasts the possible meaningfulness "today" of the phrase, "proceeds of labour," with its meaninglessness in the future "collective society."

What seems to undermine this interpretation is the fact that immediately after the above paragraph, Marx gives his account of what he calls the *first* phase of communist society:[30]

> What we are dealing with here is a communist society, not as it has developed on its own foundations, but on the contrary, just as it *emerges* from capitalist society, which is thus in every respect, economically, morally and intellectually, still stamped with the birth-marks of the old society from whose womb it emerges.

This passage clearly expresses Marx's dialectical conception of socialism. The new society arises out of the old one, and is stamped by its origins "in every respect." And yet this passage directly follows the one in which Marx declares that "the producers do not exchange their product." How could such a situation of non-exchange emerge directly from capitalism? One might be excused for believing, on the basis of this text, that there was a radical change in Marx's views regarding the post-revolutionary society, a change which seems little compatible with the dialectical approach of "emergence" that is otherwise defended. The passage suggests that the revolutionary workers' government should, practically overnight, seize all the instruments of production and direct their operation with no dependence on market exchange.

But such an interpretation overlooks another famous passage from *The Critique of the Gotha Program*:[31]

> Between capitalist and communist society lies the period of the revolutionary transformation of the one into the other. Corresponding to this is also a political transition period in which the state can be nothing but *the revolutionary dictatorship of the proletariat.*

The phrase "dictatorship of the proletariat" has so mesmerized readers that the significance of the entire paragraph may be easily overlooked. The following points are made: (1) *before* the emergence of the communist society described above there will be a distinct period of revolutionary transformation from capitalist into communist society; (2) this transitional period should be viewed in two respects: a) in respect to the political power of the proletariat, and b) in respect to the nonpolitical, i.e., socio-economic, process to which the political or state power "corresponds."

This paragraph in fact delineates the historical space to which the program of the "Principles" and the *Manifesto* belongs. Moore's main mistake is to confuse this period of "transformation" with that of the first phase of communism. Marx never changes his mind that a noncommodity producing, communist society does not appear overnight with the proletarian revolution, but only after a transitional period of transformation from capitalism into communism. This transitional period, Marx unfailingly stresses, requires the "dictatorship" or state power of the proletariat. Without political power in the hands of the working class, the sprouts of the new society already developing in capitalism will not be permitted to develop their full potentiality. But this means that the transitional period is not exhausted by its political character. In the dialectical framework of Marx, the role of the proletarian state is not to *create* a new society, but "to set free elements of the new society with which old collapsing bourgeois society itself is pregnant."

PROGRAM OF THE PARIS COMMUNE

A fuller citation, from Marx's work on the Paris Commune, *The Civil War in France,* deserves noting:[33]

> If co-operative production is not to remain a sham and a snare; if it is to supersede the Capitalist system; if united co-operative societies are to regulate national production upon a common plan, thus taking it under their own control, and putting an end to the constant anarchy and periodical convulsions which are the fatality of Capitalist production—what else, gentlemen, would it be but Communism, "possible" Communism?
>
> The working class did not expect miracles from the commune. They have no ready-made utopias to introduce *par décret du people* [by the people's decree]. They know that in order to work out their own emancipation, and along with it that higher form to which present society is irresistibly tending by its own economical agencies, they will have to pass through long struggles, through a series of historic processes, transforming circumstances and men. They have no ideals to realize,

but to set free elements of the new society with which old collapsing bourgeois society itself is pregnant.

No revolutionary decree after the seizure of power is going to create an ideal, i.e., communist, society. Writing here of the work of the proletarian government of the Paris Commune, Marx essentially repeats ideas of the *Manifesto,* more fully elaborated in the "Principles." The proletarian revolution will inaugurate a period of transformations—transformations of economic conditions and of human beings. This is the period of revolutionary transformation briefly mentioned a few years later in *The Critique of the Gotha Program.* The practice of the Commune verified Marx's earlier analysis in *Capital.* The socio-economic starting point of these processes are those sprouts of the new society that have been developing within the old, the cooperative production of the workers. These are cooperative societies producing for a market. Cooperative production, liberated from the constraints placed upon it by the capitalist state and encouraged by measures taken by the Communal government, develops more rapidly.

The Commune did not abolish the market or even capitalist production. It moved to make market production subservient to human needs, by regulating and moving to abolish the market in labor. Marx mentions some of these regulations. Night work for journeyman bakers was abolished. Employers lost their dictatorial power to fine workers. Workshops and factories that were closed by owners, either because they absconded or were engaged in capital strike, were made over to workers' associations to be run as cooperatives. The peasantry was to be freed of onerous taxes and debt, and, thanks to the worker-based salaries of politicians, provided with one of its favorite traditional demands, "cheap government." The financial measures taken by the Communal government were "remarkable for their sagacity and moderation."[34]

Marx was particularly impressed with the political reforms undertaken by the Commune. The Commune brought the state closer to the people by limiting salaries of representatives and introducing the right of recall. Here, Marx stressed, the Commune went significantly beyond the program of the *Manifesto.* But the general principle underlying the economic program of the *Manifesto* remains. The first steps are taken to launch society in a new direction. A whole series of later developments will have to be worked out in step-by-step fashion as these changes call for additional ones.

Significantly different is the greater degree of worker self-management compared to what Marx and Engels projected for 1848. The direction of revolutionary change consists in facilitating those sprouts of the new society already developing in the old one. Rather than the "state market socialism" of the *Manifesto,* this is a "cooperative market socialism" which deliberately limits the powers of state inherited from the old society. Rather than fundamentally shifting power to the state for purposes of managing the economy, as in the "state command socialism" of the later Soviet period, power is turned over more fully to workers both to defend themselves against arbitrary decree of their employers and to manage their own economic associations in a regulated market context. The ready-made machinery of the bourgeois state must be substantially changed so that there is greater control over the political representatives whose job in the economic field involves facilitation of this growth of worker-managed cooperatives. This is a far cry from the state socialism that Stalin installed in 1929. But it is also not a system of democratic central planning, as others have suggested:[35]

MARXIST MARKET SOCIALISM

In the "Principles" and the *Manifesto* two "stages" of the post revolutionary experience could be distinguished, the first being generally transitional to the second, which is the goal of the post-revolutionary transformations. I used the expression "stages" so as not to coincide exactly with what Marx calls, in *The Critique of the Gotha Program*, the two "phases" of the communist society. Marx in fact has three "periods" in his prognostication of the post-revolutionary society: the period of revolutionary transformation, and the two phases of the communist society that emerges out of this transformation. Proletarian state power is necessary only during the first of these periods, when distinctly capitalist elements will continue to exist side by side, and in competition with, socialist elements. Such competition should be peaceful economic competition after an initial period of possibly violent clashes.

How do the two "stages" of the "Principles" and the *Manifesto* relate to Marx's later delineation of three "periods"? It would seem that the first phase of communist society is not yet that of the *Manifesto*, in which "the free development of each is the condition for the free development of all."

The state of affairs that characterizes the first phase of communism is one in which work continues to be a necessity imposed on workers for the sake of earning a living. It has not yet become "life's prime want," as Marx says of the second phase of communism. In the language of *Capital* are still dealing with "the realm of necessity":[36]

Freedom in this field can only consist in socialized man, the associated producers, rationally regulating their interchange with nature, bringing it under their common control, instead of being ruled by it as by the blind forces of Nature; and achieving this with the least expenditure of energy and under conditions most favourable to, and worthy of, their human nature. But it nevertheless still remains a realm of necessity. Beyond it begins that development of human energy which is an end in itself, the true realm of freedom, which, however, can blossom forth only with this realm of necessity as its basis. The shortening of the working-day is its basic prerequisite.

So the first phase of communism would seem to fall within the first stage of the post-revolutionary society as suggested in the *Manifesto*, but perhaps outside of the transitional stage described in the "Principles" which concludes with the common management of production.

In the post-revolutionary society, two processes are occurring side by side. On the one hand, capitalist enterprises are diminishing in number, while the socialist ones are increasing. At the same time, a different dynamic is taking place. Workers are developing the skills and education necessary for them to comprehend and direct a complex modern society. A third element should be factored into these processes. Technological development is advancing, greatly increasing the productivity of labor, freeing workers from the drudgery of machine labor, and making possible free labor. We might add that technological development also tends to create growing interconnected complexes of production that replaces production by technologically independent entities.

The pace of class transformation does not necessarily coincide with that of technological and social-psychological development. Marx's distinction between two phases of communism supposes that class divisions will be overcome before the development of a level of productivity that makes possible a predominance of free, creative work. And yet during this period "the associated producers" are capable of "rationally regulating their interchange with nature, bringing it under their common control." *I.e.,* the first phase of communism involves the "common management of society" of the Principles, which we see as a less lofty goal than that of fully developed communism. But if we follow Engels' argument, such common management depends on the development of the abilities of workers to manage their own affairs, in conjunction with technological development.

These technological and subjective conditions for such common management of society may not be in place with the end of class divisions. It seems reasonable, therefore, to suppose that a period could exist after the disappearance of significant capitalist ownership, yet before common management of production has developed to the point of replacing significant market production. Such a period of "pure market socialism" coming after the "mixed socialist-capitalist society" that immediately follows the revolution would be consistent with the dialectical logic of post-revolutionary developments. The period of "transformation of capitalism into communism" might therefore itself have two "phases" one in which capitalist enterprises are important, and one in which cooperatives predominate, but still having significant capitalist qualities and relying significantly on market production.

SIX MOMENTS OF COMMUNIST DEVELOPMENT

Central to the Marxist dialectical method is the idea of historical change and development. Marx did not elaborate a fixed notion of communism to place in contrast to capitalism. He saw these two antitheses in dynamic opposition. Between the two extremes there are intermediate connections. Our presentation here has in fact identified five stages of communist development in Marx's work—with the possibility of a sixth stage of pure market socialism interpolated at one point. Let us enumerate these moments of the single process of communist development. (1) The Factory Acts were the "first conscious and methodical reaction of society against the spontaneously developed form of the process of production." These and comparable forms of regulating market exchange can be said to sow the *seeds* of the new society. (2) The "first sprouts" of this society were cooperative enterprises, including factories and farms, in which workers became employers of their own labor, and proved that they can compete successfully with capitalist enterprises in a market framework.

(3) The third stage is that of the post-revolutionary period of transformation of capitalism into communism. This is a time of rapid growth of the new society, which gains strength in its contest with the old one, a contest taking place under the new rules enforced by the proletarian state. This contest is not only a political fight, but a socio-economic competition as well. Viewed narrowly this stage ends with the elimination of capitalist ownership of the means of production. (4) With the eventual elimination of capitalist ownership, a fourth stage is possible. Capitalist production no longer exists, but at the same time commodity production continues to play a significant role because more directly conscious methods of organizing production have not yet emerged. Workers may not have the abilities to direct their affairs themselves, or

conditions of technological development have not required direct society-wide cooperation.[37]

(5) Communist society now stands as a systematic totality. Cooperative production has developed to the national, and perhaps international, level. But this society still has many "bourgeois" defects (as Lenin later stressed).[38] It is still stamped "in all respects" by its capitalist origins, according to Marx. This characterization of the first, immature phase of communist society recalls Marx's similarly deprecatory characterization of the sprouts of the new society as reproducing "all the shortcomings of the prevailing system." We should pause to examine this moment more carefully.

THE COMMUNIST MARKET

It would be a mistake to regard the "bourgeois" features that still characterize the new society as purely negative vestiges of the past, as the term "birthmarks" might suggest. Marx focuses on the necessity of "bourgeois right" as a standard of justice during the first phase of communism, by which he meant that workers should receive compensation according to the quantity and quality of their work. This "bourgeois" feature is of positive importance for the development of the new society. Just as capitalist society made use of institutions of feudalism during its early development, until it was capable of replacing these with institutions appropriate to its own nature, so communist society continues to make use of institutions inherited from capitalism until it is able to replace these with methods of organization that more fully reflect its own essential nature. Why then should not communism, in its infancy, make use of the market?

"Within the collective society based on common ownership of the means of production, the producers do not exchange their products . . ." Marx apparently dismisses market production altogether, even for the first phase of communism. And yet Marx goes on in fact to describe a *de facto* system of exchange. Workers receive "certificates" based on their labor, and with these they purchase goods on some sort of market. Marx insisted that "labor money" "is no more money than a ticket for the theatre."[39] And yet if it is not money in the full sense of the term, it does fulfill some of the functions of true money. Similarly, if there is no market in the full sense, there is a limited or restricted market in communist society during its first phase.

Marx explains that because we are dealing with a cooperative society the labor of the individual is not validated indirectly, through the relatively autonomous "decisions'" of the market. What does this mean? In the fully developed market society of capitalism, producers operate independently of one another, and only when they come to sell their goods do they learn, by the fact of selling their product, whether their production has been socially useful. What then will be the situation for the cooperative society? Instead of being dependent on the sale of goods, the labor of the individual is directly validated at the workplace. Workers receive certificates indicating that they have earned the equivalent of so many hours of labor. The "money" they receive is probably not like a theater ticket, or a ration book, earmarking the purchase of certain types of goods. Rather it is more like a certificate of merit, stating that a certain person earned by work the equivalent of so many units of value, which, for old times sake, may be called dollars. Here it has become illegal for individuals to accumulate money from the work of others. Hence "money" is personalized. One can only spend what one has earned by one's own labor. The bearer of the certificate, or computerized purchase card, then spends this limited form of "money" on whatever he or she wants.

Suppose that despite all efforts to foresee eventualities some item has been produced in larger quantities than desired, or even proves to be altogether undesirable. In a commodity producing society in the strict sense, such a result can be calamitous. Under conditions of commodity production strictly speaking, the labor spent on the production of such goods has no real social value. Such labor turns out, *post factum,* to have been worthless. The small commodity producer gets nothing and, without the aid of friends and relatives, perhaps starves to death. The capitalist producer may face bankruptcy, but before that workers at least are laid off. The fired worker bears the full impact of this failure of production to coincide perfectly with consumption.

In the cooperative society, by contrast, the labor of the individual is directly considered to be part of the total social labor. The fact that some of this labor will be useless is an anticipated cost to the society as a whole. This cost, which is more or less inevitable, is not to be wholly borne by the unfortunate individuals directly involved, but by the society as a whole. So there is no calamity for the producers of these unwanted or economically unfeasible goods. Their labor is still "good." Of course adjustments in production will have to be made in the light of such signals coming from this "market," so that the amount of such socially useless labor is reduced to the minimum. Some new mechanism will be necessary to replace that which had once operated like "the blind forces of Nature," bringing unemployment and even death in its wake. New mechanisms of adjustment will be needed so that the interchange of human beings with nature will take place with "the least expenditure of energy and under conditions most favourable to, and worthy of, their human nature."[40]

Consequently, in the communist society in its lower phase, while there is no money in the full sense, and, in the strict sense of Marx's definition, there is no commodity exchange, there is still a restricted form of money and a restricted form of exchange. Similarly, if the state in the full sense no longer exists, because classes have been eliminated, there are still "state-like" functions, ensuring for example that necessary work is performed and rewards are distributed according to that work. These two vestiges of the old society, money and the state, continue to play a positive role in the newly emerged communist society.

(6) Eventually we will reach a sixth stage of fully mature communist development, when the free development of each person will be the basis of the free development of society. We might be tempted here to rest our efforts to find traces of market production in post-capitalist society. The forms of exchange of free labor, no longer constrained by necessity, will have little in common with the alienated mediations of Wall Street. But if we take Marx's dialectical approach seriously we should recognize that this stage does not merely follow the others but permeates the entire process. Communism is "the real movement which abolishes the present state of things." The final goal of communist development is not a future utopia. It is the maturation of an on-going process of humanity struggling to free itself from its own self-alienation, and using that very alienation as a means of its liberation.

NOTES

1. James Lawler, "Lenin and the Dialectical Conception of Socialism", in *Socialist Future*, London: April, 1995, 11–19.
2. Karl Marx, Frederick Engels, *Collected Works*, Volume 6, Progress Publishers, Moscow, 504. Afterwards, this collection will be abbreviated as MECW, with the volume number.
3. Stanley Moore, *Marx Versus Markets*. University Park, Pennsylvania: The Pennsylvania State University Press, 1993. Cf. 66–67.
4. MECW, Volume 6, 504.
5. *Ibid.*, 505–6.
6. Engels to Marx, 23–24 November, 1947, from MECW, Volume 38, 149.
7. Engels, "Principles of Communism," in MECW, Volume 6, 351.
8. *Manifesto*, in MECW, Volume 6, 498: "In this sense, the theory of the Communists may be summed up in the single sentence: Abolition of private property." Significantly, this phrase is qualified in the previous paragraph. Marx and Engels are anxious to join with the existing communist movement, while giving to it an interpretation that may in fact contradict that of other would-be communist

leaders. See James Lawler, "Marx's Theory of Socialisms: Nihilistic and Dialectical," in Louis Pastouras, ed., *Debating Marx*. Lewiston, New York: Edward Mellen Press, 1994.

9. "Principles," MECW, Volume 6, 351.

10. *Manifesto,* MECW, Volume 6, 505.

11. As argued by Moore, 7.

12. *MECW,* Volume 6, 350. Stanley Moore translates: "compensation in the form of bonds." *Op. cit.,* 7.

13. *MECW,* Volume 6, 350

14. Karl Marx, *Capital,* Volume 1 (New York: International Publishers, 1967), 645.

15. "Principles," MECW, Volume 6, 353–34.

16. For my distinction between nihilistic and dialectical socialism, see Lawler, 1994, *op. cit.*

17. *Capital,* Volume 1, 480.

18. *Capital,* Volume 1.

19. *Capital,* Volume 1, 368.

20. Karl Marx, *Capital,* Vol. III (Progress Publishers, Moscow, 1966), 440.

21. The higher profit levels of cooperatives are cited in *Capital,* Vol. III, *op. Cit.,* 388.

22. MECW, Volume 20, 12.

23. MECW, vol. 5. 49.

24. MECW, vol 22, 335.

25. Moore, *Markets Versus Markets.*

26. Lenin wrote, in support of the market socialist system introduced by the New Economic Policy, that it was possible "to build a complete socialist society out of co-operatives, out of co-operatives alone, which we formerly ridiculed as huckstering . . ." Lenin, V.I. 1971. *Selected Works.* Vol. 3. (Moscow: Progress Publishers), 761. See Lawler, 1995.

27. Engels, Frederick. 1949. "The Peasant Question in France and Germany." In Karl Marx and Frederick Engels, *Collected Works,* Vol. II (Moscow: Foreign Languages Publishing house), 397.

28. MECW, Volume 23, 175.

29. MECW, Volume 24, 85.

30. MECW, Volume 24, 85.

31. MECW, Volume 24, 95.

32. By contrast to the position of the *Manifesto*, Moore argues that "According to the *Critique,* an immediate task of proletarian revolution is to abolish commodity exchange." (8) He writes that Lenin's later terminology identifying Marx's first phase of communism with "socialism" "obscures a major a difference between the classless transitional economy described in the *Critique* and that suggested by the *Manifesto*. The latter, like capitalism, is an economy of commodity exchange. The former, like the other economies described as free from fetishism, is not." (40) Moore concludes that Marx changed his mind about the nature of the transitional economy. But this is to overlook Marx's indication of a place for a transitional economy prior to the "emergence" of the communist society, in its first phase. It is Moore who calls this first phase of communism a transitional economy, not Marx. If the first phase of communism can also be regarded as transitional, this is a kind of different transition from that "between capitalist and communist society." Showing the consistency in Marx's work, however, does not reply to Moore's

main point, that Marx failed to demonstrate the necessity of a non-commodity producing society. A reply to that argument is implicit in our presentation: Marx's strict definition of commodity production does not rule out the existence of socialist or communist forms of exchange, where commodity fetishism is overcome, while communism cannot be characterized in terms of central planning, as Moore suggests (e.g., on p. 30).

33. MECW, Volume 22, 335.
34. MECW, Volume 22, 339.
35. E.g., Darrow Schecter, *Gramsci and the Theory of Industrial Democracy* (Brookfield, Vermont: Gower Publishing Co. 1991), 17–18. See Lawler, 1994, 174–79. Schecter dwells on a contradiction between democracy and alleged central planning by the council system, which he mistakenly supposes to have been installed by the Commune and recommended by Marx.
36. Marx, *Capital,* 820.
37. Stanley Moore suggests such a fourth stage in his presentation of the projected developments in the *Manifesto.* He sees a period in which socialist and capitalist sectors coexist, and one in which there is a classless "socialist economy, combining markets with planning." (67). This is speculation, in both his own and my reconstruction, though a reasonable projection about the period which I identify as a gap left open in the text of the *Manifesto.* But it is unnecessary to compare this projected fourth stage to the non-commodity society of the *Critique of the Gotha Program.* In the theory of the *Manifesto,* the logical eventuality of this fourth stage still falls short of the goal of the *Manifesto,* the society based on free labor. In the theory of the *Critique,* both stages identified by Moore can be situated in the period of transformation which precedes the emergence of Communist society properly speaking.
38. Cf., Lawler, 1995.
39. Capital, Volume 1, 94.
40. By contrast to that of Moore, my own interpretation of the first phase of communism is compatible with that of a market economy. But this is not a market in commodities in the sense identified by Marx where commodity production supposes separated or isolated units of production. This interpretation may suggest a convergence of my fourth stage of "pure market socialism" and Marx's first phase of communism. However, I believe there is plenty of room, logically and historically, for phases of development of "market socialism," with more or less proximity to the model of capitalism. A market socialist society will have to deal with the effect of the organic composition of capital on the distribution of income. Capital intensive industries will earn more income for their worker-owners than labor intensive industries. This problem might be rectified indirectly by the state, through tax policies, or directly, as Marx suggests in the *Critique,* by labor certificates. In the former method, cooperative workers in the capital intensive industries would have a vestigial capitalist relationship to other workers, which would have to be corrected by the state. The method proposed by Marx is more advanced, more fully reflective of the cooperative nature of the society as a whole as well as less "state-interventionist." But it may not be practicable before a more or less lengthy experience with more "primitive" forms of cooperation in which many workers see themselves as private owners of their own companies, and perhaps are liable for the consequences of such ownership in possible bankruptcies.

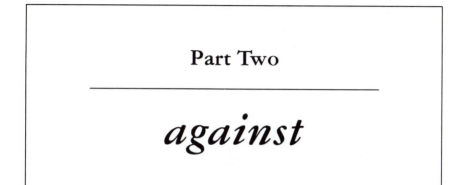

Part Two

against

3

The Problem is Market Socialism

HILLEL TICKTIN

INTRODUCTION

By 1996 Market Socialism was almost, but not quite, dead as a doctrine. It originally emerged under another name as the form of the transitional period between capitalism and socialism in the twenties, when it was supported by Bukharin and Stalin. It was more rigorously formulated in the thirties and was then espoused by Social Democrats in the post-war period and by Stalinists in late Stalinism. The failure of both Stalinism and Social Democracy might be regarded as a clear indication of the failure of the theory of market socialism. Nonetheless, the apparent victory of capitalism has led many former Marxists to adopt the market as an inevitable feature of any and all economies.[1] The doctrine, therefore, continues, if in a somewhat less supportive environment. This article argues that market socialism is a practical impossibility, undesirable, and certainly has nothing to do with socialism.

HISTORY

As the term "socialism" has been widely and loosely used for close to two hundred years, it would be easy to argue that the idea of having a market under socialism was present from the very early days. Proudhon, the anarchist and inveterate foe of Karl Marx from the mid forties of the nineteenth century, had put forward a conception of society, which is probably the first detailed exposition of a "socialist market." Marx, it should be noted, wrote much of his best work in opposition to Proudhon's views.[2] From the *Poverty of Philosophy*, published in 1847, to the *Grundrisse*, written in 1857, Marx was refuting Proudhon. When Marx speaks of a system of wage labour as a system of economic force,[3] he is clearly demanding the abolition of the market in labour and with it of capital itself. At the same time, he ridicules Proudhon's attempts to remove wage labour and capital while retaining the market.

Marx's basic enterprise may be regarded as showing the way in which exchange value stands in contradiction to human need and how it will necessarily be superseded. That at any rate was the orthodoxy within Marxist circles until two things occurred. The first was the arrival of a current, which became dominant among the German social democrats after 1914, that believed in working within the system. The term social democracy came to denote those who believed in gradually reforming capitalism. This could only mean that the market and socialist elements would have to co-exist for a time if not forever. When Sir William Harcourt, the British Liberal politician and one time Chancellor of the Exchequer, declared at the end of the nineteenth century that we are all socialists now, he was surely talking of something which could be called market socialism. In other words, the twin concepts of a gradual movement to socialism and that of welfare statism were acceptable to sections of the less oppressed layers of the population from the end of the nineteenth century on. There was then a merger between these elements and those who had formerly been Marxist. At the same time, while we may trace the antecedents of market socialism in this way, it did not become a serious intellectual or political enterprise until the emergence of Stalinism.

The second event was the arrival of the Soviet Union. There all sides accepted the need for a market to exist for a period of time after the overthrow of capitalism. The real question, which was hotly debated, was whether such a market was necessarily hostile to socialist forces and so to planning. The left, with Trotsky and Preobrazhensky, argued that market and planning were at war with each other. There was a conflict which one side or the other would have to win. Bukharin and Stalin from 1923 onwards saw plan and market co-existing in some kind of symbiosis. Stalin, of course, broke with Bukharin in 1929 and then declared war on the market. Even Bukharin rejected the view that there would be a market in a socialist society, as he made very clear. Preobrazhensky and Bukharin both maintained, as indeed all Marxists had until then, that the law of value will cease to exist under socialism. In the debate on this question in the Communist Academy both right and left agreed totally on this matter. They most vigorously opposed the truly confused viewpoints of Stepanov-Skvortaov, Pokrovsky, Bogdanov, and others, who seemed to be arguing that some form of the market would continue forever.[4] Nonetheless, Bukharin has a place as the father of market socialism in view of his determined defence of the co-existence of market and plan and his vicious opposition to the views of the left opposition who held

that they were necessarily conflictual. That the above cited Soviet socialists took a more conciliatory view of the market indicated the growth of
a more deeply rooted market socialist tendency under conditions of a
Stalinist turn to the market and its ambiguous theorisation by Stalin and
Bukharin. It was this tendency which re-emerged under Gorbachev,
when he rehabilitated Bukharin as his forerunner, but its high period was
brutally cut short by its own contradictions.

The detailed economic theorisation of the concept of market socialism
was put forward in the Lange-Lerner discussion of the mid thirties. There
Oskar Lange, in particular, argued that Ludwig Von Mises was incorrect
in arguing that socialism could not calculate, and without it planning
could not exist. His argument remained at the level of orthodox economics and hence accepted the permanence of the market both in his use
of concepts and in his actual model. He demonstrated that market socialism could use a form of money and prices. He thereby established a
model of market socialism. The main reason that the participants in the
discussion were able to discuss the issue lay of course in the existence of
the Soviet Union and of large social democratic and communist parties.
The argument had little relevance to Soviet practice of the time, but it
did inform social democratic debates and later Stalinist thinking.

When the Stalinist countries of Eastern Europe began to explode, sections of the intelligentsia there came to propound a new variant of market socialism. In essence, it was a reform of the then extant Stalinist
system by introducing money, profit and loss accounting, and denation-
alisation for the non producer goods sector of the economy. Investment
would be regulated from a centre and the government would place limits on the labour market. The intelligentsia would be protected under
this system, as well as most of the old elite. It, therefore, amounted to a
compromise between the elite and capitalism. The best known author
advocating such a compromise was Alec Nove.[5]

The situation has changed in the period since the USSR began to dis-
integrate in that many in the West who looked to the Soviet Union as a
model of some kind have been disillusioned in socialism itself. They have
concluded that socialism as conceived by Marxists cannot work and hence
that the market must be retained. Most of those in the East who had formerly supported market socialism concluded that it had failed and that
only full-blooded capitalism was possible. In the Soviet Union itself the
situation is confused. Many economists support the market, but, few of
them would call for a socialist market. As one participant in a Moscow
conference that dealt with an earlier version of this paper put it: The conception of a market under socialism is like "fried ice."[6]

Thus, two clear lines of thought that have existed over the history of socialism. One, Marxism, has opposed the market, while the other has compromised with it. At the same time, some "Marxists" have also accepted the market at times. These have gone on to found new schools of thought which many consider to be non-Marxist or even wholly anti-Marxist and inhuman, as in the case of Stalinism.

DEFINITIONS OF MARKET AND SOCIALISM

We will begin by defining the market and socialism, and then the differences between the market socialist and the Marxist. Marxism's antagonism to the market is based on the view that capitalism is in the process of decline and with it, value, and so too the market. Furthermore, the rise of bureaucracy, in the present period, is not due to socialist forces but rather to the market itself. In short, my contention is that bureaucracy arises in a period when the old is dying and the new form cannot yet establish itself. The exact nature of bureaucracy depends on the particularity of the transition. In the transition from capitalism to socialism, bureaucracy is formed by the imposition of market-type criteria on an administration that would otherwise be based on need.

The market is defined by orthodox economists, who support it, as a competitive economic environment in which there are buyers and sellers. A Marxist economist could not define it in that way. He would have to define it as the sphere of action of the law of value, or the point at which values are realised. There is, therefore, an immediate disagreement or misunderstanding. For a Marxist, for instance, exchange in itself is not a market unless value is involved. Thus the issue of tokens to a population, who can only exchange those tokens for specific items, is no indication of a market. For a market to exist there must be money, exchange value, and value. A barter regime in which factories exchange their manufactured products for the food of the collective farms is also a non-market regime. For an orthodox economist, however, the crucial issue is the existence of buyers and sellers, irrespective of the nature of the exchange involved.

There is a similar disagreement over the nature of socialism. For an orthodox economist, socialism is usually defined in terms of nationalisation. In this respect neo-classical economists and Stalinists are in agreement. For an anti-Stalinist Marxist, socialism is defined by the degree to which the society is planned. Planning here is understood as the conscious regulation of society by the associated producers themselves. Put differently, the control over the surplus product rests with the majority of the population through a resolutely democratic process. For Stalinists and orthodox economists, however, planning is simply a form of a priori coordination of producers intentions. It is a technicality and not a social relation.

The crucial difference between pre-socialist and socialist society lies in the position of labour. For Marxists, labour in socialism becomes humanity's prime want instead of mankind's burden. The sale of labour power is abolished and labour becomes necessarily creative. The division of labour is overcome in two senses. Everyone works at more than one occupation and everyone participates in running their institutions and society as a whole. No one controls anyone else.

It is clear that market socialism means very different things to Marxists and non-Marxists. For non-Marxists, market socialism refers to an economy with large-scale nationalisation and a market between the enterprises, which then work on the basis of profit and loss. For a Marxist, socialism implies the abolition of the sale of labour power and hence workers who control both the economy and the enterprises. This means that the market does not control labour and there cannot be a capital market. Value and money cease to exist. In short, market socialism is definitional nonsense to a Marxist.

Some argue that the market existed before capitalism and hence that it will go on existing after capitalism. The market, in this interpretation, can be separated from an economy based on accumulation and profit. From the point of view of Marxism, the market did indeed exist before capitalism but only in immature forms. These forms developed to maturity only under capitalism. Before capitalism the market was extremely limited. The social systems then existing used the market as a secondary feature of the economy. For market socialists, the market is not a secondary feature of the economy but its main method of functioning. Before capitalism came into existence there were retail and wholesale markets of different kinds but no mass commodity production. Buying and selling was a sporadic affair. As a result, it is clear that, while exchange value existed, value, by and large, did not. This only expresses the fact that the market cannot be divorced from its social relations, capital and labour. Systems based on the manor or on household production and imperial tribute cannot have a market form suitable for mass production. The post capitalist society has a division of labour so advanced that market relations can be overcome. Thus, pre-capitalist market forms offer no precedent whatsoever.

The present forms which have emerged in post-Stalinist Russia are indicative of what happens when an essentially utopian market is foisted on a society in disregard to its social relations. It necessarily operates only in finance and in bureaucratic and criminal forms elsewhere in the economy. The market can only operate when the forces of production have developed up to a certain point and not beyond that point.

THE DIFFERENCES BETWEEN MARXISM AND MARKET SOCIALISM

The disagreements centre around two essential points. Firstly, for a Marxist, socialism must involve the abolition of abstract labour and of the reduction of the individual worker to an appendage of the machine or of the production process. For a Marxist, the worker must be the master of production. Here, the worker works because he feels responsible for the system, the enterprise, and the individual unit, and because his work becomes increasingly individual and creative. His work time becomes a means by which he fulfills his humanity. Such a regime is egalitarian, in terms of income and control, and humanist in its social relations.

Under a market regime, the worker is subjected to the reign of accumulation and the rate of profit. He is compelled to compete against his fellow workers for a job, for a higher standard of living, and for promotion within the job situation. For the marketeer, the worker is primarily a consumer who acquires a higher standard of living through the market. Competition and the drive for profits ensure efficiency. The manager or the owner of the enterprise receives a higher income to reward his responsibility. Market socialism is anti-egalitarian and anti-humanist in reducing the worker to the level of a competitive machine.

The market socialist will argue that the above is a caricature of his viewpoint. Market socialism, he says, will ensure full employment and equal opportunity for all through free and universal education and a free health service. The rising level of skill required for production will also permit an increasing number of workers to enter more rewarding jobs. Movement between jobs would be meritocratic. This society would be efficient and provide job satisfaction. The market socialist insists that his solution is the only viable one under modern conditions. Anything else is rejected as utopian. As a result of its utopianism, the Marxist alternative, he warns, would open the way to Stalinism or worse. Bureaucracy, elitism, inefficiency and permanent conflict, we are told, are the fate of any society which abolishes the market.

The Marxist answers that market socialism cannot exist because it involves limiting the incentive system of the market through providing minimum wages, high levels of unemployment insurance, reducing the size of the reserve army of labour, taxing profits, and taxing the wealthy. As a result, the capitalists will have little incentive to invest and the workers will have little incentive to work. Capitalism works because, as Marx remarked, it is a system of economic force. In market socialism, that force is insufficient to provide an incentive to make the system work. At the same time, the basic social relations are unchanged. The worker is still controlled by the functional capitalist and must work according to the speed of the machine.

More fundamentally, a socialist society must be one in which the economy is run on the principle of the direct satisfaction of human needs. The word "needs" must be interpreted broadly to include all aspects of human requirements from leisure to creative; it is certainly not confined to simple consumer satisfaction. Exchange value, prices and so money are goals in themselves in a capitalist society or in any market. There is no necessary connection between the accumulation of capital or sums of money and human welfare. Under conditions of backwardness, the spur of money and the accumulation of wealth has led to a massive growth in industry and technology. This has meant enhanced power and material gain for those who controlled the means of production. Gains for the non-wealthy were only obtained by enormous struggles. To make the making of money a goal, therefore, is to so distort human values as to destroy the humanity of the society. The argument can be made more specific.

The making of money stands opposed to direct democracy, in so far as it requires a capitalist or manager who gives orders. Competition compels those competing to subject themselves to the aim of making money as opposed to using a more humane labour process or producing a better product. The argument that somehow competition leads to consumer satisfaction is dubious. The goal of making money can only mean that prices will be as high as possible, given the market. The perfect competition of the orthodox economist has never existed and could never exist. The result can only be that the manufacturer will shape his own market. He markets only those products that give him a profit and then differentiates them so that the rich receive high quality goods and the ordinary worker shoddy goods.

In so far as society is unplanned, its goals are achieved in an anarchic fashion. The making of money and so the accumulation of capital can only lead to a betterment of society itself, as opposed to the ruling group in that society, under very specific conditions. That Adam Smith saw an invisible hand bringing about a rise in the wealth of the whole society is well known. Would Adam Smith have seen this same invisible hand operating under conditions where the making of money leads to enormous arms sectors, deliberate mass unemployment, and the destruction of food surpluses, so-called, while millions starve? The answer of the market socialist or the welfare economist is that the market must be tempered with social responsibility. Then, supposedly, the aims of society will be achieved.

The question is whether the coincidence of exchange-value and use-value of the time of Adam Smith is repeatable under modern conditions. It is indeed an odd argument to say that the making of money and individual greed automatically lead to the good of all. Clearly for it to be true at all there have to be special conditions present. The accumulation of capital, which is not identical with greed, is itself a peculiar phenomenon.

Why should intelligent human beings subordinate themselves to the building up of agglomerations of capital as opposed to producing knowledge or directly useful objects? A massive office block or the Concorde aeroplane do not necessarily add anything to the real wealth of mankind. In fact, their impact on our real wealth may actually be negative by ruining the environment. It is no answer to reply that Stalinism was worse. It may have been, but then it was neither capitalist nor socialist. At a certain point in the history of mankind the accumulation of capital served the purpose of industrialising the world. It cost the lives of millions, but it achieved an object that, at that stage, could be fulfilled in no other way. The conclusion to be derived is that only exceptionally is the wealth of mankind enhanced through exchange-value. Under other circumstances, our real wealth may be diminished by the very same procedures.

It is possible to go further and argue that exchange-value and use-value, or the making of money and human needs, stand directly opposed to each other. This is true in a number of ways:

1. Resources are necessarily distributed both unevenly and against the needs of the majority. It may pay more to produce false icons rather than more food, making food scarce. This will always be the case if incomes are polarised. Thus the rich can afford to pay exorbitantly for false icons while the poor cannot afford to pay much for their food.
2. The making of money itself wastes resources. Its apparatus absorbs huge resources as shown by the pretentious buildings in which financial intermediaries are housed. The expansion of exchange value leads to the production of use-values that do not satisfy mankind.
3. The goal of expanding capital can only be achieved in modern times through the development of commodities which are totally useless, although they have an abstract use-value, or are actually harmful

when looked at from the point of view of majority interest. Arms are a commodity of this type. Narcotics are another.

Use-values under capitalism are re-defined by capital itself, but human needs remain. As a result there is an increasing contradiction between the use-values produced and the actual needs of mankind. This contradiction found a parallel under Soviet-type production, where the poor quality of the product reflected the contradiction between the formal nature of the product and its actual nature.

4. Competition may be better than monopoly or bureaucracy, but it is still a duplication of resources. It seems an odd argument to say that a capitalist will only be efficient in producing use-value of a good quality when trying to make more money than the next capitalist. It would seem easier to rely on the planning of use-values in a rational way, which, because there is no duplication, would be produced more cheaply and be of a higher quality.

Where the market dominates, a region, factory, country, etc. can make a lot of money for trivial reasons, such as the fact that the entity in question is close to the market or has considerable resources of raw materials. This may seem reasonable until it is counterposed to rewards. The capitalists in the rich region will receive high rewards and those in a poor region low ones. In both cases, the same product is produced and workers labour the same number of hours at the same intensity. Still, the result would be that business and money would flow to the one region rather than the other, even if the so-called poorer region was environmentally or otherwise more suited to produce this particular product.

From the above, it might appear as if there can be no discussion between our different theoretical viewpoints because they lack a common ground. Indeed, when the question involves the nature of a truly socialist society, the ultimate goal of any socialist, then there is no common ground. For a Marxist, under modern conditions, market cannot exist outside of capitalism, except under very special conditions and for brief periods of time, such as in China today. The market is not a technicality or a mechanism but a specific social relation of labour and capital. Hence, the market socialist solution is not even on the agenda. There are only two viable systems possible: socialism and capitalism. There may be many non-viable system, of course, in the transition period from capitalism to socialism. If market socialism were possible, therefore, its forms of control over the worker would only produce a society that is the very opposite of socialism.

In the end, the consistent socialist must be an essentialist. In other words, he has to argue that socialism has its own necessary features, of which planning is the most fundamental. The market is its opposite in that it does not permit conscious regulation of the economy by the workers. It relies on spontaneous or anarchic actions in which those who control capital play the greatest role. The real argument at this point becomes one about the nature of capitalism itself.

WHAT IS CAPITALISM?

If one regards capitalism as an accidental agglomeration of features, then it becomes a pragmatic issue as to whether some features of the market can be removed from capitalism and grafted onto socialism. Another marketeer might regard capitalism as composed of essential elements but not see any way that they could be changed. In that case, the rational solution to improving capitalism is to try to limit its worst effects. If, on the other hand, capitalism is regarded as a contradictory system which grew, matured and began to decline, then the issue appears differently. Then the problem is posed in terms of the decline of the law of value and so of the market itself. The market from this point of view is declining, decaying and without a future. Socialism cannot be combined with a moribund form. At this point we must address the whole question of decline.[7]

THE TRANSITION PERIOD

There is, however, one point where the two sides in this debate can meet. The historical period between capitalism and socialism is unexplored territory. The transition period to socialism must of necessity partake of both the past and the future. Would this not be market socialism? In the transition, the market would continue from the previous period, although most classical Marxists believed it would be progressively phased out. The difference between those who favour market socialism and socialists who oppose it begin at this point. The debates between Bukharin and Preobrazhensky, or Stalin and Trotsky, in the 1920s, first expressed much of the theory underlying these different viewpoints.[8] In a conference of the Communist Academy in 1925, in which Preobrazhensky, Bukharin, Bogdanov, Stepanov-Skvortsov and Pokrovsky took part, most participants agreed that under socialism there could be no market.[9] Nonetheless, there was a clear difference on the role of the market. Bukharin did not see the market as necessarily antagonistic to planning or to progress towards socialism. Trotsky, on the other hand, who was not present, saw it as "the arena of struggle between us and capital."[10] This was also the viewpoint of Preobrazhensky.[11] The problem was not one of history of institutional mechanics but of the underlying forces involved during a real transition period.

To begin with, Trotsky did not deny that a market solution was possible. He explicitly agreed that it could succeed but he argued that it would be antagonistic to socialism. The growth of peasant capital would lead to capitalism in the countryside. Peasant capital would need merchant capital under conditions of isolated peasant agriculture, and merchant capital would trade with international capital. Under conditions of relative backwardness, international capital would inevitably dominate.[12] The same argument *mutatis mutanudis* can be made for the towns. This point can be made less specific.

The market inevitably builds up capital, and capital is international. In so far as capital dominates the world market, it will dominate the would-be socialist country. Furthermore, even if the whole world is socialist, a market sector will attempt to create other market sectors. It must find suppliers and customers who will supply or buy its goods for money, under competitive conditions. The market firm can go bankrupt or lose its position within the market; whereas a state firm will remain, since it is financed by the state. For that reason, social democracies have limited their state sectors in order to permit the private sector to compete. Each sector has its own advantages and disadvantages, and each is international. Hence each must try to establish its own network. The situation, however, is even more complicated: each must try to drive out the other.

When the two sectors work together the result is the worst of both worlds. The state sector becomes corrupt, giving contracts on the basis of bribery, while the private sector operates on the basis of a guaranteed income and hence lacks competition. Corruption at the interface between the public and private sectors was not an issue raised in the twenties. They did not have sufficient experience to observe the long-term effects of the co-existence of the two sectors. Since that time, however, so-called "scandals" of public sector corruption have become endemic. Where rewards are limited in the public sector and almost unlimited in the private sector, it is inevitable that the public sector employees will be open to "sweeteners" from their private contractors. In the United States, the absurdly high prices paid to the private defence sector for items like screws have become a national joke. From Italy to Japan politicians have been indicted for accepting money for favouring particular contractors to the state. The fact that a lot of this money is used for the politicians' own political party only indicates the level of overall political corruption. The standard and inevitable example is that of construction, where local government officers inevitably enmesh themselves in a corrupt web of intrigue and favouritism. The theoretical point is that all this is inevitable under conditions where bureaucrats have to make decisions which lead to large profits for others.

The market socialist might try to invent forms of collective decision-making and public sector policemen to control this corruption, but the history of the last seventy years shows the limitations of these procedures. The enforcers are themselves subject to bribery, while committees are usually dominated by their Chairmen, or at the very least by a few members. There is also no way of preventing the private sector from rewarding civil servants upon their retirement with lucrative positions on the boards of companies. Because of this implicit future reward, private companies receive favorable treatment until the official's retirement and then, after he joins the board of directors, they are able to use his inside knowledge and contacts to continue receiving favourable treatment.

THE MARKET LEADS TO BUREAUCRACY

The growth of bureaucracy has meant that these forms of corruption have become endemic in the private sector as well. The ordinary executive makes decisions on contracts often involving millions if not billions of dollars. It is not difficult for the bidder to provide gifts and favours which ensure the success of his bid. It does not have to be direct bribery. He can find the unhappy executive a better job in his or another company after a decent interval has elapsed. The growth of bureaucracy creates the very same conditions in the private as in the public sector.

The market socialist can only reply that bureaucracy must be eliminated through competition, and corruption through the police. This is an argument of the same order as King Canute telling the waves to go back. The history of the twentieth century is one of continuous bureaucratic growth punctuated by corruption scandals in the public sector. Wherever there are bureaucrats and private enterprise, the former will be subordinated to the latter through the power of money or, more strictly, of capital. Even when factories are broken up, the enterprise that owns them simply grows larger. Ford, General Motors, Du Pont, ICI, Glaxo, and IBM are all examples of companies which are gigantic, though their individual plants may get smaller and smaller. Competition destroys both the advantages of large scale production and "planned" organisation of that production. The costs of research, the nature of long production runs, the effect of investment over long periods of time, and long gestation periods make small competitive firms uneconomic and wastefill.

The concept of a large number of small firms each competing in a market over which none has a decisive influence is utopian. Apart from the well-known example of peasant agriculture, such a market probably never existed. Since the emergence of giant, long-lived firms, such as General Motors in America, Daimler-Benz in Germany, Mitsubishi in Japan and the large, enormously powerful banks, such as Deutsche Bank in Germany or Citibank in the United States, competition is a form limited to only a few companies in each industry. The fact that IBM and General Motors are now in decline only signifies that new market leaders will appear over time. It is true that there is more international competition, but this appears to be a temporary phenomenon. The logic of the present situation in the world economy is carrying us towards global monopoly rather than more competition. A few airlines and a few car companies, for example, will dominate their respective industries. Under these circumstances, the idea that competition will remove bureaucracy and corruption appears other-worldly.

The argument of the marketeers that bureaucracy is inevitable under socialism or in the transition period would appear to apply to market socialism as much as to non-market socialism. This criticism is very important, for, if it is correct, it deals a fatal blow to the concept of socialism itself. The devolution of power to the level of the local unit and so ultimately to the individual is the only means of controlling bureaucracy, and, if this is not possible, then neither is socialism.

The most famous argument in favour of eliminating bureaucracy in the transition period is one based on the concept of Soviets or councils. In the Russian Empire, between February and October 1917, before the Bolsheviks took power, the Soviet of Workers and Peasants Deputies had become an alternative source of power. Since then, every popular revolution has thrown up similar workers' councils. If socialism is a society, without abstract labour, where the worker is no longer compelled to work for others under a common regimen, then the worker must be in charge of his own work. This is only possible if there are ways for the worker to control the management of his enterprise and the political life of the country. Elections to central bodies every five years achieve little. It is necessary to have much more frequent elections both to a central democratic structure and for all posts where there is someone in charge of others. Only then will bureaucracy be abolished. The whole question of bureaucracy needs to further explored.

BUREAUCRACY, ELITISM, AND DEMOCRACY

What is bureaucracy? The market socialist will answer that it is an age-old phenomenon present in the Roman Empire or even earlier in Ancient Egypt, something that has existed for as long as there have been governments. No one can doubt its ancient origins but that in itself does not provide an answer. Why do governments, large corporations, and particularly central governments spawn bureaucracy? Bureaucracy can be defined in different ways. If it is simply defined as a hierarchical social apparatus governed by strict rules, then the market socialist can find it everywhere. That, however, does not exhaust the phenomenon. The key feature of bureaucracy is the existence of an independent authority, apparently removed from nominal control, which has the power to make decisions within its particular area of competence. It arises where and when the surplus product cannot be controlled in any other way. In modern times, the elected government is supposed to control its own bureaucratic apparatus, but that apparatus has usually acquired such power that the government's ability to control it is limited. The reason is that the bureaucracy has become an extension of the ruling class in an even more direct way than the government itself. In other words, the commanding section of the civil service is simply another aspect of the ruling class, and as such enjoys some independence of the elected government.

I would argue that bureaucracy arises wherever and whenever the administrators of the surplus product supplants those who are supposed to control it. This happens at specific times in history. During transition periods from one mode of production to another, for example, the form of control over the surplus product is also changing. Under these circumstances, the administration of the surplus product often loses its old form before acquiring a new one. This allows those involved in the administration to become relatively independent. At the present time, we are witnessing the decline of capitalism and thus of value. As a result, the surplus product is no longer simply controlled through value. Administered measures have to be undertaken to ensure that the surplus value is extracted and appropriated. Taxation, centralised and nationalised money forms, nationalised industries, punitive forms of control over labour and labour power are all forms of administration which are necessary to ensure extraction of the surplus product under these conditions. Meanwhile, inside the corporation, accountants, computer analysts, industrial relations departments, etc. all become part of a management team that is essential to maintain control over profits. Firms may also shift their micro-aims from profit extraction to particular named targets, such as volume sold, in order to arrange an overall result which will keep the shareholders happy. Throughout all this, the role of the capitalist is steadily declining. In the case of the Soviet Union, the administrators became the ruling group because there was no other group in a position to take power. The administration there became uniquely independent of those who were supposed to control the surplus product. This is not the only time in history that this has happened.

The Asiatic Mode of Production is another case where a whole mode of production had an indeterminate form of control over its surplus product. In so far as the direct producer possessed his land, he could control his surplus product. But the legal owner of the land, the Oriental despot, taxed the possessor of land in order to obtain part or even all of the surplus. The despot, in turn, had to pay the priests and the administrators of the public works who were essential to production. The bureaucratic apparatus that extracted the surplus product through taxation and spent it on the public works used its position to acquire a degree of independence from all classes. Even the Oriental despot had a weak form of control over them since he could only obtain the surplus with their help.

The upshot of this discussion of bureaucracy is complex. On the one hand, it follows that during the transition period to socialism aspects of bureaucracy are inevitable. On the other hand, what is needed to control the bureaucracy is equally dear. Only through forms of direct democracy operating throughout the society can bureaucracy be avoided.

The transition period is of necessity one of incomplete movement from the old form to the new. Hence, full, direct democracy, which is an essential feature of socialism, is impossible. At the same time, the removal of value will leave decisions on the surplus product to be made through conscious forms of regulation. If these forms are not democratic, then inevitably they must be bureaucratic. The whole nature of the transition is that of the gradual removal of value in favour of planning. At this point, the market socialist may argue that he has been proved correct in two ways. He can say that he is right because direct democracy is only applicable to small institutions like the kibbutz, not to large, complex countries, and certainly not to the whole world. To this, my reply is that I am not talking of total decision-making, but am only interested in the decision-makers being held accountable. This can be established in a number of ways. Elections can be frequent. Holding elections every four or five years gives enormous power to the party elected, but if they were elected for one year only they would have to carry out their promises or not be reelected. Annual parliaments is an historic demand that was first made over one hundred and fifty years ago. Secondly, all elected representatives can be made recallable by their constituents. Thirdly, all positions of responsibility can be made to rotate, so that everyone, in principle, could enter some post of responsibility. Fourthly, higher education can be made available to everyone capable of benefiting from it. This last point is essential to deal with the argument that ordinary people cannot govern because they do not have the necessary skills.

The market socialist is necessarily elitist for he must argue at this point that some bureaucratic skills, like those of economists, are too esoteric for ordinary people to master. However, one would not need to acquire the skills of the economist in order to understand what is happening in the economy. With substantial inequality economists also tend to be more conservative and favourable to a ruling group, while less inequality gives us economists who are more egalitarian. It is also questionable whether the skills of the economist are really that esoteric.

As a democrat and socialist, it is difficult for the market socialist to argue this elitist case, but he can still point to the very real problems which will continue to exist before such direct democracy and high levels of education are introduced. A country with a low standard of living will have to maintain forms of rationing, and that will require some kind of sanctions. A country with a high standard of living may have enough consumer goods to avoid rationing, but it may not have the machinery that is needed to replace routine work. As long, therefore, as scarcity remains and work retains its alienated aspect, sanctions and a bureaucratic apparatus would have to continue. The little truth that there is in market socialism rests here. The market as an apparatus of economic force can compel people to work and establish a form of unequal monetary rationing. Such a market has nothing to do with socialism, but it might be necessary in the initial phases of the transition period in order to raise the overall level of productivity to a point where the market can be abolished. The crucial question, at this point, is whether such a phase might not strangle the baby at birth.

With the final failure of the Russian Revolution, this question has come up for renewed debate. Some claim that the Bolsheviks strangled their own baby by failing to introduce democratic forms which would contain and destroy the growing bureaucracy. Lenin and Trotsky consciously argued for capitalist methods of raising productivity including Taylorism. Democratic forms of control hardly existed by 1920, and those that survived were suppressed in the period of NEP. Perhaps Lenin and Trotsky may be absolved of blame on the grounds that they regarded socialism in one country as impossible, particularly in a country as backward as Russia. On this view, they were merely staking out a territory to assist the more real revolution that they believed was about to break out in Germany. With hindsight, however, we may ask whether it might not have been better for them to have gone down as a democratic social formation rather than as one overwhelmed by a bureaucratic apparatus.

At this point, the difference between a market socialist and a Marxist is clear. The Marxist argues that the bureaucracy arises out of the market itself. It is a social group of administrators, who establish themselves as a force independent of the working class. Deriving their position and power from administration of the market, the bureaucracy is part of the old society and has no place in the new one. Hence, the failure to destroy the bureaucracy was fatal to the socialist project in the USSR.

There appears to be an insoluble dilemma here. In order to overcome the old society and its own emergent bureaucracy, the new regime needs to adopt strong measures. But these same measures hand over power to the bureaucracy. In a developed country, with other developed countries moving the same way, strong measures will only be necessary in the immediate seizure of power and for self-defence. Democracy can be introduced immediately. This situation is the best possible one. In a backward country, however, or in a developed country surrounded and invaded by hostile neighbours, or in conditions of civil war, democracy can only be limited. Hence, the failure of the Soviet Union may well be repeated. In other words, the transition period must be one in which the bureaucracy is defeated, precisely because it represents the old society and not the new.

THE NECESSARY CONFLICT OF THE MARKET AND SOCIALISM

I have argued that in market socialism there would inevitably be a conflict between the two sectors. The market sector would control workers through unemployment and monetary incentives while the planned sector would gradually phase out those forms of incentive in favour of creative work, job rotation, and the participation of all in management. In principle that would mean that the market sector would be more efficient at first but less efficient over time. Workers would then prefer one or the other. The regime, however, would necessarily work to end unemployment and the public sector would do its best toward that end. At the same time the regime would ensure that all workers would receive a minimum wage, unemployment insurance would be at a high level, factory environmental controls would be strict, salary differentials would be greatly reduced through a system of taxation which would work towards an egalitarian society, and the position of women would be safeguarded through an extensive system of creches, nurseries, child leave both before and after birth, and preferential promotion to ensure greater sexual equality. The result would be that the market sector would necessarily be uncompetitive internationally. Its real payment levels would be high. At the same time, workers could not be compelled to work through unemployment or lack of money. Inevitably, workers in the market sector would demand the same rights that workers in the public sector have to elect their managers and decide policy.

On the other hand, an unsuccessful transitional regime might find that it had low productivity in the state sector and much higher productivity in the market sector, because the workers in the state sector have no incentive to work while the workers in the market sector have monetary incentives. It should now be possible to see very clearly the differences in attitude of the market socialist and the socialist. A transitional regime could succeed as long as it was egalitarian, because it would have the support of the population as a whole—that is as long as it maintained maximum democracy and tried to raise the overall standard of living—even if it was unsuccessful in some respects. It would have support, since it was democratically elected on a recallable basis; everyone would be involved with the country's problems. Only then would the government be able to take the necessary measures to raise productivity. These measures would initially mean the extension of limited forms of the market qualified by the conditions enunciated above.

If, on the contrary, the regime did not have popular support, the situation would only get worse. The market socialist approach could only be one of extending the market and so the control of the unelected management. Management will not manage unless it is better rewarded than workers and hence this solution amounts to an extension of inequality and a reduction of democracy. Such a policy might succeed in the short term in raising productivity, but it would lose the support of the majority who were being forced to work harder for lower returns.

EFFICIENCY AND MARKET SOCIALISM

This is the nub of the argument. After the collapse of Stalinism, it appears as if socialism is necessarily inefficient but that it does ensure full employment, social services, welfare benefits, education and a minimum wage. On the other hand, it seems as if the market is efficient and can raise the standard of living of all, given time. Hence, the marriage of the market and so-called socialism appears to offer the best of both worlds. In fact, the marriage, like many marriages, is based on a series of illusions.

In the first place, the so-called socialism which is predicated is that of the Soviet Union. It had little to do with socialism and is more properly called Stalinism. A socialist society is one in which the direct producers govern. The existence of an elite controlling or partially controlling the surplus product, as in all the Stalinist countries from China through the former USSR to Cuba, is an indication that the society has little in common with socialism. The aspects which now appear to be positive, in relation to the regime it succeeded, were deeply flawed. The health service was differentiated according to social group, included a private sector, and was at a low level for the majority. Education was similar. The lack of unemployment only existed because of the inefficiency of the regime. Furthermore, a strong case can be made that it was popular pressure against the regime which ensured that such benefits came into being and were retained. It was not a necessary feature of the Stalinist system but something maintained as a means of survival. It is, of course, better to be employed than unemployed. Such a choice, however, only poses itself as between Stalinism and the market, not between Stalinism and socialism. For the latter, full employment of the labour of the society is a necessary goal, which can only be properly achieved when full employment is obtained through the creative employment of all. It was Trotsky who pointed out that full employment obtained through inefficiency is a false full employment.[13]

Because Stalinism did not have genuine money, (and so, ultimately, value and what lies behind that, abstract labour) calculation was extremely difficult if not impossible. As a result, all economic decisions were taken on very limited information. It is, therefore, assumed that socialism will be similar and, hence, equally inefficient. In contrast, it is said that the market, through money and the laws of supply and demand, does provide a reasonable method of calculation and so an efficient system of determining and supplying needs.

Market socialism cannot deliver efficiency, however. Apart from the other arguments provided above, market socialism suffers from the problems of the market itself. A market in a developed economy necessarily creates the problem of conflict between the capitalist and worker, between employer and employed. Under conditions of full employment, monetary incentives become blunted, especially when the work itself is uncreative or even injurious to mental or physical health. This is true of modern capitalism and not just of a hypothetical market socialism. As a result, a worker will do as little as he can get away with. Modern capitalist economies do not produce the kind of high quality mass-produced goods consumers want. The cheaper goods are of poorer quality. More expensive goods either have unexpected defects or built-in obsolescence.

Even the food produced for consumption has a series of problems induced by the need to maintain profits. The recent BSE food disaster in Britain is a good example. It is believed to have originated from the effects of deregulation. The government allowed the processing companies to reduce the temperature and remove solvents which had acted to keep the poisons from entering the human food chain. As a result, BSE was given to cattle, and they have passed the disease to humans. The government has further reduced the number of inspectors operating in abattoirs and on farms in order to cut its costs and get off the back of the farmer. The need to reduce costs, sell more, and so raise profits inevitably creates a conflict between the interests of the consumer and those of the farmer-producer. No government can successfully deal with this conflict. The catastrophe in the UK is only the most extreme example of what occurs everywhere. The use of harmful hormones, pesticides, fertilisers, and feed is part of industrialised farming in the market. If the government really defended the interests of consumers by having a large number of efficient inspectors, skilled in snooping, and insisted on approving all farming inputs, profits would be so reduced that farmer, would go out of business. It would be far more efficient to set standards and plan agriculture on the basis of need. The worker/consumers could then decide what they prefer, if the choices were put before them.

While this point may be conceded, it can be argued that the market supplies appropriate signals to producers and consumers which can ensure the efficient allocation of resources. This is not true for a number of reasons. The market only provides signals in response to money. Hence those people who do not have money cannot signal their needs or wants. Those who have a lot of money are willing to spend it on the objects of their desires. As a result, prices are distorted upward. The market will always produce for the wealthy because that is the best way of making money and healthy profits. The entire structure of the economy gets distorted towards satisfying the desires of the rich. Profit-making enterprises then use advertising to sell still more to the rich. They also demand that the state keep them in production whenever they are in trouble, because they employ so many workers. The Concorde is such an example. It was maintained in production by a Labour government to keep the manufacturer going. Since its completion, it has served the rich exclusively. Important resources were effectively wasted on the rich.

The market necessarily produces a series of forms of waste. It must have unemployment to function at any level of efficiency. It must have periodic depressions when there are high levels of unemployed people and unused machines. Competition duplicates effort and resource utilisation unnecessarily. It stands opposed to a more rational division of labour. Competition between countries must lead to a large military machine and periodic wars. It also underutilises and ruins the talents of those who are employed.

THE ARGUMENT FOR A PSEUDO MARKET

The economist, Michael Albert and Robin Hahnel have argued that a series of non-monetary prices, or costs, can be derived and used in a socialist society or in a transitional form of society. They also argue that, instead of competition, peer pressure can be used to bring out the best in people. They see competition as destructive and solidarity as a positive good which should be encouraged.[14] Since the derivation of costs remains open to question, however, it is not surprising that some have accused them of reintroducing the market. In a sense, this is exactly what they have done in so far as they base their costs on market-type techniques. What is clear is that their assumptions are very different from the classical Marxist ones.

It has to be emphasized that Marxism does not place special value on solidarity. It is opposed to competition, of course, but not from a solidarist or collective angle. For the Marxist, social labour is not a moral good but an objective necessity. Competition is necessarily phased out by the increasing socialisation of labour. Marxism also starts from the proposition that relative abundance is possible, and hence that the cost calculation can be gradually abandoned. When machines make machines and technology can ensure an abundance of sources of power and raw materials, costs are reduced to zero. Under these circumstances, competition becomes meaningless. The argument that mankind will necessarily waste resources so that peer pressure will be needed sounds Orwellian. It conjures up a picture of atomised workers being spied on by peers or, alternatively, of everyone afraid of offending others just in case it would have a deleterious effect on themselves. Albert and Hahnel start from a moralistic collectivist perspective, which may or may not be admirable. The problem is that the majority of society may disagree with them. People may prefer the impersonal power of money and the market. There has to be a more powerful reason to cooperate fully and efficiently than moral suasion.

COMPETITION AS A NECESSARY COMPONENT?

That reason for cooperation is that cooperation and planning are necessary to achieve the goals of each individual. Competition then appears as irrational, wasteful, and destructive of the ends of the particular individuals involved but not for the reason that Albert and Hahnel have noted. From this point of view, competition appears to be so outdated that its use would be equivalent to using the manorial system or slave labour. It would simply be unproductive and inefficient.

Before the advent of Stalinism, competition looked to most people, other than functionalist economists, to be an irrational form whereby different capitalists ensured that they received part of the profits produced in their industry. Economists justified this as a means of keeping down prices and hence costs. The logical evolution of competition into different forms of monopoly, however, was not accepted by the state. The reason lay in the threat posed to capitalism itself by the ruin of the small capitalists. After World War I and, even more so after World War II, the preferred strategy of the capitalist class was to build up or save the competitive capitalist sector. If capitalism had grown as slowly after World War II as it did before the war, the competitive sector would have been doomed in any case. Propelled by capital's tendency toward monopoly, the post-war period saw an enormous concentration of industry in Germany, Japan, and the United States. Hoping to check this trend, the promotion of competitive industry became a conscious goal, and this involved the retention of the small farmer as well of small-to-medium size industrialists.

In other words, competition today is artificially maintained and must disappear over time. It follows that modern competition is not truly competition, if it is artificially maintained. That is obvious to anyone in business. In the reserved sectors of agriculture and retailing, competition which was once widespread is now confined to particular areas like corner shops or specialist consumer goods. While the ethics of those who support the morality of the jungle must of course be questioned, that is a secondary issue. Modern economics has occupied itself in a totally scholastic way with the nature of monopoly and competition. It has looked at their advantages and disadvantages. It has introduced graphs and equations into an analysis that has become so refined that it has lost its substance. It has created the absurd notion of Perfect Competition, which is something that has never existed and could never exist. Then it has compared such idealized competition with reality and concluded that reality was wanting. Modern economics does not analyse that reality to discover how our system actually works. Indeed, it cannot do so. The real world of "kick-backs" and corrupt deals, on the one hand, and bureaucratic functioning combined with the profit motive, on the other, would involve a critique of capitalism that it is not ready to make.

STALINISM AS A TRANSMUTED FORM OF "MARKET SOCIALISM"

The strength of the market socialist argument has usually rested on the view that it is a more liberal, decent and successful form of socialism than Stalinism. Few have looked at the underlying nature of Stalinism and considered whether its origins do not lie in a failed market socialism. Historically, Stalinist industrialisation followed the previous Stalinist-Bukharinist policy of conceding to the peasantry and Nepmen. Stalin was essentially pragmatic and effectively took over the aspects of the market congenial to his policy. The rule of an elite, payment with rubles, wide income differentials, hierarchy, and competition or so-called emulation are all derived from the market. Labour power ceased to be a commodity under Stalin, but that was not entirely due to him. He would have preferred to have workers competing for jobs and levels of pay. That this did not occur was a result of working-class resistance. Under Stalinism, the forms of the market remained together with the forms of planning. In reality, there was neither plan nor market. Stalinism was a form of non-market market.

The idea of building socialism in one country, which is the essence of Stalinism, was always utopian. Paradoxically, it was the Stalinists who accused Marxists who refused to adapt to the Stalinist version of Marxism of being utopian. Socialism is a world system or it is nothing. It cannot come into being by accretion, step by step, any more than a baby can be born with a leg on one day and then with an arm on another day. The fact that it is difficult for a new society to be born does not mean that there is an alternative, a lower-grade form, which must be accepted.

CAPITALISM IN DECLINE AND THE IMPOSSIBILITY
OF THE SHIFT TO THE MARKET

Can there be a return to the market in the Stalinist countries?[15] Can capitalism in decline be restored to countries which have lost commodity fetishism? I have already laid the groundwork for answering this question in pointing out that modern capitalism lacks the forms of mature capitalism. Competition is limited, governments play crucial roles in running the economy, the needs-based sectors are large and increasing in size, the reserve army of labour is either small or non-existent, and money is nationalised and controlled by the state, even where there is a nominally independent bank. The question needs to be reposed, therefore, in terms of the possibility of moving from Stalinism to a declining form of capitalism. The relevant model of the latter can only be modern America, because that is the country on which the rest of the capitalist world is based. There the arms sector is absolutely central to the maintenance of the economy. The critical sectors of the economy, such as computers and cars, are run by a small number of companies. Competition is controlled. Most shares are held by insurance companies and pension funds, and the largest companies and banks are run by bureaucrats.

The shift to an economy of this kind from the economy that existed in the former Soviet Union would involve the maintenance of the arms sector as well as of the other large firms now existing. The only real difference would come from the millions of workers who would be dismissed as surplus. Such an enormous level of unemployment and indeed a reserve army would make Russia very different from the United States, which has official levels of unemployment around seven percent. In fact, the United States can only maintain its levels of unemployment by segmenting the work force into ethnic groups with controlled and patrolled areas of major towns. This condition does not exist in the former USSR. Therefore, it would be politically impossible to introduce such levels of unemployment there. Furthermore such a move risks destroying large sections of the elite itself and possibly the independence of Russia.

The shift to the market cannot but be injurious to the working class in Russia precisely because the market ideal is impossible in the modern world. It might be argued that a market must be retained until it is phased out under socialism, but such a market could only have any possibility of working to the degree to which its opposites were also present. In other words, the workers would have to establish control over the society and the elite, abolishing all forms of privilege. Under these conditions, a limited market might function provided it was gradually phased out. The alternative of a true capitalism must lead to confrontation with the working class. That is probably inevitable. Any programme which proclaims the need for the market without first discussing the abolition of the elite and all forms of privilege as well as the formulation of a rule that no one should receive more than the income of a skilled worker is both a utopian capitalism and anti-socialist.

CONCLUSION

Planning and value do not mix. In so far as they have done so, through Social Democracy and Stalinism, the mixture has lasted an historically short time. Though these two systems had different kinds of mixtures and produced different results, they have arrived together at the end of the road. Neither of them has any future. The market is utopian and its day is over.

NOTES

1. See for instance Diane Elson: "Market Socialism or Socialisation of the Market," *New Left Review*, 172, November–December, 1988, 3–44. Diane Elson has tried to develop a model of a socialist society using prices. It is clear that her view of a socialist society is one where a controlled market functions with wage labour.

2. J. P. Proudhon: *General Idea of the Revolution in the Nineteenth Century*, Pluto Press, 1989. See in particular the Introduction by Robert Graham, xxxiii. "Market socialism is but one of the ideas defended by Proudhon which is both timely and controversial." In the book itself he clearly defends the market even to extent of supporting a purer form of competition. He says: "To suppress competition is to suppress liberty itself." 50.

3. Karl Marx: *Grundrisse, Collected Works*, Vol 28 251: "... *wealth made in general exists only through direct forced labour, slavery, or through mediated forced labour, wage labour.*"

4. "Debate on the Subject of Political Economy," *Vestnik Kommunuisticheskoi Akademii*, no. 11, 1925, Moscow, 1925.

5. Alec Nove: *The Economics of Feasible Socialism*, Allen and Unwin, London, 1983. Nove was a Professor at Glasgow University who came with his Menshevik parents to the West in the early twenties when he was eight years old. Although brought up in the West, he was in close contact with liberal intellectuals in the East.

6. An earlier version of this paper was translated in Russian and published with a reply by M. Voyeikov preparatory for a seminar around the paper and reply at the Institute of Economics of the Academy of Sciences in Moscow, in December 1995.

7. See my paper on decline, in *Critique 26*.

8. See E. A. Preobrazhensky: *The New Economics*, Cambridge University Press, Cambridge, 1965.

9. See *Vestnik Kommunuisticheskoi Akademii*, vol. 2, 1925, pp. 357 ff.

10. *Dvenadtsatyi S'ezd PKP/b, Stenografischeskii Otchet*, Izd. Politicheskaya Literatura, Moscow, 1968, p. 313. Trotsky's speech at the 12th party Conference on the Scissors crisis described NEP as follows: "NEP is our recognition of a legal order for the arena of struggle between us and private capital." Earlier he claimed that the market was essential for all countries undergoing a transition to socialism. At the same time he made it crystal clear that it was the use of "methods and institutions of the capitalist system" which would be phased out as quickly as the new socialist methods of planning, centralization and accounting could be introduced. (P.310) For an account of Trotsky's views at the time and later, see: Ticktin and Cox: *The Ideas of Leon Trotsky*, Humanities Press, 1995.

11. Preobrazhenski, above citation.

12. L. D. Trotsky: "Speech at the 12th party congress." L. D. Trotsky: *Dvenadtsatyi S"ezd RKP(B)*, Stenografischeskii Otchet, Izd. Politicheskoi Literatury, Moskva, 1968 1968, p399–401: Trotsky argues that the Asiatic nature of Russia was crucial in establishing the importance of merchant capital, and that under NEP there is the ever present danger that merchant capital will provide the basis of a return to capitalism.

13. L. D. Trotsky: "Speech at the 12th party congress." L. D. Trotsky: *Dvenadtsatyi S"ezd RKP(B)*, Stenografischeskii Otchet, Izd. Politicheskoi Literatury, Moskva,

1968, p324–325: "We will face the need to dismiss male and female workers. . . . There can be no doubt that the disguising of unemployment represents
the worst, least real, and the most costly form of social security" (my translation).

14. Michael Albert and Robin Hahnel: *Looking Forward: Participatory Economics for the
Twenty-First Century*, South End Press, Boston, 1991 66–74.

15. For a more detailed discussion of the market in the USSR and the transition after
Stalinism, see H. H. Ticktin: *Origins of the Crisis in the USSR: Essays on the Political
Economy of a Disintegrating System*, Myron Sharpe Inc. New York & London, 1992;
"The Road to International Chaos." *Critique* 23, June 1991, 9–32; and "The
Growth of an Impossible Capitalism," *Critique* 25, May 1993, 119–32.

4

Market Mystification in Capitalist and Market Socialist Societies

BERTELL OLLMAN

I A LACK OF TRANSPARENCY

Amidst all the turmoil and exultation that marked the final days of the German Democratic Republic, an East German worker was heard to say, "What bothered us most about the government is that they treated us like idiots." In the capitalist lands, of course, people are first made into idiots, so when they are treated as such few take notice. The difference is one of transparency.

One major virtue of centrally planned societies, then, even undemocratic ones, even ones that don't work very well, is that it is easy to see who is responsible for what goes wrong. It is those who made the plan. The same cannot be said of market economies, which have as one of their main functions to befuddle the understanding of those who live in them. This is essential if people are to misdirect whatever frustration and anger they feel about the social and economic inequality, unemployment, idle machines and factories, ecological destruction, widespread corruption and exaggerated forms of greed that are the inevitable byproducts of market economies. But to the extent this is so, only a critique of market mystification will enable us to put the blame where it belongs, which is to say on the capitalist market as such and the class that rules over it, in order to open people up to the need for creating a new way of organizing the production and distribution of social wealth.

Most of the debate over the market has concentrated on the economy, particularly on the economic advantages and disadvantages (depending on who is talking) of organizing exchange in this manner. Relatively little attention has been given to the ideas and emotions that arise in market exchanges and their role in reproducing capitalism's problems, as well as in limiting the possibilities for their solution. Without wishing to minimize the importance of this economic debate, this essay is addressed to the latter lacuna. By viewing market ideology as the subjective side of a thoroughly integrated organic whole, however, I also hope to cast a clearer light on the nature of the market overall.

There are, of course, many institutions, conditions, and practises that serve as "factories of ideology." Among the busiest of these are the state, the media, the army, the family, the church, school, the workplace, and wherever it is that sport, entertainment and gambling go on. Capitalism uses all this to make the abnormal appear normal, the unjust appear fair, and the unacceptable appear natural and even desirable. To be sure, not all the ideas, values, etc. that come out of these other sites are compatible with market ways of behaving and thinking. Yet few people have allowed whatever contradictory pressures they feel—arising from religion, for example—to interfere with their buying and selling, or with how they rationalize either. With the explosive expansion of consumerism—of the amount of time, thought, and emotions spent in buying and selling, and in preparing for (including worrying about) and recovering from these activities—the market has become a dominant, if not *the* dominant, influence on how people act and think throughout the rest of their lives.

The market also stands out from the other sites on which ideology is constructed, with the possible exception of production itself, in relying more on actual experience than on teaching with words in producing its effect. We learn through what we see, hear, and feel, and especially through what we do and what is done to us, that is through our experience. This is because experience usually combines activity with perception and a stronger dose of emotions than accompanies just seeing and hearing on their own. In addition, the ideas that derive from our buying and selling appear to be privately confirmed every time—and that can be several times a day—such behavior succeeds in obtaining what it is we want. While the fact that everyone seems to be acting in the same way provides a certain public confirmation of their truth. Why else would they behave in these ways? How else could they behave? Few of the ideas we acquire during our socialization can count on this much support. The mystifications associated with the market, then, result mainly from people's experiences of buying and selling (and witnessing others buying and selling) from early youth, with the thousands of ads we absorb every year as children putting down the first foundations. The lies, omissions, and distortions laid on by what some have dubbed the "consciousness industry" only confirm and give finished form to the world view and more particular beliefs forged by personal involvement with the market.

II MARKET EXPERIENCES CREATE A MARKET IDEOLOGY

What do these market experiences consist of ? Before answering, we need to make it clear that what is called "the market" really refers to four inter-related markets, one for finished goods or commodities, one for capital, one for currency and financial instruments of various kinds, and one for labor power. In all four markets, individuals compete with each other to get as much money as they can for what they have to sell, and to pay as little as possible for what they wish to buy. Furthermore, it is obvious that there are important class differences in how people participate in these markets. Only capitalists, for example, buy and sell capital and currency, while labor power is sold exclusively by workers and bought chiefly by capitalists. And while everyone buys finished goods (naturally, not the same ones and not for the same price), most of the selling is done by capitalists, including, of course, small capitalists. Despite such dis-crepancies, however, there are remarkable similarities in the market expe-riences of people from all classes.

Among these are (1) buying is experienced as the only legitimate way to acquire what you want, and selling—whether labor power, capital, currency, or commodities—as the main way to obtain the money needed to buy anything. (2) Each person acts in the market as an individual rather than as a member of a group (corporations, though legal individ-uals, may be an exception, though their shareholders are not). (3) Each one decides for himself what he wants to buy and sell. (4) Choices are made largely on the basis of personal interests and felt needs. (5) Every-one can buy something, if he can pay for it, and everyone can sell some-thing, if he owns it. (6) No one actively restrains another when making or carrying out his or her choice. (7) The human quality that gets most attention in the market is thus the act of choosing, however watered down, and the rational calculation that goes into it.

(8) Everything that is sold is recognized as something that is not only owned by someone but separable from him (if he does not own it, he cannot sell it; if it is essential to his identity, he cannot part with it). (9) Everything and virtually everyone (if not yet everything about them) is found to be available for sale, as evidenced by the fact they all carry a price. (10) Because there is not always sufficient demand for the good one has to sell at the price one would like to get (or perhaps at any price), and because there are not always sufficient goods that one would like to buy at the price one would like to pay (or perhaps at any price), one is forced to compete with others in selling and buying anything. (11) To engage in such competition, let alone be effective in it, people become indiffer-ent to the human needs of their competitors—otherwise, learning that

another person's need for food, a job, a home, or a sale in business is greater than one's own would inhibit one's ability to compete.

(12) Workers, capital, landed property, and money are all seen to earn money which is then called "wages," "profit," "rent," and "interest" respectively. (13) As the medium by which prices are paid and goods obtained, money becomes everyone's prime want and the immediate object for which anything is sold. (14) With everything carrying a price, quite different things get compared on the basis of their relative cost. (15) People seek to amass as much they can, not only to buy what they want (whether now or in the future) but also to enjoy the power, security and status that money brings. (16) Given the generally inadequate amount of money that each of us has and the kind of competition we face, the outcome of most of our efforts in the market is highly uncertain (people can never be sure of getting what they want, no matter how badly they need it); the result is a deep seated anxiety that never completely disappears. (17) Yet, despite all the competition and individual decisions involved in buying and selling, a surprising equilibrium gets reached, so that the market not only appears to be just—because no one interferes with our choices—it also appears to work.

While not the sum total of what everyone experiences in the market, I take this list to contain what typically occurs in the buying and selling of capital, labor power, currency, and especially commodities. Repeated daily, long before most people hold their first job, these experiences produce a very distinctive view of the world. With the market occupying such a central place in people's lives, it is not surprising that how people behave there gets taken for what human beings are really like, and the same misuse of induction determines how most people understand the nature, the fundamental nature, of whatever else they encounter in the market.

Thus, human beings get thought of as atomistic, highly rational and egoistic creatures, whose most important activity in life is choosing (really, opting); because people choose without interference what they want (really, prefer), they are thought to be responsible for what they have (and don't have); the main relations between people are taken to be competition and calculated utility, where each tries to use others as a means to his ends; the world is thought to consist of things that can be bought with money, so that things come to be viewed largely in terms of what they are worth; the ability of capital, landed property and money to earn more money is considered a natural property of each of these economic forms, as evidenced in the expression "money grows interest" in money is understood as power without which nothing is possible, so that greed for money becomes perfectly rational; being allowed to do anything for money when you need some and buy whatever you want to when you have some serves as the paradigm for freedom (the market mystifies freedom by making one believe that one can do what one can't, and, when one does what one can, it makes one believe that one has done what one hasn't); equality is when others can do the same; people who fall out of the market, and to whom, therefore, these notions of freedom and equality cannot apply, are considered to be less than human; and the market is viewed as a marvelous, albeit mysterious, mechanism with a life of its own that works best when tampered with least.

What stands out sharply from even this brief summary of market thinking is that nothing that takes place in society outside the market or in the past history of society is introduced to account for any of the phenomena mentioned. But society is composed of a number of interrelated structures and functions. It is a system, and like any system, the parts, its functions, are mutually dependent. At a minimum, therefore, exchange must be examined in its interconnections with other economic and social processes to see how they effect one another. Similarly, society, as the sum of these processes, has a history; society has not always been what it is now, and learning how and when it acquired its present characteristics can reveal a good deal about it. In the case of market ideology, this would include learning what makes it so different from what proceeded it and from the beliefs and values advocated by virtually every religious and ethical system. Now, all this strikes me as being pretty obvious. It only requires restating because, without ever making it explicit, these are some of the elementary truths that the explanations of market phenomena which are suggested by people's experiences in the market would seem to deny. Welcome to the world of market mystification.

III MYSTIFYING PRODUCTION

By "mystification" I am referring to the kind of broad misunderstanding that results from the combination of hiding things, distorting them, misrepresenting them, confusing them, and occasionally simply lying about them. All these processes are to be found in the operations of the market. While everything in our lives can be said to be affected to some degree by our experience in the market, some things suffer far more mystification than others. The mystification of human nature, social relations, money, and freedom, which were mentioned above, are widely recognized, if not well understood. Less well known is the pervasive mystification of the whole sphere of production, which, in terms of its extended effects, may be the most harmful mystification of all.

As regards production, market mystification occurs in part by occluding the whole sphere of production from view, so that exchange seems to go on in a world by itself. We have just seen how the market gives rise to its own in-house explanations for whatever people experience there. To be sure, everyone knows that whatever is exchanged must have been produced. Yet, in the way most people are brought to think about this subject—with the aperture of our internal camera set extra-small—the market appears to be self-contained. Products are viewed as already "on the shelves." Production goes on, of course, but in the next room, as it were, and the door between the two rooms is closed. Hence, there is no need, no felt need anyway, to make use of what is happening in production to help explain any features of the market. And, even though the same person is both producer and consumer, one's life as producer would appear to be irrelevant to one's life as a consumer, so that the media often gets away talking about consumers as if they were not the same people who hold jobs in industry and offices.

The mystification of production doesn't end with ignoring its presence and downplaying, if not dismissing outright, its influence on what occurs in the market. Whenever production cannot be ignored completely, adopting the vantage point of the market for viewing it, dressing the actors in production in the clothes they wear in the market place, has a similar mystifying effect. In this way, work becomes something we only do in order to earn money to consume. Just as the capitalist, by hiring us, is seen mainly as someone who gives us the opportunity to do so. That work might have other uses connected to creativity and to transforming nature to satisfy human needs is never considered, because from within this perspective they don't appear. Viewing production exclusively from the vantage point of the market also makes it appear that the whole of production is directed to satisfying the wants of consumers, which makes production completely dependent on the market (hence, the theory of "consumer sovereignty"). It also makes it appear only natural that our form of society should take its name from the market, as in "free market society," rather than from production, as in "capitalist mode of production." Economics itself becomes a way of manipulating the factors that affect the market, and banks and stock markets, rather than the assembly line, become the main symbols of the economy.

A third way in which the market mystifies production is by foisting a model based on market relations onto production, so that people think of the latter inside a framework only suitable to the former. Do people confront one another in the market as individuals? Then the same must apply to production. Are individuals free to buy and sell as they want in the market? Then, the same must apply to their actions in the sphere of production. Operating with this model, each worker appears to be free to accept or reject any particular job, just as each capitalist appears to be free to hire or not to hire him. And the same freedom carries over once production has begun: a worker can quit and the capitalist can fire him. What is important here are individual preference, having a choice, and not being physically or legally constrained in exercising it.

If we examine production directly, however, without using the market either as a model or a vantage point, what do we find? We find people working together cooperatively to transform raw materials into useful goods, and experiencing most of their successes and failures collectively. The shared conditions in which production occurs move to the front of our consciousness. Marx is very emphatic that "If you proceed from production, you necessarily concern yourself with the real conditions of productive activity of men. But if you proceed from consumption . . . you can afford to ignore real living conditions and the activity of men."[1] Starting out from production, we also find a complex division of labor that ensures that people working on a wide variety of jobs all contribute to the common good. Yet, and this too emerges clearly: not everyone seems to be working. Some people, the owners of the means of production, are only giving orders, and doing that from afar.

Of all the main social groups to which we belong, class is the only one that is not immediately apparent and therefore obvious, which is why it is often confused with divisions based on income, status, culture, or consciousness (all of which are heavily, though not exclusively, affected by class). Referring essentially to the place a group occupies and the function it performs in a system of production, class is only observable and sense (Marxist sense) can only be given to its covering concept once that system of production is introduced.

What stands out, then, when production is approached directly is (1) the social nature of human life (it is our shared situation and qualities, and not our individual differences and preferences that come into focus); (2) the social division of labor along with the cooperation it requires and enforces; and (3) the class division of society between owners of the means of production and those who work on them, together with the domination of the former over the latter. By contrast, all of this appears very murkily, if at all, from the vantage point of the market or within a model based on market relations.

Production, too, of course, is not without its mystifying features. Under conditions of capitalism, it could not be otherwise. Competition for a job as well as on the job, for example, contributes to an atomistic view of self; just as selling one's labor power by the hour, in the absence of any appreciation of its value creating potential, helps stoke the illusion of equal exchange and therefore of "fairness" in economic relations. Compared to the market, however, production is an oasis of important economic truths, but taking the road that passes through the market is a sure way to miss them all.

Approaching the study of production directly, it is clear that workers and capitalists are locked into particular patterns of behavior by the very structure of their group relationship, and that this structure provides the essential context for examining whatever individual variations that do occur. Thus, while each worker may be free to decide whether to work for a particular capitalist, all workers are not free to decide whether to work for capitalists as a class, that is for those who control most of the jobs. The same thing holds true for the capitalist: though an individual capitalist may decide whether or not to hire a particular worker, all capitalists are not free to decide whether or not to hire workers as a class, that is, those who have the labor power needed to run their industries. Hence, Marx's insistence that workers are not employed by individual capitalists, but by the capitalist class as a whole. It is the relationship between *classes* and not *individuals* that preoccupies him.[2] If we examine the relation between these two classes as it unfolds in production, without passing through the distorting lens of the market, what strikes us immediately is just how unfree workers really are, how dominated they are by the capitalists.

While no one is actively restraining individual workers from doing what they want, the main conditions in which they live and work supply the real alternatives among which they must choose and apply the most intense pressures that incline them to make the choices they do. And the most important of these conditions apply to the entire class. Consequently, Marx can say, "In imagination, individuals seem freer under the domination of the bourgeoisie [i.e. the market] than before, because their conditions of life seem accidental; in reality, of course, they are less free, because they are subjected to the violence of things."[3] The impact of conditions is all the greater—hence, the "violence"—whenever, as is generally the case under capitalism, the extent of their influence is unrecognized.

IV HIDING EXPLOITATION AND ALIENATION

Only now are we in a position to grasp the account Marx gives of the workers' domination in capitalism in the overlapping theories of exploitation and alienation. Very briefly—though sufficient for our purposes—exploitation can be said to deal with the workers' loss of part of the wealth they create, while the theory of alienation deals with the workers' loss of self that occurs in and through the process by which exploitation takes place. Both theories focus on the common situation of the workers, on what they share as a class, and the same holds true for the capitalists.

For Marx, all the wealth of society is created by workers, who transform the stuff of nature into things that people want. In capitalism, workers receive a wage that allows them to buy back in the market a part of the wealth that they produced. The remainder, which Marx calls "surplus-value," stays with the capitalists and is the basis of their wealth and power. With their interest in maximizing surplus-value, capitalists do whatever they can to get workers to work harder, faster, and longer for less, since it is always the difference between the amount of wealth workers produce and the amount returned to them as wages that determines the share of wealth that goes to the capitalists. In our day, "exploitation" is usually used to condemn those employers who pay their workers too little or are otherwise very harsh with them, on the assumption (whether explicit or implicit) that if they were more moderate their behavior would be acceptable. Marx's criticism is directed against the entire class of capitalists, and is more in the nature of an explanation of how they acquire their wealth, which makes everything they do unacceptable, than a condemnation of occasional lapses in their behavior.

Individual workers and capitalists enter this picture only as members of their respective classes. To say, on this account, that a particular capitalist does not exploit his workers could only mean that he does not obtain any surplus-value from them, and this would signal the end of his career as a capitalist. So even kind capitalists are exploiters; they have to be if they wish to remain capitalists. Likewise, even well paid workers are exploited, necessarily so in so far as they are employed by capitalists, who—in order to stay in business—must extract surplus-value from them.

As a way of characterizing the relation of workers and capitalists in production, Marx's theory of exploitation offers a counter-model to the one provided by the market as well as an alternative vantage point for perceiving and thinking about the rest of society. Starting out from the market with its single-minded focus on the moment of exchange, the unequal relation of the class of workers to the class of capitalists never comes into view, so that from this perspective exploitation can only be treated as a matter of some capitalists taking unfair advantage in their dealings with some workers. Since what is "unfair" is a highly subjective judgment, the criticism contained in this use of "exploitation" is easily deflected. According to Marx, however, only in the "hidden abode of production" does exploitation occur.[4] Unfortunately, the approach that starts with the market hides the very elements in production that serve as the building blocks of Marx's theory of exploitation, making it impossible to perceive, let alone understand, what Marx is talking about.

While the theory of exploitation highlights the workers' relationship to the capitalists in the process of production, the theory of alienation focuses on what happens to the workers, to their human nature, in this same process. Marx's conception of human nature goes beyond the qualities that lie beneath our skin to include the set of distinctive relationships we have with our productive activity, its products, and the people with whom they involve us. As the necessary means of expressing and developing who and what we are as human beings (for what distinguishes us as a species also evolves), these relations are all part of Marx's broad notion of human nature.

What occurs in capitalist production is that the qualities, and mainly these relations, that mark us out as human beings are transformed in ways that diminish our humanity. Essentially a wedge is driven between key elements of an organic whole, so that they seem to exist and function independently. Thus, instead of controlling his own productive activity, this vital aspect of the worker's being is controlled by others who tell him what to do, how to do it, how fast to go, and even allow him to do it, or not (hire him and fire him). Instead of using his products as needed— and no matter how great that need is—everything the worker produces is controlled by those who use him to serve only their own interests. It follows that the worker's relationship both with capitalists, who control his activities and their products, and with other workers, with whom he is forced to compete for scarce jobs, cannot exhibit any of the mutual concern of which our species is capable. Separated in this manner from their productive activity, products, and other people, workers end up also being cut off from the potential inherent in our species (and therefore also a part of human nature) for evolving still further along the road away from our animal origins. Thus, capitalist production steals from workers not only part of what they are but also part of what, as human beings, they have in them to become.

Alienation, then, is domination in the form of dehumanization. It is a form of dehumanization that is particularly acute in the capitalist era. As with exploitation, it is the situation workers are in as members of a class, and not the special circumstances of an unlucky few, that accounts for the workers' loss, of surplus-value in the case of exploitation, and of self in the case of alienation. As in Marx's theory of exploitation, through mystifying the process of production, the market hides the class relations that frame the theory of alienation. With its emphasis on individual consciousness, market ideology offers in its stead a vague sentiment that anyone can have of being isolated and lonely, to which it attaches the label "alienation." Separating such feelings from their source in capitalist relations has led, on one hand, to treating the source as a mystery, and, on the other, to enormous efforts at quantifying these feelings in what passes today as social science. More importantly, by referring to a subjective reaction to our condition by the name that Marx gives to his explanation of it, the criticism contained in the latter is wholly diffused.[5]

If alienation, exploitation, and class itself are so thoroughly mystified by the market world view, we should not expect a better fate for class interests, and with one blow Marxism is deprived of the main bridge on which it crosses from critical analysis to revolutionary politics. Humanly diminished and materially deprived by the conditions of their life and work, workers have an objective interest in overturning these conditions, and a good deal of socialist politics takes the form of helping to raise workers' consciousness in this regard. For this effort to succeed, however, workers must be able, at a minimum, to view themselves as a class constituted by just such conditions. Otherwise, the subject that is said to possess these interests either disappears or assumes a form ("class" grasped as a category of income or culture) that directs workers' attention away from the conditions in which their objective interests are found. The capitalists' victory here is not achieved through argument. Working from a model of the market, the series of steps that lead to Marx's revolutionary politics are simply occluded from view.

V DISTORTING THE WHOLE OF SOCIETY, ITS REAL PAST, AND POTENTIAL FUTURE

Production isn't the only economic process mystified by market experiences and their accompanying ideology. Distribution and consumption suffer a similar fate. Distribution is the process by which each person acquires his share of society's wealth. As such, it determines not only what one brings to market to sell but what one must buy to satisfy pressing needs and interests. The existing division of wealth is largely a function of the class one belongs to in production, and whether that class earns a wage or extracts surplus-value. With production safely out of sight, however, distribution seems to depend on one's success in the market, a personal matter due mainly to effort, skill and luck. Being wealthy appears to be a result of having made a series of good choices in trading capital, labor power, or commodities, and being poor just the opposite.

Consumption stands at the end of the economic chain. It is when what is produced, distributed and exchanged is finally put to use. Approaching consumption from the vantage point of the market rather than that of production, consumption takes on the alienated form of "consumerism," where the creation of wants has priority over the satisfaction of needs, and use comes to be viewed as a means to exchange rather than its goal. Market thinking also tries to conflate exchange and consumption, going so far as to refer to the "exchanger," the one who buys and sells, as the "consumer." But exchange always involves money, and it is never money that is consumed. Neglecting to distinguish between exchange and consumption leads many people to miss the fact that a growing amount of exchange occurs in order to amass money and not to consume anything. Furthermore, what one consumes is largely a function of how much wealth one has acquired in distribution, which is mostly dependent on the position one occupies in production. With production hidden, however, and distribution viewed as a byproduct of the market, consumption too appears dependent on one's personal success (or failure) in exchange.

After distribution, consumption and especially production, it is probably the state and politics that suffer most from a generally unrecognized market mystification. People do a lot of thinking in areas they know relatively little about through analogies with subjects about which they know more. The market serves many people in this way when they consider politics. Thinking by analogy with the market—confident that their experience in the market, and the clear perceptions and strong emotions it gives rise to, have provided them with basic truths that can be applied anywhere—people tend to emphasize some features of our political life, while distorting and totally ignoring others. The role that each individual plays in voting (picking a candidate, just as one chooses a commodity in the market), the need for there to be more than one candidate to choose from, even if they are different versions of the same thing (as often happens with different brands in the market), and free elections, understood as being able to vote without being openly restrained, even if nothing of importance gets decided in the election (just as one has the formal right to buy in the market, even if one can't afford what one wants)—these are taken to be the main features of our political system.

The most respected voices in the academic world can only echo this popular wisdom. A leading representative of the currently in vogue

Rational Choice school, for example, maintains that "Voters and cus-tomers are essentially the same people. Mr. Smith buys and votes; he is the same man in the supermarket and in the voting booth."[6] The part that money plays in politics is seen, of course, if only dimly, but its power—as in the market—is taken as both inevitable and not such as to require any basic alteration in our democratic script. Current political dogmas, such as free trade and de-regulation, are also understood on the market model of removing restraints on individual choice and initiative, with little attention given to the inequalities of power and wealth that predetermine most outcomes.

What gets a free ride in this account of politics, unmentioned because unseen in any model derived from the market, are the class relations that underlie our political practises, and how most of our laws (including the Constitution), judicial decisions, and administration of laws are bent to serve the interests of the capitalist class. Instead of learning how the state benefits from and simultaneously helps to reproduce both exploitation and alienation, we get a civics lesson on the theme of one man, one vote. According to Marx, it is the relations between the owners of the means of production and the producers that "reveal the innermost secret, the hidden basis of the entire social structure" and with it "the correspond-ing specific form of the state."[7] In occluding production, the market hides the relationship between these classes in production and the crucial "secret" that this relationship reveals—that, despite all signs and assur-ances to the contrary, the game is thoroughly rigged.

Nothing is more important to the effective functioning of the state than the illusion that it belongs equally to all its citizens and is a neutral arbiter of justice. By encouraging each citizen to view himself as a dis-tinct individual without any necessary ties to anyone else, to understand freedom as the exercise of choice in the absence of overt restraint, to think about equality in terms of formal rights to exercise just this kind of free-dom, and above all, by neglecting class and the class differences that emerge from production, market thinking also plays a crucial role in producing as well as legitimating this illusion. Both our political processes and their real world outcome seem to be what people have freely chosen, rather than the biased results of unequal relations of power between the classes. It is the restricted range of possible laws that are given in the one-sided rules of the game by which we live, even more than their equally biased applications, that make our society—for all its democratic pretentions—a class dictatorship, the dictatorship of the cap-italist class. And in politics, as in the economy, the real limits set by rul-ing class interests on the actual alternatives between which we are forced to choose can never be investigated, because the class context in which they exist is itself invisible. Once again, capitalism's lack of transparency makes it virtually impossible for the people living in it to see who and what are responsible for the larger order problems in their lives.

By hiding and distorting what occurs in production, as we saw, the market interferes with our ability to grasp the social nature of man, the division of labor, and the constitution of classes. This in turn makes it impossible to understand either exploitation or alienation (and the workers' objective interest in doing away with both), to say nothing of distribution, consumption and politics. But the theories of exploitation and alienation also provide us with the best explanations for some of the more mystical ideas that arise from people's experiences in the market, so in mystifying production the market ends up by mystifying itself. For example, the quasi-human power that some things exhibit in the market, where capital produces a profit and money grows interest, in what Marx calls the "fetishism of commodities," is also attributable to the wealth that is first created by and then taken from the workers in alienated production. Where else would the new wealth embodied in profit and interest come from? When money is seen to grow interest, Marx says, "The result of the entire process of reproduction appears as a property inherent in the thing itself."[8] By hiding what occurs in production, it is made to appear that this new wealth arises as from within the very social forms that are responsible for how it is distributed.

Even the mysterious power of money to buy people's varied activities and products in the market is a function of the alienated productive activity that separates workers from parts of their own human nature. Marx refers to money as "the alienated ability of mankind."[9] More than a medium of exchange, its power reflects the abilities that workers have lost in transforming nature under alienated conditions of production. Though lost to workers, these abilities do not disappear. Instead, they become metamorphosed into a social quality of their product, its price, and an equally social quality of another material object, money, its ability to pay that price. As the ghostly form of living labor past, carried to its abstract limits and now in the hands of others, money can do what workers no longer can, which is to acquire all that workers have lost control over. Money's power grows with the extension of alienated relations, as the amount of production destined for the market and hence separated from its producers increases, and with it develops the social and political power of the class that possesses the most money. In capitalism, unlike earlier class societies, the chains that bind those who produce to the means of production are invisible. Indeed, most workers today believe they are free. Except in regard to money. There our chains do show, but where they originate and how they are applied remain a mystery. If the market often presents us with things that seem to dance on their own, a major objective of Marxist analysis is to specify with whom they are dancing, so we can place responsibility where it belongs.

The list of mystifications produced by the market is still not complete. For if exploitation and alienation account for some of the most puzzling features of the market, then the origins of the market are to be found in the history of these two conditions. It is in the development of exploitation and alienation, which Marx usually treats as essential parts of the rise of the capitalist mode of production, that we can discern the market's own past. But if exploitation and alienation are rendered invisible, it would appear that the market never originated, that it has no history, that it is frozen in historical time like a natural phenomenon.

Alternatively, abstracting the market from its roots in the capitalist mode of production can lead to doing a history of its lowest common denominator, which is trading. If one includes all human societies in which any kind or degree of trading occurs, the story stretches back a very long way. Andre Gunder Frank, who has made important contributions to our understanding of capitalism in his earlier writings, has recently traced market society understood in this way back five thousand years.[10] But by emphasizing the modest similarities between markets in all kinds of societies, the unique characteristics of the capitalist market are underplayed and left unexplained. As we saw, in capitalism most goods are not only sold on the market but produced with this aim in mind; huge markets also exist for labor power, currency, and capital; competition between buyers and sellers in all four markets has become the way people typically relate to one another; and money is blessed with the power to buy everything. The origins of these distinctive characteristics of our capitalist market are not to be found in the history of markets in general. How the market acquired its capitalist specific form is what we want to know, and for this we must look beyond exchange into the developments that took place in what has retrospectively been called the transition from feudalism to capitalism. This is why Marx calls our society the "capitalist mode of production," and why those who refer to it as "market society," or even "capitalist market society," by down-playing production in this way, are inhibiting us from acquiring an accurate understanding.

But the past contains the roots not only of the present but also of the future. So, still another mystification of the market is that by hiding production, which effectively hides exploitation and alienation, which in turn distorts our understanding of the market's own distinctive features

as well as their origins in the past—by hiding and distorting all this—
the market also hides its own potential for becoming something other
than it is. Everything that has its beginning in historical time is destined
to end as the conditions that gave rise to it can no longer be reproduced.
This applies to social systems as well as to people (and, as we are learning much to our horror, to natural systems too). By examining the conditions that led to capitalism and how difficult it is becoming to
reproduce them, Marx casts a prophetic light on the worsening problems
that will eventually cause—especially when combined with the disappearance of old solutions—the demise of the present system. At the same
time, he wants to draw attention to a variety of new conditions, opening
up new alternatives for society as a whole, that have emerged as part of
the same developments, which could become the basis of the system that
will follow.

Whatever force lies in Marx's projection of the death of capitalism and
the birth of socialism comes from his study of the capitalist mode of production organized around a set of overlapping contradictions, or mutually supporting and mutually undermining tendencies, that reach back to
the origins of the system. To have chosen another topic, or vantage point
for examining it, or way of relating what he found, or a shorter time
span—as so many critics of capitalism have—would have left Marx with
little more than hope for a better future. Instead, tracing the unfolding
contradictions in the capitalist mode of production, the most important
of which is that between social production and private appropriation
(sometimes referred to as the contradiction between the logic of production and the logic of consumption), Marx can expect, albeit modestly,
what other socialists can only hope for.

Marx's projections of where the contradictions he uncovered were
headed are only possible because his present was extended far enough
back into the past to include the trends and patterns of which the present
moment partakes and the pace at which change has occurred. Without
any analysis of the capitalist mode of production, of exploitation and
alienation, however, the market is deprived of a past, so that contradictions in the present appear as tensions or temporary disfunctions, and
lead nowhere. They don't get worse or better; they just are, and there is
no reason to expect them to change. Viewed statically, and apart from its
necessary ties to production, the market, then, doesn't seem to have a
future, in any case, not one fundamentally different from its present.
Conceived in this manner, whether we look forward or backward, the
market seems to be eternal, and socialism becomes an impossibility.

Finally, by mystifying the possible future of the market, as well as its present character and its real past, the market mystifies the kind of politics required to deal effectively with its own worst problems, to wit, social and economic inequality, unemployment, overproduction (relative to what people can buy), corruption, pollution, and recurrent crises. Working with an a-historical notion of the market, itself detached from developments in the sphere of production, these problems seem to exist independently of one another as well as of the system in which they arose. Capitalism's lack of transparence is greatest just where our need for transparence is most acute. With nothing more to go on than the form in which each problem presents itself, the solutions that are advocated usually involve getting those with power to change some of their practises, particularly as buyers or sellers of commodities, labor power and capital—to increase investment in poor communities, hire more workers, bribe fewer government officials, cheat less on quality and prices, etc.

The fact that Blacks, women, the handicapped, Native Americans, immigrants, the very poor, and workers are the chief victims of the problems mentioned has led many progressive non-Marxists to fight for more substantial changes in how the market operates, such as minimum wage laws, guaranteed jobs, community input into investment decisions, affirmative action, and so on, that would offer special protection or benefits to these people. The aim is not to get rid of the market, since this is considered impossible, but to reform it, to make it work for everyone, with the implication that this ideal state is attainable. Since the focus is on outcome—and suffering is so difficult to measure—there is no obvious way to privilege the claims of one aggrieved group over those of the others, unless, of course, you happen to belong to one of them. Class divisions, if mentioned at all, are understood mainly in terms of what people get rather than what they do, so that workers are viewed as simply one group among others that gets less than it should. Since many workers, especially unionized workers, are better off than a lot of people in other oppressed groups, there is no reason to give workers any special priority. Politically, this has led to the "Social Movement Strategy" of trying to create a coalition of all oppressed groups in order to secure a more just division of the pie for each of them.

Not so with Marx. Starting out from production, he is involved immediately with the interaction of classes and its effect on what happens in the market, including all the interrelated problems that arise with their accompanying injustices. The same analysis enables him to catch a glimpse of a non-market alternative germinating within capitalism itself that would resolve these problems and do away with these injustices. To alter, radically and permanently, the inequities associated with the market, therefore, requires overturning the workers' subordinate relation to the capitalists in production. Nothing else will do, or will do only a little bit, and that only for a short time before it gets reversed (as we see today). The political strategy derived from this approach gives priority to the working class—not because it suffers more than other victim groups—but because the particular form of its oppression (exploitation and alienation) gives workers both an interest and, through their position in production, the power to uproot all the oppressions currently associated with capitalism.

To abolish the conditions underlying their own exploitation and alienation requires that the workers do away with all forms of oppression. Treating everyone as equals is the only way the workers themselves can be treated as equals, without which no thorough-going reform is possible. Here, the workers simply cannot help themselves without helping others. This then is the politics of class struggle. Our final complaint against the market, then, is that it mystifies the politics of class struggle, both its centrality and its potential, as well as what's needed to make the workers (our side) more effective in carrying it out.

In drawing up this bill of particulars against market mystification, I may have made it sound more like a seamless whole than it really is. There are, after all, major contradictions in the operations of the market narrowly construed, such as that between the individual's freedom to choose and the restraint that comes from not having enough money to buy what one wants; or between wishing to sell one's labor power and not being able to find anyone who will buy it. Such contradictions bring many people to question market verities. Likewise, as I mentioned earlier, the experiences people have in other areas of their life, particularly in production—though always contributing something to market ideology because of the alienated context in which it occurs—also establish counter models and alternative rules of the game. These often stress the importance of cooperation, and clash head on with ways of thinking promoted by the market. And, of course, criticisms of the market, whenever they break through the sophisticated forms of censorship thrown up by our ruling class, can also help to undermine what we learn as buyers and sellers. If all these "countervailing forces" were not present, capitalism would not need such an imposing consciousness industry to reinforce the mystification that arises as a matter of course from our immersion in the market. Yet, overall, with the spread of market relations to all walks of life and their growing importance for our very existence as well as for an increasing number of our joys and sorrows, the market has become the chief mold in which most of humanity's worst imperfections are cast, just as the mystifications associated with the market have become the major ideological defense for the status quo.

VI WOULD MARKET SOCIALISM DO AWAY WITH MARKET MYSTIFICATION?

With the market responsible for so much mystification, which, in turn, contributes to so many of capitalism's worst problems, it would seem that socialists would be of one mind in wanting to abolish it as quickly as possible. Not at all. Instead, one of the strongest trends in current socialist thinking would retain a substantial role for the market in any future socialist society. To what extent does my critique of market mystification under capitalism apply to what its advocates have labeled "market socialism"?

There are different versions of market socialism. What makes them market societies is that buying and selling, however restricted, continue to go on for commodities and labor power and, in some versions, even capital. And money continues to mediate between people and what they want, as under capitalism. What makes them socialist is that the capitalist class has been removed from its dominant position in society. In the more popular version, workers own and/or control their enterprises and collectively, or though the managers they elect, make the decisions now made by the capitalist owner and his manager. The capitalists, as a distinct class, are either abolished or, in cases where a small private sector remains, have their power severely restricted.[11]

As co-owners of their enterprise, the workers, like any capitalist will buy raw materials, hire labor, and sell finished goods. Except for managers, these activities won't take much time, but the experiences they provide workers will be completely new. Selling their own labor power and buying commodities, on the other hand, will continue to take a lot of time and will offer many of the same experiences that workers have today. Furthermore, when the worker first applies for a job and is treated by the collective as an outsider, the fear and insecurity he will feel is all too familiar. The collective, after all, will only hire new people if it believes their work will increase its profit, or secure or improve its market share (ultimately reducible to profit). With this approach, the collective is unlikely to show more concern for the human needs, including the need for a job, of the unemployed and others in the community than businesses do under capitalism.

Even on the job, the interests of the individual worker and the interests of the collective do not coincide, for while he may wish to work shorter hours at a reduced pace the collective may force him to work longer and faster so that it can keep up with the competition, which will still be viewed as an impersonal power beyond human control. And, as in capitalist society, it will be the owner of the enterprise whose interests predominate. The worker's desire to reorganize his job in function of his interests as a worker will carry little weight in comparison with the profit maximizing interests of the collective, backed as it is by the logic of the market. In which case, the worker's actual experience in selling his labor power, even where he is part of the collective that buys it (and whatever soothing label is used to hide the reality of this exchange), will not be very different from what it is now.

The political scientist, Robert Lane, studied a number of worker-owned enterprises in capitalist society, and found that, while there was some increase in empowerment and in overall morale, this change did not produce the expected effect on the workers' quality of life or on their general satisfaction. What people actually do at work, their ability to use initiative and their own judgement, and how much of the process they control turn out to have a much bigger effect on their satisfaction than simply acquiring a new status as co-owners in a context that doesn't allow for major changes in work conditions. "Marx was right," Lane concludes. "The market economy is unfavorable to worker priority [treating workers' needs first] . . . because any costs devoted to improving work life in the competitive part of the economy make a firm vulnerable to reduced sales and profits because of the violation of the efficiency norm."[12] There is no reason to believe that the situation in market socialism, where enterprises are owned by workers—even with considerable democratic control—but market relations continue to operate, would produce a very different result.

In all versions of market socialism that I have seen, it is the market for commodities that changes least, but this is the market that is most responsible for the long laundry list of mystifications that I sketched earlier. The new relations of ownership do not affect the fact that it is individuals who will decide what to buy, and—like now—will compare goods on the basis of their price, and compete with others to get the best deal. They will constantly desire more money so that they can buy more, or have the power and status of someone who could. As now, they will worship money as something that gives them this power. And, in order to be more effective in the competition for goods and money, they will develop an indifference to the human needs of those with whom they are competing. Accordingly, they will view having a lot of goods and money as success, as now—never thinking they have enough; money will retain its mystery; and the greed and indifference people display in their dealings with each other will continue to be misconstrued as human nature.

Even the mystification of the production process, which leads to a whole series of mystifications under capitalism, would have its parallel in market socialism. Starting from the vantage point of the market or thinking with a model based on the market, production would still appear to be a relation between the worker as an individual and the owner of his enterprise, modified to some degree—to be sure—by the worker's additional role as co-owner. Consequently, grasping one's identity as part of a society-wide working class would continue to be an uphill struggle for most workers. If, today, the market's occlusion and distortion of production (and hence of class) makes it virtually impossible for people to acquire an adequate understanding of capitalism and to develop the class-based politics needed to overthrow it, under market socialism, the same cause will make it extraordinarily difficult to raise the workers' class consciousness, and especially their class solidarity, to the level required for socialism to work anywhere in society. It may be the oldest idea in socialism: each of us is his brother's keeper. For people to act upon this, however, they must really think of others as their brothers (and sisters), or, in this case, as members of the same class whose common interests makes them brothers (and sisters). Expanding a worker's sense of self to include others in his enterprise is a poor substitute for perceiving one's identity in an entire class, especially in light of the no-holds-barred competition between enterprises (and therefore between groups of workers) that would mark this arrangement.

The mystery surrounding money also gives no signs of disappearing under market socialism. Money, we will recall, only has the power to buy goods because the workers who produced them have lost all connection to them. In capitalism, having produced a good conveys no right to use it, no matter how great the need; nor do workers have any say in who can; nor can they easily understand why this is the case. The context in which workers have lost control over whatever it is that their labor has transformed is hidden behind the apparent independence of the final product on the market and the power of money to acquire control over it. All this applies equally to capitalism and market socialism. Even if a case can be made that exploitation no longer exists under market socialism because workers, as co-owners of their enterprise, belong to the collective entity that retains the surplus (the alternative interpretation is that the collectivity exploits the individual workers), it is clear that alienated relations of labor would remain substantially intact and with them the mystification and deification of money. The modifying influence that one would expect to come from workers electing their own manager is more than offset by the regime of production for the market and its pitiless logic of profit maximization.

What is new in market socialism, as I've said, are the experiences workers have as co-owners of their enterprise, and to the extent their relations with their co-workers are cooperative and democratic these experiences could be very empowering. As co-owners of an enterprise, however, their relations to those outside, whether they are people who are applying for a job, or those who represent other enterprises with whom they are in competition, or the final consumer of their product, are those that of a collective capitalist. Marx spoke of the cooperative factories of his day as turning "the associated laborers into their own capitalists."[13] With the aim of maximizing profits, workers, as collective capitalists, are likely to behave very much like capitalists do today, i.e. producing what sells, producing for those who have the money to buy and ignoring the needs of those who don't, cutting corners on quality and safety whenever they can get away with it, creating needs for their products—or for more products or for their brand of product—where they don't yet exist, and besting the competition in whatever ways the laws allow (and often in ways that they don't).

To the extent that workers participate in these activities directly, or even indirectly, they will share in far more than the profits that typically go to the capitalist class. By making workers into collective capitalists, market socialism adds capitalist alienation to their alienation as workers, and only modifies the latter slightly. Now, they too can experience the lopsided perceptions and twisted emotions, the worries and anxieties that derive from competing with other capitalists; they too can manipulate consumers and themselves as workers in quest of the highest possible profit; they too can develop a greed for money abstracted from all human purpose; and they too can turn a blind eye to the human needs of others. There is not much room here for acting as one's brother's keeper. Marx aptly characterized competition between capitalists as "avarice and war between the avaricious."[14] The same description would apply to competition between workers as collective capitalists in market socialism.

To be sure, there are some important differences between what is projected for market socialism and our own market capitalism. Any market socialist society is likely to distribute many goods, such as education, health care, and perhaps even some capital for investment, on the basis of social need and not enterprise profit. Likewise, one would expect "fairer" treatment for groups that are currently discriminated against, and a greater degree of cushioning for those who lose out in market competition. Still, the experiences people have selling their labor power and buying commodities, combined with the new experiences they have as co-owners of their enterprise, are likely to create ways of thinking and feeling that are very similar to what exists under capitalism. Also, as happens today, this mystification will spill over into other areas of life, into the family, into politics, into culture, and into education. The attempt to educate the people of this time in socialist values can have only modest results in the face of daily experiences in exchange that teach them other lessons. Confused about money, competition, human nature, and the market itself, about its real past and potential for change, people will neither be able to build socialism nor to live according to its precepts in any consistent manner.

Granting that a certain amount of capitalist mystification would continue under market socialism, defenders of this arrangement have argued that a balance of pro- and anti-socialist qualities could still be reached, and that the end result would be at least partly socialist. To decide this, we need to understand just what kind of mix is being proposed here, and how volatile it is. There are, after all, some things that mix quite well, like salt and pepper, and others that don't mix at all, like fire and water. As an attempt to mix opposite qualities, is market socialism more like salt and pepper, or is it more like fire and water? The same question can be directed at social democrats who favor a mixed economy, i.e. some private ownership operating under market rules and some public ownership operating under a national plan. In both cases, their advocates believe that a more or less permanent coexistence between socialist and capitalist forms is possible.

Neither market socialists nor social democrats, however, take sufficient account of the logic of the market and of what might be called the "dynamics of cognitive dissonance." The market, as I've tried to show, is not only a place and a practise but also a set of rules for a game that embodies this practise. As rules, it lays down goals, ways of attaining them, and a series of rewards and punishments for keeping players in line. Winning requires amassing money, which people can only do by investing capital and selling labor power and commodities. Competition with others turns what seems like standing still into falling back, so those with capital seek to expand it, moving into new areas whenever possible. This is necessary not only to increase their profit but, in the face of heightened competition, to maintain it. While everyone looks for what more they can sell. Acting otherwise is severely punished by material deprivation, unemployment, and bankruptcy. Worse, it makes no sense. The inevitable result is the spread of the market and market rules to take in more and more of what was previously declared out of bounds, including, in the case of mixed economies, areas once considered part of the public domain.

The market operates on the basis of what people are able to sell and can afford to buy, while the public sector is dependent on some estimate of social need. In a mixed economy, however, it doesn't take long before maintaining the health of the private sector gets interpreted as the most important social need. Wherever the market is given a privileged place and role in society, whenever the firms operating on market criteria are expected to provide society with a sizeable proportion of its jobs and goods, the state has no choice but to do whatever is necessary to enable the market to fulfill its role. Thus, in all mixed economies, the state assumes many of the costs of doing business (through subsidies, tax benefits, low interest loans, publicly financed training and research, i.e. "corporate welfare" of various sorts), minimizes some of its risks (through providing—often via the public sector and guaranteeing or simply protecting the most profitable opportunities for investing, buying, and selling), and tries to keep potential threats to profits under control (through anti-labor legislation and administration, and a foreign policy directed against competition from abroad). Private companies, whether owned by capitalists or by their own workers, have always required this kind of help, and have generally gotten it from social democratic as well as from liberal and conservative governments, since the need for a strong private sector has gone unquestioned.

More recently, with the enormous growth in production throughout the capitalist world, and therefore of capital to be invested and commodities to be sold, what was once enough help has proven insufficient, and governments in countries with mixed economies have been busy rearranging the mix to increase still further the size and advantages of the private sector. The progressive dismantling of the welfare state, deregulation, and the privatization of many previously public enterprises are the main forms taken by this rearrangement. For all the party battles won and lost in the political arena, this development has taken place essentially because of what the market is, because of its logic, the same logic that argues against the possibility of market and socialist features enjoying long term stability in any future market socialist society.

What of our market-inspired mode of thinking—is it compatible with the way of thinking, feeling and judging required for socialism to work? At its simplest, can people develop the mutual concern needed to cooperate effectively while maintaining the mutual indifference and lust for private advantage that makes them good competitors? While at any given moment, it is probably possible to find such contrasting qualities inside the same personality, the mix is an extremely volatile one. The time set aside to think "market thoughts" will simply spread to take in the entire waking day, not only because the problems toward which these thoughts are directed are never wholly resolved but also because the emotions that accompany them—especially the greed, the fear and the anxiety—cannot be turned on and off at will. Neither beliefs nor values nor emotions are easy to compartmentalize, and when they come into contact with their opposites a battle for dominance generally ensues. Cognitive dissonance evolves, and at least in this contest the victor is not in doubt. The political theorist, Robert Goodin, has argued convincingly that people's ability to respond to moral incentives (the kind that make socialism possible) diminish with the increase of material incentives, money and the like. "Base motives," he concludes, "drive out noble ones."[15] China provides us with a recent example of just how quickly and, it would seem, thoroughly this transformation can occur. As long as market ways of thinking and feeling receive daily reinforcement through people's experiences in exchange, the development of socialist sentiments, and hence socialist practise in any sphere, cannot proceed very far.

If market socialism cannot lead to socialism, how should we characterize those who advocate it? Before answering, it is important to recognize that the school of thinking that calls itself "market socialism" is further divisible along three different lines: (1) whether its goal, market socialism, involves only worker-owned enterprises, or a mix of enterprises, some worker-owned, some privately owned, some nationalized, etc.; (2) whether market socialism will eventually be followed by communism, or is itself the final stage of social development, and therefore as far as society can progress in a cooperative direction; and (3) whether market socialism can begin to develop now inside capitalism, or whether it requires a socialist revolution of some sort and a workers' government to get started (even though some socialist experiments exist today). Those who understand market socialism as a mix of worker and privately owned enterprises, consider it to be all that human beings can attain, and believe that we can begin building such a society right now inside capitalism are best viewed as reformers and not socialists, since their market socialism is really capitalist reform. A more accurate name for their goal is "economic democracy," and for them "radical democrats."[16]

On the other hand, market socialists who want an economy dominated by worker-owned enterprises, who view market socialism as a transition to communism, and who believe that a change of this magnitude requires a socialist revolution and a workers' government are clearly some kind of socialist.[17] But if the solution they intend is unworkable, they are best understood as utopian socialists and their goal a variety of utopian socialism. One of the leading market socialists, the philosopher David Schweickart, denies that market socialism is utopian, in part, because "it recognizes that at this stage in our development, none of our values can be perfectly realized."[18] The accusation, however, has little to do with how extreme one's vision is (dramatic changes do occur in society as in nature), but with whether it is realizable. The moderation of the market socialist vision doesn't save it from being unrealizeable and, hence, utopian.

VII SOURCES OF MARKET SOCIALISM'S PRETENDED SOLUTION

What remains to be explained is how market socialists, radical democrats as well as utopian socialists, have come to favor a solution that is both overly modest and unworkable. I believe that both faults arise out of their inadequate analysis of capitalism as well as of communism (as a post-socialist society), of socialism (as a post-capitalist society), and of the socialist revolution that serves as a bridge from capitalism to socialism. As for capitalism, I have tried to show that market socialists don't realize just how much of capitalism, of its practises and ways of thinking and feeling, and of its problems, are contained in its market relations, and, consequently, how much retaining a market, any market, will interfere with the building of socialism. Here, the fundamental error in their analysis is to identify capital with capitalists, the current embodiment of capital, and not see that capital, as a relation of production, can also be embodied in the state (as in state capitalism) or even in workers' cooperatives (as in market socialism). Capital is self-expanding wealth, wealth used not to satisfy wants but to create more wealth, satisfying wants only where this does so and developing new, artificial wants where it doesn't. What is decisive is its goal, and not who owns it. It is how capital functions in pursuit of this goal that gives our society most of its capitalist character and problems. The market, through which newly created wealth circulates allowing what initially takes the form of commodities to return to the owners of the means of production in the form of capital, is a more important feature of capitalism than is private ownership. Thus, ownership may be transferred to the state (as has occurred with national-ized industries in many countries) or to workers' cooperatives, but if the market remains essentially intact, so too will most of the problems asso-ciated with capitalism. Market thinking, as we saw, is produced by peo-ple's experiences in any market without regard to who owns the values that are exchanged.

As for communism, radical democrats and market utopian socialists are insufficiently aware of how different socialism as a transitional form must be from capitalism if it is to lay the foundations for the extraordinary achievements of full communism. To make this case, however, one would have to sketch out the communist future in more detail than is appropriate on this occasion, and, since most market socialists do not believe that communism is possible in any case, this line of argument is not likely to have much effect.[19] Not appreciating the necessary ties between communism and socialism, however, remains an important reason for the moderate reforms offered in the name of market socialism.

As regards socialism, market socialists, like most non-socialists, have generally confused planning in this era with the central planning that existed in the Soviet-style economies. Occurring after capitalism, a major pre-condition for the success of socialism, socialist planning has the advantage of advanced industrial and organizational development, a highly skilled and educated working class, relative material abundance, and a widespread tradition—however distorted and abused by the power of money and those who have most of it—of democratic decision-making. Unlike the situation that existed in the Soviet lands, there is a plentiful supply of goods and the material means, scientific knowledge, and skilled workers needed to make more. Consequently, most planning decisions, at least initially, are likely to be in the nature of revisions of the distorted priorities bequeathed by the market (to wit, too many large mansions and not enough public housing). There is no overriding need to build an industry from scratch. Advice from a cooperating public, computers and other modern communication technology, and, of course, repeated trial and error and correction of error will permit quick adjustments whenever necessary. Hence, there is little likelihood of making major miscalculations or of suffering much material deprivation when errors are made. I would also expect socialist planning to occur at various levels—nation, region, city, and enterprise as well as world-wide—so that many of the decisions that were taken by central planners in the Soviet Union would be relegated to planners on levels more in keeping with the actions required for the plan to succeed.

Equally important is the nature of socialist democracy as it affects the economy of this time. For the workers to function as the new ruling class, it is not enough that the government act in their interests. They must also participate in making crucial political decisions, and none are more crucial than choosing the economic planners and establishing the main priorities of the plan. I would expect debates on these matters to be an essential part of politics under socialism, as workers overcome their political alienation by realizing their powers as social and communal beings.

At this point, many readers are probably thinking—"But workers are not like that. They wouldn't want to get so involved, or, if they did, the result would be chaos." Enter the revolution—a successful revolution, since we are discussing what comes after capitalism. Market socialists don't seem to realize what an extraordinary educational and transformative experience participation in a successful revolution would be and consequently what workers in socialism will want to do and be capable of doing that most workers today do not and cannot. Like most people, market socialists are simply projecting the same personalities they are familiar with from their daily lives into the future. New conditions and experiences, however, bring out new qualities in people. Perhaps no lesson from Marx's materialism is more obvious; yet, there can be few things that are more frequently overlooked. Marx believes that taking part in a revolution is a mind and emotion expanding experience of the first order, with its greatest impact in just those areas that are crucial for the success of what comes afterwards.[20]

Given the enormous power of the capitalist class, for a socialist revolution to succeed, the majority of workers will have to become class conscious, which involves, among other things, understanding their common interests, developing greater mutual concern, becoming more cooperative, and acquiring a keener interest in political affairs as well as a stronger sense of personal responsibility for how they turn out. But these are the same qualities that make building socialism after the revolution, including democratic central planning, possible. Naturally, the more transparent society is at this time, a feature on which Marx insists, the easier it will be for people to carry out their socialist functions.[21] While mystified social relations, the result of continued market exchanges, will only confuse and otherwise undermine their efforts.

When we consider the favorable conditions in which socialist planning will take place and the altered character of the workers who will be involved in it, we can see just how spurious is the comparison that is so often made with Soviet planning. Would the workers in a post-capitalist socialist society give the planners the accurate information that they need? Would workers at this time exhibit the mutual concern necessary to provide help to those who are worse off? Would they have sufficient flexibility and understanding to make the needed compromises among themselves? Would workers then do their best to make sure that the plan, which they have played a role in making, succeeds? In his widely influential book, *The Economics of Feasible Socialism,* Alec Nove answers all these questions in the negative.[22] But his answers are drawn entirely from the experience of the Soviet Union, where workers had no input into the plan or into choosing the planners, and never felt themselves fully integrated parts of the social whole. There is little, if anything, however, to learn from the fate of undemocratic central planning functioning in a context of extreme scarcity, and with an increasingly skeptical and uncooperative working class, for a situation where none of these conditions will apply.

What market socialist analyses of capitalism, communism, socialism, and the revolution, almost without exception, have in common is the treatment of each period in virtual isolation from the others. Yet these periods are internally related. They are stages in a historical development, which is not to say that a socialist revolution, socialism, and communism are inevitable, but that they cannot be adequately understood, as possibilities, hived off from one another and from their origins in capitalism. This is as true looking back from each stage to what gave rise to it as it is looking forward to what comes after, understood as the realization of a potential (to be sure, not the only one) already present in the preceding form. What each period has drawn from earlier stages and the potential it contains for what is to follow are as much a part of what it is as its more directly perceptible qualities. Indeed, past, present, and future are so interlinked in all that conditions us that they cannot be completely separated from one another without serious distortion. Hence, no attempt to fully grasp capitalism or any of its succeeding stages can forego examining all of these stages in their interconnections.

If capitalism, socialism, and communism are internally related stages in a historical evolution, the preferred vantage point for beginning an analysis of socialism, or any of its important features, is capitalism, giving special attention to the problems it poses for socialism and the material preconditions it establishes for solving them. An approach to socialism that begins with an analysis of the market under capitalism involves one immediately with the market's organic ties to the accumulation of capital, exploitation, alienation, and class struggle. Having established the essential identity between capitalist relations and market relations, it is impossible to conceive of the market as a neutral means for carrying out social policy under market socialism. The same approach makes it very clear how the market, so construed, is responsible for many of our society's worst problems—economic crisis, unemployment, extremes of wealth and poverty, ecological destruction, exaggerated greed, corruption, etc.—and that these problems will remain and continue to grow until another means is found for distributing our social wealth.

Marx stands out from virtually all other socialist thinkers, however, in insisting that capitalism not only makes socialism necessary, it also makes socialism possible. Starting out to investigate socialism from the side of capitalism, therefore, has an additional advantage in that it enables us to give due weight to the enormous achievements of capitalism as well as to its failures in influencing the shape of the future. In the area of the market, the most important of these achievements include advanced distribution and communication networks and the technology needed to make them work, established patterns of resource allocation, extensive planning mechanisms within private corporations and public agencies, the organizational skills of all the participants, and, of course, the vast amounts of wealth already in the pipeline as well as all the material factors required to produce much more. The possibility of economic planning in socialism cannot be fully understood, let alone evaluated, apart from its necessary preconditions, which, like the main problems to which such planning is addressed, are an inheritance from the capitalist society that preceded it. All this, and more, leaps out at anyone who begins an analysis of socialism from the vantage point of its origins in capitalism.

Market socialists, on the other hand, almost without exception, approach the question of the market in socialism from the vantage point of the failures of the Soviet-style regimes. It is no coincidence that market socialist thinking has become so widespread at just this moment in history. Starting from an analysis of what went wrong in the Soviet Union (even when the point is not belabored), they move directly to economic reforms that, in their view, would avoid the worst of the errors that were made there. If planning seems to have been at fault, the solution can only be to replace the plan with the market.

Though mention may be made (usually late in the discussion) of the problems associated with the market in capitalism, market socialist reforms are not directed to these problems, or are only to a modest degree. But why should reforms that were tailored on the measures of the Soviet Union fit our own very different reality? Only on the assumption that all the problems treated are of an equally general character does this make sense. To make it appear that market socialist solutions to the problems of a faulty socialism would apply to our situation, the historically specific character of the Soviet-style system gets abstracted out, leaving a flattened landscape of social features that are found everywhere. With this methodological sleight of hand, the problems of distribution in general are then seen to require the same market-oriented reforms, irrespective of the distinct needs and possibilities of each social system. All the advantages that we would possess in trying to build socialism in a post-capitalist society are simply ignored, because from the vantage point from which the market socialists begin their investigation these advantages do not appear. Contra market socialist doctrine, it is not a faulty socialism that needs to be replaced by a well functioning socialism, but capitalism that needs to be replaced by socialism, and the only place to look for what this can mean is within capitalism itself.

But it is precisely these temporal connections along with more systemic ones that exist on each stage of society that are hidden and/or distorted by market-induced ways of thinking. By obscuring, altering and otherwise trivializing the essential links that constitute our social whole, market mystification—whether of the capitalist or market socialist variety—dooms the individual to misunderstand what is, was and could be. Market socialists, it would appear, are victims of the very market thinking—formed by their own experiences in the market, with the addition, no doubt, of some academic frills—that they would perpetuate into the future. They have succumbed to capitalism's main ideological defense, which is the price they pay for having been too successful in ignoring it.

None of the above should be taken to mean that capitalists are any less fearful of market socialism than they are of the real thing. The owners of capital don't distinguish between different kinds of "thieves." They don't care how the people who want to take away their wealth say they will use it. If their criticisms of socialism sometimes indicate otherwise, this is because it is difficult to defend what one has with the argument that one simply wants to keep it. Yet market socialism has often been presented as if retaining a market and taking people as they are would reduce capitalist antipathy and make the transition to socialism an easier one. While organizing a few worker cooperatives, especially in previously bankrupt firms, is acceptable, replacing the present class of capitalists is not. Hence, market socialism will meet the same total opposition that capitalists have always directed against socialism. It follows that only a socialist revolution (using democratic processes wherever possible) that removes capitalists from political power could bring about the kind of change that market socialists desire.

In revolutions, however, people undergo dramatic changes, and, if a revolution in an advanced capitalist country is to succeed, people will have to develop, as I've argued, many of the same qualities that are called upon in building a socialist society. Thus, the kind of reforms that may appear sensible today, based on people remaining pretty much as they are, will appear much less so then. The market socialist suit tailored for today's measurements will no longer fit. New human beings who know how to cooperate and want to do so will make full socialism possible. The same developments will also make it infinitely preferable to any market socialist alternative which could only strike the people of this time as an unwieldy compromise with the past. So, if today market socialism is merely impossible, tomorrow (or the day after) it will also be unnecessary.

Unfortunately, what is unnecessary and even impossible is not without its effect on people's thinking and, therefore, on the class struggle. At the present time, capitalism's central problem of finding sufficient opportunities for profitable investment and new markets for the rapidly growing amount of value that is produced has reached critical proportions. This has forced the capitalist state to expand its role in serving capital not only in the traditional areas of repression and socialization, but in such economic tasks as the accumulation of capital and the realization of value—to the point where President Bush can make a special trip to Japan to boost American auto sales. However, by making the state's necessary ties to the capitalist class that much more evident, this has greatly increased the state's and, indeed, the whole system's need for effective legitimation. And nothing legitimates capitalism as much and as effectively as the mystifying rationales generated by our daily activity in the market. In this context, advocating market socialism, with its suggestion that there are good markets and bad ones, can only confuse people further, and undermine their efforts to perceive the market in its internal relations to production, exploitation, alienation, and politics, which is the only way they will ever be able to grasp the full nature of our problem, its origins, and its possible solution.

A frontal, no-holds barred attack on the market and all its ills, which now includes the horrific experiences of the newly marketized societies, is an absolutely indispensable means of developing socialist consciousness. People's turn to socialism will only emerge out of the rejection of all market relationships. No one lacks for painful experiences in the market, and more and worse are on the way, but a clear understanding of the responsibility of the market in its internal relation with capitalist production still eludes most people. Our task, therefore, is not to blur the edges of what the market is and does, as occurs with the proposals for market socialism, but to offer an analysis of the market that helps people make the connections that are necessary to engage in effective class struggle. Leaving most market mystification in place, market socialism cannot be viewed as just another form of socialism, or even a compromise with capitalism. It is a surrender to capitalism which for historical reasons continues to fly the socialist flag. It is an ideological facet, however well intentioned in the minds of individual market socialist thinkers, of the social problem for which we seek a solution, and must be criticized as such.

A brief word on the applicability of my critique to third world countries that have tried to construct their own versions of market socialism. There is no question but that all my criticisms of the market—if only a few of my complimentary remarks (since these were all directed at the more democratic features of market socialism)—apply to these countries, as the recent experiences of China and Vietnam make abundantly clear. But it is also evident that these countries do not possess the material and social preconditions, such as we do in the advanced capitalist world, that would make socialism possible. The intentions, however admirable, of some socialist political leaders cannot substitute for a practise that history has placed beyond their reach. The real choice for these societies, therefore, would seem to be between a dictatorial form of savage capitalism, with socialist trimmings (China), and a progressive, egalitarian, anti-imperialist dictatorship, with different socialist trimmings, that is neither capitalist nor socialist (Cuba). If the political dictatorship is not too severe, I favor the latter option if only because social and material benefits are shared more equally under such regimes, other social problems associated with the market are either missing or minimal, and the anti-imperialist foreign policy that these regimes generally follow creates difficulties for the worldwide rule of capital. Only socialist revolutions in the advanced capitalist lands, however, could create the conditions that would enable the underdeveloped countries whose regimes have declared in favor of socialism to make substantial progress in this direction.

VIII MARX ON CO-OPS BEFORE AND AFTER THE REVOLUTION

It would appear that in making the case against market socialism I am simply elaborating on the position already taken by Marx, but even this is now contested. The arguments of market socialists seem to have progressed from claiming that the market is more efficient than central planning, to claiming, in the aftermath of the collapse of the Soviet Union, that nothing else will work, to claiming, because of the presumed relationship between planning and bureaucracy, that the market is more socialist, and—most recently—then to claiming that Marx himself was a market socialist.[23] For those who discount Marx's views on socialism, of course, this latter claim may be of little interest, but we who accept Marx's broad analysis of capitalism, including its potential for socialism, cannot dismiss it so easily.

The assertion that Marx, himself, was a market socialist seems to derive mainly from a confusion over two matters: Marx's generally favorable reaction to workers' cooperatives in capitalism, and his belief that a restricted market would continue to operate for a brief period after the socialist revolution. In so far as workers' co-ops gave workers more power over their work lives and strengthened the ties of solidarity between workers in the same enterprise (and in this way reduced some of their alienation), co-ops were obviously a good thing. In capitalism, those who own enterprises decide what to make, what to charge, who to hire, what to pay them, and so on, and this applies whoever the owners are. As we can see, the market is assumed here. If one tries to retain these powers for workers in each enterprise under socialism, the market would remain, and there would be little scope for large scale economic planning. Is this Marx's vision of a socialist society?

Marx did say that "To save the industrial masses, cooperative labor ought to be developed to national dimensions and, consequently, to be fostered by national means."[24] But he also claimed that cooperative enterprises "make the associated laborers into their own capitalists, i.e. by enabling them to use the means of production for the employment of their own labor."[25] Just earlier, in this same work, he noted that the organization of workers' cooperatives "reproduces and must reproduce . . . all the shortcomings of the prevailing system."[26] Does this sound as if Marx is speaking about socialism or capitalism?

Marx recognized that late capitalism might develop an extensive network of workers' cooperatives. Both the rise of the credit system and the greater efficiency of workers' co-ops (workers as collective capitalists were very effective in exploiting themselves as workers) made such a scenario possible.[27] To the extent co-ops were established, they would also provide important evidence that workers are capable of running the economy on their own, and that the capitalists, as a class of owners, are not essential to the production process. Not only could industry be run without them, but, this being so, capitalists deserve none of the wealth and power that now go to them for doing what they insist only they can do. In this way, workers' co-ops help bolster arguments to the effect that socialism is both possible and "just," but, apart from the workers' greater participation in economic decision-making, they provide few indications of what socialism would actually be like.

What we have in Marx's comments on workers' cooperatives is an alternative scenario to the one he usually presented for late capitalism. As we know, Marx believed that capitalism was already sufficiently developed for a socialist revolution to occur, if not in his lifetime then shortly thereafter, and it is this possibility that received most of his attention, both scholarly and politically. If the revolution did not take place in what was for him the near future, he foresaw the further development of a number of trends that were already well underway. One was the trend to monopoly capital, another to corporate capital, another to managerial capital, another to capital becoming more and more of a world system, and another to workers' co-ops, as increasing numbers of workers became their own capitalists. None of these developments did away, or could do away, with exploitation, alienation, economic inequality and recurring crises—overall these problems got worse—or the need for a socialist revolution to resolve them.

While the new status a worker acquires in becoming part of a cooperative does nothing to alter his need for a socialist revolution, it could seriously dampen his desire to join in it. Aware of this, Marx was very critical of his socialist rivals Ferdinand Lasalle's plan to have the state finance workers' co-ops.[28] And when the German Chancellor, Bismarck, indicated he might support the idea, Marx polemicized against it, saying it is "of no value as an economic measure, while at the same time it extends the system of guardianship, corrupts a section of the workers, and castrates the movement."[29] Later Engels suggested that Lasalle's proposal of state-aided co-ops originated with the bourgeois republican, Buchez, who first put it forward in France in the 1840s as a way of undercutting the socialist movement.[30]

Marx's worry was that, in placing workers in the same relation to capital as capitalists, workers' co-ops provide workers with many of the same experiences as capitalists, and thus with many of the same ideas and emotions, however modified by their other experiences and interests as workers. The resulting mix—except perhaps on those occasions when as collective capitalists they go bankrupt and as workers they lose their jobs—is not conducive to their engaging in revolutionary activity. Our overall experience with the political activity of workers in workers' co-ops over the last hundred years suggests that Marx's fear was not unjustified. For all the progressive qualities Marx saw in workers' co-ops and for all the support this economic arrangement gives to some important arguments for socialism, Marx did not believe it provides us with either a model for socialism or a useful strategy to pursue in the class struggle against capitalism.

Besides misunderstanding Marx's qualified praise for workers' co-ops in capitalism, the claim that Marx was a market socialist rests, as I have indicated, on a misreading of his treatment of the market under socialism. Here, market socialists who claim Marx for their side appear to have run together the answers to three different questions: (1) Is the market to be completely abolished immediately after a workers' government assumes power? (2) If some kind of market continues to exist at the start of socialism, how will it be dealt with and how long will it last? (3) Will the market continue to exist throughout the socialist stage as the socialist form of allocating resources and exchanging goods? What has happened, in effect, is that the answers Marx gives to the first two questions have been mistakenly treated as answers to the third question, which refers to the long term (and not so long term) compatibility of the market with socialism.

As regards the first question, it is quite clear that Marx foresaw substantial sections of the market continuing to function right after a socialist revolution. In the *Communist Manifesto,* for example, his suggestions for what the new socialist government should socialize immediately are surprisingly modest—banks, means of transport and communication, and unused land.[31] This leaves most of the economy in private hands, at least initially, but the owners' decisions on all matters would be strongly affected by the economic plan (which is established at the same time), the newly nationalized banks, new laws on such things as wages, conditions of work, pollution, etc., an administration and adjudication of these laws that is now biased on behalf of the workers, and by their own workers.[32] The only forceful expropriation Marx advocates—indeed, his only explicit reference to the use of force in this period—is of "rebels" (people who take up arms against the government) and "emigrants" (those who leave the country). It is clear that at this at point in time, markets for commodities, labor power, and even capital, though already regulated and modified, continue to operate.

The crucial question, then, is how will the socialist government deal with this private sector? Marx says that in the first stage of communism, his preferred manner of referring to socialism, a worker will receive, "after deductions have been made for new investment exactly what he gives . . . his individual quantum of labor."[34] It is the workers, we will recall, who through democratic planning help decide what these deductions will be and how they will be used. Contrast this projection with how profits are distributed under market socialism, where there is no direct connection between the number of hours worked and the amount of wages earned, and where, consequently, workers who put in the same number of hours in different enterprises can earn widely varying amounts.

With equal pay for equal time at work as the economic goal, every effort is made to enable people to develop a broad range of abilities and to make full use of those they have. But, as we have seen, at the very start of socialism, there are still some people who will be allowed to take from what society produces according to their property and not according to their work, which will also allow them to participate in production with something less than their full ability. This major exception to the economic principle that governs socialist society will probably last as long as it takes for a transfer of their private property to public ownership in a manner that will not disrupt the production process. To achieve this end, the socialist government will set up public enterprises to compete with the remaining private ones (not to help subsidize them as usually happens in capitalism), as well as to put pressure on the latter through targeted bank loans, high taxes, and strict laws.[35] The combination is likely to drive most capitalists to bankruptcy or to sell their companies to a public authority in a relatively short time. One of the major reforms Marx believes will occur immediately after the revolution is the abolition of inheritance in wealth producing property.[36] When the current generation of private owners dies out, therefore, their companies would all revert to the public. As a result of this and the other strategies mentioned, within forty to fifty years, at most, the entire economy will be socially owned. Pressure brought by workers in the private sector to socialize their enterprises would, if anything, speed up this process.

What emerges from even this brief sketch is that a substantial private sector would continue to exist for a short while after the revolution and that it would allocate resources and exchange goods through some kind of market. Like all markets, it would create a market mode of thinking, with its accompanying range of mystifications, and people's activities in this market would be the main source for whatever alienation still exists. Fortunately, people's experiences in other areas of their lives at this time will produce many ideas and emotions of an opposite kind, and, with the constantly expanding socialized sector of the economy, it is these experiences that are becoming dominant. In the unstable mix of perceptions, ideas and emotions that survive into the beginnings of this new era, what ensures the eventual ascendance of a fully socialist mode of thought is an increase of communal and cooperative experiences of all sorts, the replacement of humanist for capitalist values in education, the extraordinary developments throughout society that are making socialist goals ever more practical and therefore easier to envision, and the steady momentum maintained in the movement toward these goals.

It is only after all property in production is brought under the control of the entire working class that socialism can be organized according to the principle, "From each according to his ability, to each according to his work." We are still a long way off from the time when the applicable principle is "From each according to his ability, to each according to his need."[37] In short, it is only now that socialism, or what Marx usually refers to as the "first stage of communism," really begins. If socialism is a transitional stage to communism, the conditions for which it progressively lays out, the first few decades after the socialist revolution can best be understood as a transition to socialism. As a transition, it contains something of both capitalism and socialism, but it is too short and it changes too quickly to be considered a separate stage. This period might also be viewed as a distinctive "moment" at the very beginning of socialism, a moment when the final prerequisites for socialism are being put into place (based on the conditions brought about by a successful working-class revolution), or, alternatively, as a continuation of the socialist revolution itself, a kind of mopping up operation directed against the last vestiges of capitalist power and privileges using tactics in keeping with the fact that the state is now in the hands of the workers. Carrying the class struggle into this first moment of socialism, in each country and around the world, is what Marx had in mind by the "permanent revolution."[38] Does Marx believe, then, that some form of market will continue to exist throughout the socialist period? Clearly not. Readers who took my critique of market socialism as reflecting Marx's own position on this subject can rest assured. Their first impression was the right one.

IX CONCLUSION

In the first half of this essay, I argued that, as compared to all other civilizations, capitalism suffers from a remarkable lack of transparency. While slaves, serfs, and even workers in Soviet-style command economies have no difficulty seeing who is doing what to them and why, the same cannot be said of those who produce the wealth of capitalism. Mainly responsible here is the capitalist market's role in developing a set of beliefs and way of thinking which—while highly functional in acts of exchange—also succeeds in mystifying most of the rest of capitalist society, emphasizing, in particular, a sense of freedom that hides far more than it reveals. The most serious impact is felt in the sphere of production, since it is there that the class character of society stands out most sharply, and in the exploitation and alienation that underlies the current operations of the market as well as its real history and potential for future change. I tried to show that by distorting and occluding this whole range of phenomena, market mystification serves as the main ideological defense mechanism of capitalist society.

The second part of this essay critically examines the idea that it is possible to build a socialist society while retaining the market as the chief means for distributing goods. In summary, I have made ten criticisms of market socialism, understood as a theoretical and political project within capitalism as well as an alternative vision of socialism. (1) Market socialism makes an unjustified and mischievous separation between the market and the rest of society, especially production, and between socialism and the periods immediately preceding and following it. (2) By retaining a version of the market in socialism, the lack of transparency so characteristic of capitalist conditions is carried over into socialism, and the mystification that comes from people's experiences in the market is left untouched. Without a clear understanding of their social and economic relations, workers will not be able to construct a socialist society. (3) Market socialism also won't work as a form of socialism, because, in retaining a market, it continues capitalism's main contradiction between social production and private appropriation. This ensures a continuation of most of capitalism's ills, including periods of economic crisis, along with a working class too mystified to deal with them.

(4) Even if market socialism could work, or to the degree that it might, it wouldn't be much of an improvement over the current situation, since alienation would still exist, with workers, as co-owners of their enterprises, acquiring some capitalist forms of alienation to go along with the modified forms of others that they already possess. (5) Even if market socialism could work, or to the degree that it might, by continuing the practise of using money to ration goods, it would retain many of the inequalities of the present system. (6) Unfortunately, or fortunately, market socialism is impossible as a compromise with capitalism, because capitalists, who would lose out in such a reform, will fight it with the same tenacity that they would real socialism. (7) If market socialism is impossible in existing conditions, it is also unnecessary after a socialist revolution, when these conditions and the character of most workers will have changed dramatically. (8) As regards the possibility of full socialism, it is important to recognize that the market socialist critique of central planning is based almost entirely on the less than relevant experience of the Soviet Union (and usually a caricature of that), and on the unrealistic assumption that workers after a successful revolution will be no different than the workers of today. (9) As regards its political role in the current period, market socialism undermines the radical critique of capitalism required for effective class struggle by confusing people about the nefarious role of the market. (10) Finally, for those interested in Marx's views on this subject, it is clear that Marx was unalterably opposed to market socialism.

Mystified by their own experiences in the market, disappointed by the collapse of the Soviet Union that many market socialists had regarded as a form of socialism, forgetful of whatever they may once have understood of dialectical relationships within complex systems, and reaching for a quick and easy fix to problems that don't allow any, market socialists have come to treat the market as a simple mechanism that can be fashioned at will to produce a desired effect.[39] But even if we view the market as a mechanism or instrument, the crucial question is—is it more like a can opener or a meat grinder? The one is in our hands and we manipulate it; while we are in the other and it manipulates us, and worse. The sound bite version of my conclusion, then, is that market socialists have mistaken the market for a can opener, when it really functions more like a meat grinder.

NOTES

1. Marx, Karl, and Engels, Frederick, *The German Ideology*, Parts I and III (Lawrence and Wishart, London, 1943), p.164.
2. Marx, Karl, *Das Kapital*, vol. I (Dietz, Berlin, 1967), p.599.
3. Marx/Engels, *The German Ideology*, p. 774.
4. Marx, Karl, *Capital*, vol. I, trans. by S. Moore and E. Aveling (Foreign Languages Publishing House, Moscow, 1958), p.176.
5. For a fuller account of Marx's theory of alienation, see my book, *Alienation: Marx's Conception of Man in Capitalist Society* (Cambridge University Press, 1976).
6. Tullock, Gordon, *The Vote Motive* (Institute for Economic Affairs, London), p. 5.
7. Marx, Karl, *Capital*, vol. III (Foreign Languages Publishing House, Moscow, 1959), p. 791.
8. Ibid., p.384.
9. Marx, Karl, *Economic and Philosophical Manuscripts of 1844*, trans. by M. Milligan (Foreign Languages Publishing House, Moscow, 1959), p.139.
10. Frank, Andre Gunder, and Gills, Barry, *The World System: 500 or 5000 Years* (Routledge, 1993).
11. For the most forceful presentation of this position, see Schweickart, David, *Against Capitalism* (Cambridge University Press, 1993). An alternative version of market socialism that has received considerable attention favors distributing shares of larger enterprises to the entire population, and would have workers sit on the boards of their enterprises along with representatives of the shareholders and of the nationalized banks. Roemer, John, *A Future for Socialism* (Harvard University Press, 1994). For still other models of market socialism, see Roemer, John, and Bardan, Pradham, eds., *Market Socialism: the Current Debate* (Oxford University Press, 1993).
12. Lane, Robert, *The Market Experience* (Cambridge University Press, 1991), pp. 333–4.
13. Marx, *Capital*, vol. III, p. 431.
14. Marx, *1844 Manuscripts*, p. 68.
15. Goodin, Robert, "Making Moral Incentives Pay," *Policy Sciences*, vol. 12 (1980), p.139.
16. Among the leading figures associated with this approach are John Roemer (cited above) and Miller, David, *Market, State and Community* (Clarenden Press, Oxford, 1990).
17. The more socialist of the market socialists include David Schweickart and James Lawler. The clearest statement of their views appear in this volume.
18. Schweickart, David, "Market Socialism: a Defence," in this volume.

19. I have tried to provide such detail in an article, "Marx's Vision of Communism," reprinted in my *Social and Sexual Revolution: Essays on Marx and Reich* (South End Press, 1978), and in my book, *Communism: Ours, Not Theirs* (forthcoming).

20. Marx, *German* Ideology, p. 69.

21. Marx believes, "The life process of society . . . does not strip off its mystical veil until it is treated by freely associated men, and is consciously regulated by them in accordance with a settled plan." When that occurs, "The social relations of the individual producers, with regard to both their labor and its products, are . . . perfectly simple and intelligible, and that with regard not only to production but also to distribution" Marx, *Capital,* vol. I, pp. 80, 79.

22. Nove, Alec, *The Economics of Feasible Socialism* (George Allen and Unwin, London, 1983), especially Part 2.

23. See Lawler, James, "Marx Was a Market Socialist," in this volume.

24. Marx, Karl, and Engels, Frederick, *Selected Writings,* vol. II (Foreign Languages Publishing House, Moscow, 1951), p. 348.

25. Marx, *Capital,* vol. III, p. 431.

26. Ibid.

27. Ibid.

28. Marx, Karl, and Engels, Frederick, *Selected Correspondence* (Lawrence and Wishart, London, 1941), p. 147.

29. Ibid., p. 190.

30. Ibid., p. 335.

31. Marx, Karl, and Engels, Frederick, *The Communist Manifesto,* trans. by S. Moore (Charles H. Kerr, Chicago, 1945), pp. 42–43.

32. Ollman, "Marx's Vision of Communism," *Social and Sexual Revolution,* pp. 55ff.

33. Marx/Engels, *The Communist Manifesto,* p. 42.

34. Marx/Engels, *Selected Writings,* vol. II, p. 21.

35. Marx/Engels, *The Communist Manifesto,* pp. 42, 3.

36. Ibid.

37. Marx/Engels, *Selected Writings,* vol. II, p.23.

38. Marx, Karl, and Engels, Frederick, *Selected* Writings, vol. I (Foreign Languages Publishing House, Moscow, 1951), p. 203.

39. According to David Schweickart, the market is just "a useful instrument for accomplishing certain societal goals. It has certain strengths, but also inherent defects. The trick is to employ this instrument appropriately." Schweickart, David, "Economic Democracy: a Worthy Socialism that Would Really Work," *Science and Society,* vol. 56, no. 1 (Spring, 1992), p. 21.

Part Three

criticism

5

Criticism of Ticktin

DAVID SCHWEICKART

Hillel Ticktin finds the concept "market socialism" to be an oxymoron. If one defines socialism as a wholly planned society, as he does, and if one conceives of the market as the antithesis of planning, as he does, then his conclusion follows. The conclusion is so direct, in fact, that one need not bother analyzing any of the proposals market socialists put forth, nor trouble oneself with their critique of central planning, nor offer any suggestion as to what concrete economic institutions might constitute a viable socialism. One has to admire the "efficiency" of the argument.

There are, however, some problems with Ticktin's conceptual framework. If one defines socialism "by the degree to which the society was planned," it would seem to follow that when Stalin put an end to experiments with the market in Russia, he inaugurated a socialist society. Ticktin wants to resist this conclusion. He does so by redefining "planning." "Planning" means something other than doing away with the market and attempting to "plan" an economy. Planning is defined as "the conscious regulation of the society by the associated producers themselves."

Fine. One can define terms however one wants to, I suppose. But if (true) planning is going to be defined in terms of who does the planning, then one should say something about how this process is going to work, especially since the "planners" in this case may number in the tens or hundreds of millions. *Prima facie,* there are some questions that need to be answered. How exactly are the many million "associated producers themselves" going to draw up this plan? With so many agents consciously involved, how is it going to be determined exactly what "they" want? (Does everyone want the same things? Can everyone have all their needs satisfied? All their wants? How do we adjudicate disagreements and make tradeoffs?) How is it going to be determined how the things they want will be produced? (What is to be done when there are various technologies available, requiring differing amounts of labor and raw materials, and involving differing conditions of work?) How is it going to be decided who will produce what? (Which existing enterprises should expand production? Which ones should contract? Will new enterprises be set up? Will old ones be closed? Where will the new workers come from, and where will the displaced workers go?) And how will it be insured that each and every associated producer does what he or she is supposed to do as required by the consciously adopted plan? (What will the penalties be for non-compliance? Who will do the monitoring?)

Ticktin addresses none of these questions. He assures us that there won't be any bureaucracy under socialism, no "hierarchical social apparatus governed by strict rules." There will be bureaucracies under capitalism, Stalinism and market socialism, he tells us, but not under true socialism. How then will all the complicated decisions implied by the above questions be made? It's all quite simple, says Ticktin. We'll elect representatives to make these decisions, allowing them only one-year terms, and recalling them immediately if they don't do what we want.

Let's see if I have this right. We (all ten million or hundred million or one billion of us, depending on the country) will elect some representatives, charge them with deciding our consumption during the next year (taking into account our desires, of course), with determining the appropriate technologies, and with telling us which of our enterprises should expand, which should contract, and which should go out of business or be reconstituted—and if there are any foul-ups, well, we'll just recall these representatives and elect a new set. I see.

The failure to give even a minimal account of the institutional structure of true socialism is not the only problem with Ticktin's analysis. He resolutely contrasts the market with planning. This is an all-too-common move in comparisons of capitalism and socialism, but I think it a mistake.

In point of fact, much planning takes place in a market economy, even in the most libertarian of capitalist economies. All *enterprises* have to plan. Decisions have to be made as to what to produce, how to produce it, how to market the output. Thought must be given to future conditions. New technologies must be assessed. Capital has to be raised. These activities all involve conscious planning.

Once we move beyond the free market fantasies of neoclassical economics, we find even more planning going on under capitalism. The money supply must be controlled. Regulations must be put into place to cope with market externalities. Steps must be taken by the government to deal with unemployment and to keep the business cycle from getting out of hand. In the more successful advanced capitalist countries govern-ments subsidize research and engage in long-range economic planning, often making decisions as to which industries to support and which ones to cut back. There is certainly no *antithesis* between markets and planning in the real world. There are both market relations and planning under capitalism. I contend that there should be both market and plan under socialism—at least if we want a socialist economy that is both viable and desirable.

At bottom, the dispute between market and non-market socialists is not simply definitional. I object to defining socialism as a planned, non-market economy, but I do not object to defining socialism as a society in which the direct producers control the economy. Ticktin and I could probably agree on this definition.[1] But by this definition many (although perhaps not all) models of market socialism *are* socialist. At least it can be so argued. In my own model, for example, the direct producers exert con-trol via a variety of mechanisms. First of all, since Economic Democracy is a market economy, workers, who are also consumers, exert significant control over the output of the economy by their purchases. Enterprises profit if they make products consumers want, and fail if they do not.[2] Sec-ondly, workers have control over the production process in the enterprise in which they work, since they have ultimate authority, one-person, one-vote, over the enterprise itself. Managers can be "recalled" if they fail to perform adequately. Finally, workers, as citizens, have democratic input into both the size and composition of the investment fund, and hence into the overall direction of the economy. This input occurs at many levels—at the national level, since the legislative body sets the capital assets tax, at the state and local levels, since elected bodies must set investment pri-orities.

Not only do the direct producers have far more control over the econ-omy than they do under capitalism, but there is no "privileged class" under Economic Democracy, i.e., a stable class of people with more power than the combined power of the elected officials. Under Economic Democracy there are no capitalists, nor is there any other set of non-elected officials who possess anything like the power of the capitalist class under capitalism.[3]

To be sure, the control of each and every producer is not total. The economy in its entirety will not likely conform to the conscious intention of any one producer, let alone the intention of each and every one. I don't find this fact to be a fatal flaw. No human system as complicated as a real-world economy can measure up to such a standard of producer control—no matter how dramatic a change in "human nature" a revolution might bring about. If critics of market socialism disagree, or if they are convinced that some form of non-market socialism could at least come closer to such a standard, I would invite them to spell out their proposals in detail, and let us have a look. Socialism, as I understand it, is not a movement that can dispense with faith altogether, but it should not be based on faith alone.

To end on a more conciliatory note, I should make it clear that I do not dispute the contention that the market is a *dangerous* institution. Given the recent experiences of socialist countries attempting to introduce market reforms into their previously non-market economies, we can see more clearly than ever just how powerful the forces unleashed by such reforms can be, and how potentially destructive of socialist values. The critics of market socialism have not been wrong to stress these dangers. Proponents of market socialism in our eagerness to confute those who deny the necessity of market relations under socialism and in *our* impatience with empty rhetoric, have often treated the market as more benign than it actually is, and have sometimes failed to distinguish appropriate market reforms from inappropriate ones.

To conclude with a cliché: "marketeers" and "non-marketeers" should keep their minds open and listen to one another. Each side might learn something.

NOTES

1. In my own work I define socialism as a post-capitalist economy that lacks significant private ownership of means of production. This value-neutral definition allows one to distinguish between desirable forms of socialism and undesirable forms, and obviates our having to decide whether or not the Soviet Union (or China or Cuba or whatever) is *really* socialist. In my view there can be good and bad socialist societies, and some better or worse than others. Many socialists, Ticktin among them, prefer to give socialism a normative definition. I have no principled objection to such a move, so long as the definition is not so restrictive as to be Utopian.

2. Most socialists hate to admit that the market gives workers some control over the economy, because they correctly perceive that the market responds to *monetary* demand, and hence biases production in the direction of the wealthy. But if there are *not* the inordinate disparities of income under market socialism that there are under capitalism, if, instead, income distribution is reasonably fair, then this objection loses much of its force.

3. Ticktin seems not to realize that there are few or no capitalists in most versions of market socialism. He argues that "market socialism cannot exist because it involves limiting the incentive system . . . [and so] capitalists will have little incentive to invest and workers will have little incentive to work." One can't but wonder if Ticktin has examined any of the models he is so convinced are unworkable.

6.

Criticism of Schweickart

HILLEL TICKTIN

INTRODUCTION

This critique will address three major errors in Schweickart's essay. First, he says that China is socialist. Second, he argues that socialism is the first stage of communism, and third he seems to argue that central planning can never exist in any successful or, as he puts it, optimal variant, because it is necessarily inefficient. His positive outline of market socialism is already implicitly discussed in my paper, and it is not necessary to repeat the detailed argument that any market must imply the subjection of the individual to abstract labour and that there is an automatic conflict between workers' control and that subjection. I fully agree with Ollman that market socialism is utopian and, in my view, it is precisely this conflict which makes it utopian.

WHAT IS SOCIALISM?

First, is China socialist? China is authoritarian, with no element of worker's control or worker's democracy. It has a clearly defined elite who rule the society and so have a measure of control of the surplus product as opposed to the majority who have no such control. Nationalisation *in itself* is in no sense socialist. In principle one could have total nationalisation of all the means of production and still have capitalism. Such a state capitalism, a capitalism without capitalists, would not be very stable, but it would nonetheless accumulate capital in the enterprises, with workers selling their labour power. China is not simply definable as being capitalist, but neither is it socialist just because there is substantial nationalisation.

Second, the separation of socialism from communism is not Marx's doing but Stalin's. It is true that Lenin and others make such a distinction, but they do so in a pragmatic way, often using quotation marks. Even then it should be noted that they were clear that the transitional phase to a fully communist society was characterised by the gradual elimination of the market. This is explicitly theorised by Preobrazhensky in his *New Economics*.[1] It is noteworthy that Lenin called the Soviet Union "state-capitalist" rather than "socialist," while Trotsky insisted on the sharp struggle between the market and planning. There is, therefore, no respectable history for the separation of socialism from communism in such a way that market socialism becomes a phase in which the market attains a stable and non-antagonistic role.

More importantly, the distinction makes no sense unless there is an argument which says that the market is gradually dying. In its absence there is no reason to see how the move can be made to communism. If the market is dying, there must be reasons for its death, and they are not given.

Schweickart's reference to China as socialist and his sharp differentiation between socialism and communism are tightly connected. For Marx and for classical Marxists like myself, socialism in one country is inherently impossible. (One can easily make the case that capitalism in one country was also inherently impossible.) The reason lies in the fact that the division of labour has so developed that all countries are integrated into the world economy. For any new socio-economic system to succeed it must conquer the crucial heartland of the world economy. In order to do so, apart from actually taking power, it must have a higher level of productivity than the old system. Otherwise it is not sustainable. Hence a backward country which puts protective walls around its industry can only stew in its own backwardness, given the fact that it cannot participate in the international division of labour. If, on the other hand, it tries to open up its economy, it will necessarily be dominated by capital from the more advanced economies, both because of their size and because they have a higher level of productivity. It is hard to see China in another light.

On the other hand, the assumption that the revolution must occur in the advanced countries before socialism can succeed as a system permits one to explore its real nature. Such a victory would rapidly become a global victory, even if odd countries would remain as quaint islands of capitalism. Under such circumstances, socialism could only prove itself through its higher level of productivity. In the end, the economic basis of socialism lies in its abolition of scarcity through very high levels of productivity.

THE LABOUR THEORY OF VALUE AND ABUNDANCE

This may sound utterly utopian, even though it is clearly the basis of all classical Marxism. It should be noted, however, that the labour theory of value has abundance as one of its assumptions, because it holds that the fundamental variable, or the variable to which all other variables can be reduced, is labour-time. Hence, at the point where machines make machines, we reach abundance. Raw materials can be replaced by artificial materials or by greatly enhanced genetically modified forms. In other words, where the labour input is at or near zero, costs become negligible. Hence, the use of prices, specialised signals, etc., becomes otiose.

Clearly, in the initial phases of transition to a socialist economy such abundance would not exist, but the abolition of arms production, the duplication of resources through competition and other gigantic forms of waste such as mass unemployment would permit a quick rise in the standard of living of the whole population, excluding the capitalist class. Nor would the third world constitute an insuperable barrier, given its low standard of living, because the developed countries could easily afford to siphon off a proportion of the resources which formerly went into their arms production into investment for those countries. The enormous losses generated within a capitalist economy by the relatively negative forms of work would be enough to ensure that a world economy could begin its transition to abundance within a finite time, provided, of course, capitalism had not rendered the world waste in its last ditch attempt to survive.

This insight, of the tendency of value to zero, is also incorporated into the theory of the falling rate of profit within capitalism. Indeed any market economy would therefore be subject to the same tendency to its own abolition. It can be argued that human wants are insatiable and the world will run out of resources, but this is a view of human nature under capitalism, where some people set themselves the goal of owning many top-of-the-range cars, computers, and jet planes. For a rational person, however, these goals are idiotic, as one can only use one car, etc. at a time and if there still are such oddballs they could always borrow a particular car when they needed it. They do not need to own and personally garage it. In fact public transport can be so developed that it is infinitely more convenient to use than private transport for most, though perhaps not all purposes. There is no need to produce a large number of shoddy lower range goods, whether they are cars, clothes, or consumer durables, which most people are condemned to buy in a market. A socialist society can concentrate on the highest quality that it is capable of producing. Choice is not choice for most people within a market if it consists of buying cheaper goods of lower quality, which they can afford, and expensive goods of good quality, which they cannot afford. The fact that there may also be intermediate ranges does not alter the point.

CENTRAL PLANNING

Third, Schweickart's argument against central planning is implicitly refuted in my paper. He is correct that no global central planning authority can ever totally plan everything with any degree of success. At the moment there is a computer limit, in that no computer could deal with all the twenty-five million individual goods and their relations which the USSR counted in its economy. That is to say it could not produce the necessary results in a sufficiently short time. It would take years at the present time. Eventually we may expect that the computer will produce the result in minutes, but this will not necessarily eliminate the problem. It will always be possible to add items and different relations to the total, and when we start to consider the variety which humanity would want in a socialist society, it looks as if the computer would constantly have to catch up with what it was supposed to do. So he is correct at this level, at any rate for the immediate future.

But why do we need a central planner who is a god? It is a condition of socialism that there be a high degree of decentralisation, and not because of computer deficiency, but because workers' control implies that everyone have an input into decision making wherever possible. The reason why central planning did not work in the former USSR was that the workers were alienated and opposed to the elite who were the central planners. Necessarily the commands of the centre were distorted, ignored and based on deliberately distorted information. Any society, including market socialism, where there is a gap of this kind, cannot plan. Socialism necessarily presupposes that the direct producers are involved in the planning itself and hence support the directions of the central planners. Without that support there can be no planning, whether central or not.

WHY STALINIST/SOCIAL DEMOCRATIC TYPE CENTRAL
PLANNING MUST FAIL

It is worthwhile dwelling on this point. At one level it can be argued that the former USSR failed in its central planning because the centre could not impose its control on the local unit. The local unit had every incentive to lie about its potentialities, and hence its reports to the centre did not conform to the reality of the plant or institution. In turn, the centre did not have the resources to scrutinize the reports of every enterprise and then fit them into a consistent pattern. It was here that the computer also failed. Finally, the instructions that the centre saw fit to impose on the enterprise were necessarily evaded in the interests of the local unit. Under these circumstances the Stalinist system could never plan in the less theoretical sense of organising production. The Stalinist centre played the role of firefighter and innovator. It could direct investment into a particular area though the more developed the economy the more difficult that necessarily became, as the amount of unattached resources declined.

The point of this survey of so-called planning is to bring out the fact that no economy has been successfully planned until the present time. In the USSR, the economy was organised, directed, and forced along a particular route. That, however, is not the same thing as planning. Even ignoring my social definition of planning, actually existing planning has the three conflicts described above: in obtaining information, in rendering the reports consistent, and in getting the decisions implemented. Even in non-Stalinist economies the same conflicts exist.

At the heart of the problem lies the conflict of interest between the worker and the manager/capitalist. The worker has an interest in exaggerating his work and performing as poorly as possible and the manager or capitalist has the reverse interest. The same incompatibility of interests can be found between workers and managers in nationalised industries in the West. As a result, their output is often shoddy, their service poor, and their costs high. The output does not conform to the intentions of the "planners." It is not, therefore, surprising that nationalisation has lost support. Social democracy has been hung out to dry on this issue, but there is no reason for Marxists to defend nationalisation whether under capitalism or Stalinism. Only if workers are non-alienated can they be expected to identify with their plants, management, and central planners. And only if workers have direct or delegated control over the social product will they be non-alienated. That, however, goes back to the same point on the social nature of planning.

I turn now to the argument that genuine central planning is necessarily inefficient. I have made the case in more detail in another article,[2] but I will attempt to provide an outline of an efficient central planning system.

CONDITIONS FOR SUCCESSFUL PLANNING

The first principle of socialism/communism is that labour becomes mankind's prime want. This follows again from the labour theory of value. Everyone works according to the limits of their ability because that is their nature, and they fulfill that nature by engaging in social labour. That is only possible if the labour is creative social labour. A second condition is that the labour involved must not be subjected to a hierarchy in the division of labour.

In other words, everyone must participate in management at some time in their lives, as often as is possible, and in whatever form is possible. At the same time, everyone will necessarily move around in the division of labour. While a musician cannot become a good doctor without considerable training or a doctor a good musician, each could become good amateurs in the other's profession. There are many other skills, however, that can be acquired more easily, and would allow people to change their occupation should they wish to. A doctor or musician could learn to be a good carpenter, planner, or chemist, for example. Freed from their lifetime ties to a single occupation, people would no longer form interest groups that stand opposed to the rest of society.

That is the crucial node, because a society cannot work unless the majority of that society see the society as acting in their own interest. If they do identify themselves with the society, then all major economic problems become soluble. Those problems are usually discussed in terms of relative prices, quantities to be produced, and the relation of those quantities to demand. It is argued that only the market provides the necessary signals. I have argued, however, that a socialist society will be efficient because everyone will have an interest in making it efficient, and that the necessary inefficiency of capitalism and Stalinism lies in the alienation of the majority.

So-called market socialism does not overcome that alienation because workers cannot easily become managers and managers cannot easily become workers, or be given lower salaries than workers, or be subject to recall. In principle, a market-socialist society might be formulated in these terms, as Schweickart has done, but it could not possibly function. Competition is a necessary feature of the market as are profits, even if capitalists are nominally abolished. Even in market socialism, therefore, the function of a manager will consist of forcing workers to work harder to compete with other firms in the market, presumably for lower wages. On the other hand, it will be in the interest of the worker to receive the highest wage for the least work.

Managers subject to recall with lower salaries than workers wages will not have the authority or for that matter the will to enforce the kind of control required to lower costs. Either the workers will eliminate competition and profits or the manager will establish the kind of dictatorial control normal under capitalism. If there is no unemployment then the manager will certainly lose out over time and the market will be abolished.

THE NECESSARY FAILURE OF MARKET SOCIALISM

Far from the Marxist conception of socialism/communism being utopian, it is the market-socialist concept which is utopian. I have argued the point defensively by taking the cases of the old Soviet Union and China, but I can also point to the failure of so-called market-socialism in the former social-democracies in Western Europe and to the failure of the market socialist reformers in Eastern Europe, most of whom now support the unalloyed market. The reason for its failure lay in the fact that neither workers nor the elite wanted so-called market socialism. The elite felt that it could not work, while the workers felt that they had nothing to gain from it. Schweickart is a sincere socialist unlike many of the so-called market socialists. Alec Nove, who is often placed in this category, made it clear that, in spite of his Menshevik parents, he was not a socialist. Nove had no time for Marxism or concepts like alienation or abstract labour. Schweickart is different. Hence it is all the more difficult to understand how he can speak of market socialism at all. The terms, as someone pointed out, are like fried ice. How can we put together socialism, with its categories of cooperation, creative labour, replacement of the goal of exchange value by that of use-value, with competition, hierarchical forms of control and profit maximization?

NOTES

1. E. Preobrazhensky: *New Economics*, CUO, London, 1966.
2. Hillel Ticktin: "What will a Socialist Society be like?" *Critique* 25, 1993.

7

Criticism of Ollman

JAMES LAWLER

Hannah Arendt once said that her main complaint about Marx was that he was too enthusiastic about capitalism.[1] It is capitalism—the capitalist market—Marx wrote in the *Communist Manifesto,* that liberates mankind from traditional relations of dependence between persons and the kinds of mystification of human existence that these traditional relations promote. "All that is sold melts into air," Marx wrote of capitalism, "all that is holy is profaned, and man is at last compelled to face with sober senses, his real conditions of life, and his relations with his kind."[2]

Capitalism also alienates and mystifies, for sure, but at the same time it obliges people to alienate the alienation, demystify the mystification. The mysterious source of money, which Shakespeare's Timon called "Thou visible god,"[3] is finally revealed, thanks to the very development of its powers—which we eventually come to see are really the powers of human labor alienated in it. There is the fetishism of the commodity, of course, but there is also something about the evolution of commodity production that leads to the exposure and recognition of its secret source. Thanks to the full development of commodity production under capitalism, we are more and more obliged to turn away from money's spellbinding powers to recognize its real source in human labor.

In the production process in modern societies two things occur. (1) The joint labor of workers produces capital as the quasi-divine or quasi-demonic power that governs their lives, and, (2) driven by the inexorable power of capitalist market-place competition, workers develop real practical capacities that enable them to free themselves from the rule of their own alienated labor in order to rule their own lives directly. These capacities, whose development is stimulated by capitalism, are continually frustrated—more than frustrated, since untold lives are wasted and destroyed—by the capitalistic drive for profit that nevertheless continues to produce them. Marx's subtitle for *Capital* was "A Critique of Political

Economy." But if the term "critique" suggests something purely negative, the term is misleading. *Dialectical* criticism looks for the internal
criticism, the criticism that a process produces of itself, whose negativity
is the result of its positive features.

Following the dialectical logic of *Capital* step-by-step, Marx finally
comes, in Volume III, to the emergence of "the first sprouts of the new
society."[4] These are the cooperative factories owned by workers, already
coming into existence within the framework of the old society. Marx first
examines the new, communist society in concrete form in his chapter on,
of all things, "credit." Through the availability of credit, money can
come back to the workers who produced it in a form that allows them to
break the cycle of exploitation.

In his first reference to Marx's discussion of cooperatives, Bertell Ollman underestimates the significance of this development, writing that
"Marx spoke of the cooperative factories of his day as turning 'the associated laborers into their own capitalist.'" This abbreviated citation pic-
tures Marx as a purely negative critic of cooperatives. But such an
interpretation fails to capture the fact that the cooperatives are also
described as the sprouts of the new society pushing up through the soil
of the old one. Ollman's interpretation fails to reflect the idea, expressed
in the very same sentence, that "the antithesis between capital and labour
is overcome within them." Such an overcoming is, to be sure, qualified
or limited. The new society first emerges in a form that is characteristic
of the old society. It first emerges in a capitalistic mode, in a form that
will have to be shed when the new society develops its own inherent
potential to a greater extent.

Ollman's larger treatment of this issue in the eighth section of his
paper also fails to cite the crucial positive passages: that in cooperatives we
see the first sprouts of the new society, that in them the antithesis of capital and labor is overcome. This is quite different from saying that cooperatives are just another form of capital, as Ollman interprets and as the
excerpted passage by itself suggests. Ollman claims that Marx is not
proposing a definite political strategy, but only predicting one of a number of possible developments in capitalism. He contrasts Marx's alleged
projection of a possible trend for the development of workers cooperatives
developing under capitalism—a trend that Marx supposedly feared—
with an alternative scenario of socialist revolution.

Marx, however, argues that the extension of cooperatives to the
national scale is *not* a likely eventuality within capitalism, because "the
lords of land and the lords of capital" will use their political power to
oppose such a development. Marx is at pains to argue that the expansion

of the cooperative approach to the national level, so that its potential to alleviate the misery of workers will be realized, will be possible only through socialist revolution, only through the conquest of political power by the working class. "To save the industrious masses, cooperative labour ought to be developed to national dimensions, and, consequently, to be fostered by national means."[5] Ollman cites this passage, but doesn't recognize that it is an argument about the need for a socialist revolution, not a projection of one among other possible trends in capitalism. The crucial passage needs to be cited more fully:

> . . . [T]he experience of the period from 1848 to 1864 has proved beyond doubt that, *however excellent in principle* [emphasis added], and however useful in practice, co-operative labour, if kept within the narrow circle of the casual efforts of private workmen, will never be able to arrest the growth in geometrical progression of monopoly, to free the masses, nor even to perceptibly lighten the burden of their miseries. It is perhaps for this very reason that plausible noblemen, philanthropic middle-class spouters, and even keen political economists, have all at once turned nauseously complimentary to the very cooperative labour system they had vainly tried to nip in the bud by deriding it as the Utopia of the dreamer, or stigmatising it as the sacrilege of the Socialist. To save the industrious masses, co-operative labour ought to be developed to national dimensions, and, consequently, to be fostered by national means. Yet, the lords of land and the lords of capital will always use their political privileges for the defence and perpetuation of their economical monopolies . . . . To conquer political power has therefore become the great duty of the working classes.

I emphasize the point that cooperatives are excellent "in principle," as well as in practice. This is not an argument that they are only another form of capital, on a par with monopoly corporations. What prevents the cooperatives from realizing their full potential is their isolation within the framework of the *capitalist* market.

The citation is from Marx's "Inaugural Address of the Working Men's International Association" of 1864. There he writes of the victories of the working class movement in "the great contest between the blind rule of the supply and demand laws which form the political economy of the middle class, and social production controlled by social foresight, which forms the political economy of the working class." Here are the two main opposites of Marxist thought—the unfettered rule of money on the one hand, and the rule of free human beings, on the other. How do we go from the one to the other? Is it by eliminating the first, outlawing it or burying it, so as to allow the second to be created in its stead? This sort of approach is characteristic of what I call "nihilistic socialism" as against the "dialectical socialism" that tries to see how the new society grows up out of the old, which shows the *transition* from the one to the other, the intermediary links that connect the opposites.

In the great contest between these two principles, Marx sees the first major victory of the political economy of the working class against the blind rule of supply and demand in the Ten Hours Bill, which restricted the working day of women and children to ten hours. Marx evokes the theory of fetishistic religion in describing the significance of this legislation: "In olden times, child murder was a mysterious rite of the religion of Moloch, but it was practised on some very solemn occasions only, once a year perhaps, and then Moloch had no exclusive bias for the children of the poor." In modern capitalism the money god is more voracious, devouring the children of the poor on a daily basis, in vast quantities. So we see the world-historical significance of the Ten Hours Bill: "it was the first time that in broad daylight the political economy of the middle class succumbed to the political economy of the working class."[6]

Ollman says that all talk of good markets versus bad markets is confusing and politically demobilizing in face of the main task of socialists today: not to attack big corporations and their rule over society, but to mount a "frontal, no-holds barred attack on the market and all its ills." We should attack market production wherever it occurs, in state enterprises, in worker cooperatives, apparently in corner grocery stores, as well as in transnational corporations. "People's turn to socialism," he writes, "will only emerge out of the rejection of all market relationships." This is clearly not the perspective of Marx in the above passage, or in *Capital,* where he repeated this position. There is the unfettered, free market, which is the real "meat grinder." This is the market that expresses the political economy of the capitalists and the one to which capitalists are today trying to return thanks to the absence of political controls over the emerging global market. And then there is a socially controlled market, the market subject to the conscious will of society—the market as "can opener." The Ten Hours Bill was a major step in the direction of turning the meat grinder market into the can opener market.

As is all too obvious today, this process is still subject to reversal by the continued economic and political domination of capitalists—not of particular individuals, to be sure, but of the capitalist system of economic relations which results in the global power of multi-national corporations, international finance capital, etc. The dynamics of class struggle require further advances to strengthen past ones. Consequently, Marx points to an even greater working-class victory than that of the Ten Hours Bill.

> But there was in store a still greater victory of the political economy of labour over the political economy of capital. We speak of the cooperative movement, especially the cooperative factories raised by the unassisted efforts of a few bold "hands." The value of these great social experiments cannot be over-rated. By deed, instead of by argument, they have shown that production on a large scale, and in accord with the behests of modern science, may be carried on without the existence of a class of masters employing a class of hands; that to bear fruit, the means of labour need not be monopolised as a means of dominion over, and of extortion against, the labouring man himself; and that, like slave labour, like serf labour, hired labour is but a transitory and inferior social form, destined to disappear before associated labour plying its toil with a willing hand, a ready mind, and a joyous heart.

Note that Marx says that these cooperatives were established by the *unassisted* efforts of the workers themselves. In his polemic against the "state socialism" of Lasalle, Marx does not attack cooperatives *per se*, but cooperatives established by the state.[7]

Cooperatives are not just a new form in which capital embodies itself. The antithesis of labor and capital essence of cooperatives is that the market in labor (of workers and capitalists) —is eliminated. This is the next major step beyond such steps as the Ten Hour Bill (and eventual welfare legislation) that takes place still *within* the parameters of the old society. With their cooperatives, workers have taken a major step beyond capitalism, albeit in the form of workers being their own capitalists, i.e., in a capitalistic mode. Capitalism itself had emerged at first with feudal forms. Such may be the necessary dialectic of historical development. Changes do not usually take place from one position to another, fundamentally opposed one, without passing through intermediary stages. A dialectical Marxist does not claim that such a transitional stage is the "end of history," the last word in unalienated existence. But neither does a dialectical Marxist insist that there has been no positive change until the new system has been created *in toto*.

This latter position cannot be attributed to Ollman, who also recognizes a series of stages between capitalism and fully developed communism. But this idea implies that alienated labor still exists, and must exist, in post-capitalist society. There is still alienated labor under the first phase of communism—which Marx says is governed by "bourgeois right"[8]—because workers must continue work for money (in the attenuated, socially-controlled form of labor tickets). It is one thing to say that there is no permanent, lasting or secure progress until the market itself has been eliminated, and it is another to say that there is no real progress at all, that fetishism and alienation simply or abstractly persist, etc. I feel that Ollman wants to say the latter, while reluctantly admitting the former. Toward the end of his paper he recognizes, perhaps surprisingly given his earlier arguments, that even the capitalist market has done positive things for mankind. But he cannot admit that there is anything more that a restricted commodity market can do after the market in labor, and with it capitalism *per se,* has been eliminated. This is because he wants to stress the negative characteristics of the market, while being obliged as a Marxist to admit that the market also has positive features.

Will worker cooperatives, organized on a national scale under a workers government, be simply "collective capitalists" competing with one another to amass capital and exploit one another? One understands why capitalist industries are driven to maximize profits by increasing the exploitation of labor. Capital exists independently of particular enterprises and shifts ever more rapidly to where returns are greatest. And the capitalists themselves do no work. It is other people who are subject to speed-up and wage-reductions. What does it mean to say that workers exploit themselves more efficiently in cooperatives? Will a worker-owned enterprise decide to move to Mexico and work for one-tenth previous wages in order to amass ever more capital?

Worker-owned enterprises are natural responses to current capital flight that is increasingly fostered in the frenzy of global capitalism. Where capitalist enterprises are abandoned because of insufficient profit, worker-owned enterprises can survive precisely because such cooperatives, like state-owned enterprises, do not need to make any "profits" whatsoever. Faced with the prospects of unemployment and poverty, workers who succeed in gaining control over their enterprises will be quite happy just to make a decent living. If the enterprise prospers, and with no external stockholders to please, they can decide to take additional revenue in the form of greater free time. No doubt much depends on the prevailing climate of opinion and the influence of socialist ideology. In a world dominated by capitalism, with little or no support from the trade union movement or a supportive socialist political movement, isolated cooperatives may tend to behave as much as possible like capitalist enterprises, to the point even of one group of owning workers hiring another group of wage workers. But then, by definition, the enterprise ceases to be a cooperative one.

The decisive step in the overcoming of capitalism is not the elimination of exchange in general, but the elimination of the exchange of labor power for wages. This is the implication of Marx's attempt to see through the fetishism of the market into the entrails of the profit system—into the production process wherein takes place the extraction of surplus value. Capitalist profits are not, as Ollman states, the result of the exchange of labor *and* commodities, but, fundamentally, of the exchange of wages for labor power alone. This fact is masked by the exchange of commodities where the *realization* of surplus value takes place.

The market in capital and currencies must simultaneously be reabsorbed by society with the elimination of capitalists. But if the exchange of finished goods and services for money has preceded capitalism by thousands of years, we should not expect them to disappear overnight. There are two ways in which the market can be fetishized—as beneficent god, and as demon, as the source of all evil. In opposing the deification of the market, Ollman is in danger of demonizing it. In neither case is the fetishism of the market overcome.

I was impressed with Ollman's idea that the vantage point of much market socialist thinking is that of the failure of Soviet state socialism, rather than, as it should be, the vantage point of capitalism's own inherent problems. Do these problems point to the market itself as the main problem, or to the domination of the market by powerful financial and industrial powers beholden to no one and motivated by their own insatiable profit requirements? To mobilize public sentiment for socialism, should we also point to the owner of the corner grocery store, or to a beleaguered worker cooperative, or to some state enterprise that might have to earn its keep, and say—these are just as bad, these too have to go?

Ollman says that the logic of the socialist revolution will lead people to understand that the market in general has to go. But to get into the socialist revolution in the first place, there has to be some goal that is being fought for, one that people as they are now will recognize as both desirable and practical. Otherwise, no matter how bad things get, people will remain passive. Will this proposed socialist goal be the abolition of the market and its replacement, as soon as possible, with a centrally planned economy? Are we to propose goals based on what Ollman admits is the way people are now, or should we base our goals on what we project people will be like when they get into the middle of the fight? To get into the fight in the first place, don't socialists have to take people as they are, and propose goals that make sense to them now, while at the same time promoting consciousness of long-term prospects for further change?

Despite what he seems to be arguing in much of his paper about the inherent power of the market to subvert socialism, as a mixture as untenable as water and fire, Ollman agrees with Marx's post-revolutionary gradualism, suggesting a period of forty or fifty years in which market production, and even capitalist market production, continues to exist. But what about the supposed omnivorous logic of the market during that time? Other tendencies can effectively combat this, Ollman argues. So the market is not all powerful after all. It is possible to have markets and not be overwhelmed by them. They can be can openers and not meat grinders.

In my paper I argue that Marx distinguishes the "period" of transition between capitalism and "socialism," on the one hand, and socialism itself, understood as the first phase of communism. It is during the period of transition that one should locate in Marx's thought something approximating to what is commonly recognized as market socialism. For how long a time should such a system be envisaged?

Based on Marx's texts, Ollman accepts the idea of a mixed capitalist-socialist market lasting for forty or fifty years after a working-class revolution. The question arises: with state power in their hands, and a revolutionary experience promoting class consciousness and solidarity, why would not the working-class governments simply outlaw capitalism as soon as possible? If it were only a question of political power, this survival of capitalism for forty or fifty years after a socialist revolution would hardly make sense. Nor would it make sense to follow a political strategy of condemning the market *per* se, and then not only permit the market to continue after the anti-market revolution, but to allow capitalist firms to stay in business. But, as I have argued, it is not only a matter of practical politics, but of economic logic, including the logic of developed market production itself, that ought to govern the transitional period.

I'm not convinced that a draconian inheritance law by itself will get rid of capitalism. Other factors, such as the appeal and economic efficiency of cooperative ownership and a state policy of full employment, might make short shift of capitalism much sooner. But this does not exhaust the concept of a transitional economy between capitalism and socialism. After capitalist enterprises cease to play a significant economic role, the cooperative enterprises that have become predominant could continue for a significant period of time to function "in a capitalist mode." *I.e.,* wealth would continue to be distributed on the basis of the profits of individual enterprises. Unfair inequalities such as those due to differences in technological productivity (the organic composition of capital) could be compensated for by a tax system. Through such actions of the state, the economic system becomes cooperative. Before the development of a more directly cooperative system becomes acceptable, the working population may require a significant period of time in which a sense of ownership over their particular enterprise prevails.

Nationwide solidarity in the political struggle does not automatically transfer to psychological attitudes appropriate to the day-to-day operations of work, work that is not inherently interesting and so is done, not for its own sake, but for the sake of money. After the flush of revolutionary victory after an intense period of revolutionary (ideally non-violent) struggle, why should not workers relax and gain the rewards of victory from a paternalistic workers' state that doesn't demand too much of them? Before a fully developed socialist society would be possible, such attitudes would have to be overcome through "the discipline of the market," including positive market-based incentives.

What I have called the higher phase of the transitional period is indirectly cooperative through the collective will of society as expressed by actions of the workers' state. This would be followed by a directly cooperative society, communist society in its first phase, in which the compensating activity of the state would be significantly reduced. While this would be a non-market society in the sense that the product would not rule over the worker in the form of stimulus and disciplinarian, there would still be a quasi-market, a can-opener market which still requires that individuals have money, though the amount they have is based on their labor and not on the profits of their enterprises. In the "Critique of the Gotha Program," Marx argues that in the first phase of communism workers are paid on the basis of their labor in the form of labor tickets, certificates that so-and-so has worked a certain period of time. He does not explain how such a system would certify the quality of labor. Perhaps this is in part because "socialism" properly speaking presupposes a lengthy period of market socialism, the period of transition, in which habits of working conscientiously for themselves have become ingrained in workers through market-based rewards and punishments.

We should be aware of the fact that in the advanced transitional society, the product "rules over the producer" only in a relative sense. Society has for a long time consciously regulated the operations of the market. We are far from a time in which children worked long hours in factories, from a time in which unemployment reduces many people to dependence on welfare checks, from a time in which capitalists enrich themselves from the labor of others. Progressively, the unfettered market has been brought under conscious social control until, for a time, it is reduced to the function of stimulating and disciplining labor for workers who take all the benefits of production for themselves.

This market socialist period may not be a "stage," but it is a significant period of time responding to a definite socio-economic logic. It is the shape of society in the post-revolutionary situation that has to be outlined as the immediate goal of socialists. Ollman implicitly suggests a compromise with market socialists. Let's agree that for forty or fifty years after a socialist political victory we will have some kind of market socialism. Let's propose such a revolutionary goal for people as they are today. Against those market socialists who believe that the market is eternal, Ollman and I, as Marxists, will argue forcefully that the market, even the socially regulated market of the transitional society, will eventually have to go. But this will be an argument among socialists who will recognize the necessity and even the principled advantage of socialist market production, not an argument between true socialists and crypto-capitalists.

In the recent Star Trek movie, *First Contact,* time-travelers from the twenty-fourth century must patiently explain to scientifically inventive but socially benighted representatives of late twentieth-century society that in the future people will not work for money, but for creative purposes. Bertell Ollman is certainly right that this is the Marxist, and the fully humanist view of the matter. Marxists have the duty to fight to preserve this long-range and fully humanist perspective as having real operative significance at all steps in the transition to the full development of the future society. But as socialists who are still back at the end of the twentieth century, we must settle for one step at a time.

NOTES

1. "I do not share Marx's great enthusiasm about capitalism. If you read the first pages of the *Communist Manifesto* it is the greatest praise of capitalism you ever saw." Melvin Hill, ed., *Hannah Arendt: The Recovery of the Public World* (New York: St. Martin's Press, 1979), 334–35.
2. Marx, Engels. *Collected Works* (MECW), vol. 6, 487.
3. Shakespeare, *Timon of Athens,* Act iv, sc. iii. Cited by Marx at length in his *Economic and Philosophical Manuscripts of 1944*; MECW, vol. 3, 323.
4. Karl Marx, *Capital,* Vol. III (Progress Publishers, Moscow, 1966), p. 440.
5. *MECW,* vol. 20, 12.
6. *MECW,* vol. 20, 11. I have modified the translation in two places, following the German text as indicated in footnotes to the cited text. Engels had previously analyzed this bill in March of 1850, just after a court had acquitted a particular manufacturer of violating the Bill. Overgeneralizing from this momentary setback, Engels argues that there can be no significant victories over capitalism short of the revolutionary overthrow of capitalism itself. He regards the particular defeat of the Ten Hours Bill as an inevitable consequence of reforms under capitalism. However, support for the Bill was strengthened after this particular backward step, leading Marx and Engels to draw the important conclusions cited here.

7. See chapter three, "Of State-Socialism: Lassallean Model," in Hal Draper, *Karl Marx's Theory of Revolution. Vol. IV. Critique of Other Socialisms* (New York: Monthly Review Press, 1990), p. 70: "Marx distinguished his own favorable attitude toward cooperatives (an attitude most plainly to be seen in *Capital*, by the way) from the Lassallean-type plank as follows . . ."

8. From the "Critique of the Gotha Program," *MECW*, vol. 24, 86.

8.

Criticism of Lawler

BERTELL OLLMAN

Defenders of the market fall into four main categories: on the side of capitalism, there are those who view the market as endowed with moral virtue, and those who don't, but consider it a necessary part of economic life, perhaps even a natural one. While the side of socialism, there are people who also believe the market is necessary, inevitable as they are likely to say rather than natural, though much in need of humanizing reforms, and finally those who believe it is necessary but only as a transition, albeit a very long one, to communism. Jim Lawler belongs to this last group, which also means that he and I share a great many ideas on this subject. Specifying what the most important of these are should enable me to shed a sharper light on our differences.

Lawler and I agree that communism is not only a desirable goal but a possible one; that the roots of communism can be found in capitalism; that one way to understand socialism is as a period when elements already present in capitalism are "set free" to develop under the new conditions that emerge following the revolution; that right after the revolution, a lot of private enterprises, including co-ops, and a substantial market will continue to exist; that development toward full communism is a complex process with each succeeding phase made possible by what comes before; and that the political form in which the transition to communism will occur is the democratic dictatorship of the proletariat. What then are our main disagreements? These are: (1) Lawler rejects extensive central planning as a feasible option at any point in his multi-staged evolution of society toward full communism. (2) He believes that the market can be tamed once the working class is in control of the state and the economy is dominated by workers' co-ops. (3) He considers that an economy dominated by workers' co-ops would provide an effective transition to full communism. (4) He presents market socialism as a necessary development by claiming that it follows a social logic. And (5) he argues that Marx agrees with him on each of these points, in short that Marx was a market socialist.

Could central planning work in socialism? Lawler is very adamant in saying "no." He does allow for a small amount of central planning to establish "new rules of the game," but those rules are market rules, albeit ones biased in favor of workers' co-ops. His chief reason for opposing more extensive planning is that it worked badly in the Soviet Union. This is such an important piece in his case for market socialism that he begins his essay with it. Soviet central planning serves Lawler, as indeed it serves virtually all market socialists, as a house of horrors that awaits anyone naïve enough to reject the market socialist solution. In arguing for the feasibility of an economy based on workers' co-ops, however, Lawler devotes a lot of space to uncovering its preconditions in capitalism. Yet, in discussing the possibility of socialist central planning, the developments in capitalism that may have prepared the way for it are completely ignored. Instead, we get a tirade against an inefficient and undemocratic form of central planning that arose in quite different historical conditions. Leaving aside Lawler's gross exaggeration of their inefficiency (remember the Sputnik?), he cannot have it both ways. If workers' co-ops in socialism can only be understood and appreciated in light of their real history, then the same must apply to democratic central planning, whose preconditions are also found in capitalism, and the experience of the Soviet Union, where virtually none of these preconditions existed, is simply irrelevant. Viewing socialism from the vantage point of what went wrong in the Soviet Union is, as I argued in my essay, the preferred tactic of anti-socialists everywhere. In adopting their approach for his discussion of central planning, Lawler is lending legitimacy to a misuse of history that seeks to discredit all positive conceptions of socialism, including his own.

Another of Lawler's criticisms of central planning concerns the character of the planners. He refers to them as a "technological elite" and elsewhere as "economic technocrats," with the implication that they would be aloof from and unaccountable to the masses for whom they plan. Again, this was certainly the case in the Soviet Union, but would it be so in a democratic dictatorship of the proletariat, a society built on the foundations of capitalist democracy, and after a popular revolution that gave workers the desire to run their own affairs and helped develop in them the abilities to do so? I would expect that elections in such a society would revolve around the question of priorities for the plan and which groups of planners should carry them out. Also, given the spread of economic and technical education at this time, there would be a rapid increase in the number of people who could work as planners no one need serve in this capacity for his/her entire life making it even less likely that planners would become a small elite separated from the people.

My second main criticism of Lawler is that he is far too sanguine about the ability of a workers' state to tame the market short of abolishing it. According to him, once the socialist government eliminates the market in labor power by instituting a system of workers' co-ops, "what remains of the market no longer regulates production with the heartless brutality of a nature imposed necessity. The market that remains for workers who work for themselves is a market that is increasingly subject to human consciousness. It is a market that is consciously used for human welfare." This is a huge claim, and one would have expected more in the way of a defense. I am reminded of Mark Twain's response to someone who asked if there was any way to tame the submarine, the ultimate weapon of that day. If we heated all the water in the world's oceans to the boiling point, Twain replied, it would be impossible for submarines to operate. But how do we do that, his questioner persisted. Look, Twain answered, you asked me what to do; don't expect me to tell you how to do it. So, too, with Lawler, and I'm afraid with other market socialists as well. We are given the solution—"We will tame the market"—but never adequately shown what they will do and why it will work.

Lawler does not examine how a "social market," even with the elimination of labor power (and, one could add, even—as in Schweickart's model—without capital), would function under socialism. Workers' co-ops, after all, would continue to produce goods not in order to use them but to sell them and make a profit on them. Thus, they would treat competing enterprises and their consumers like firms out to maximize profits always have, and would retain all the qualities that make such behavior effective. As under capitalism, failure to move ahead in competition with others means falling behind, with its inevitable results of making less, having to work harder, and possibly even going bust. Under such threats, what would happen to the "human consciousness" Lawler speaks about? Many other problems associated with the market are also likely to exist in Lawler's version of market socialism—periodic economic crisis, inequality between workers in different enterprises, the greed for money and its accompanying corruption, consumerism, and the lack of transparence of past, present and future that I emphasized in my essay. Lawler devotes no serious attention to any of these problems, and is in no position, therefore, to tell us that they would disappear or even be attenuated in a "social market."

My third main criticism of Lawler is that he is wrong to believe that the market socialism he is advocating, should it ever come about, would or could evolve into full communism. Obviously, this point is only of concern to those, like Lawler and I, who think that full communism, as a time when classes, the state, private property and alienation have all withered away, is a real possibility. Such extraordinary developments do not come easily or quickly. They have to be prepared for. The preconditions for it which do not already exist have to be created and carefully nurtured. The crucial question, then, is this: do continuing market relations with their accompanying crises, competition, inequality, greed, insecurity, and mystification up to the very portals of full communism constitute an adequate preparation? I think not. Rather, democratic central planning along with the democratic dictatorship of the proletariat are required to construct a scaffolding of rules with which the full communist edifice can be built. Then, after material conditions have sufficiently matured and the most important of these rules have been completely accepted and internalized by people, the various institutions that embody these rules can gradually be dispensed with. Only when the communist edifice can stand on its own, the scaffolding that helped to build it is removed. For Lawler, on the other hand, the communist edifice appears to build itself against the grain of the very people who should be busy establishing its preconditions. His transition to communism is no transition at all, and cannot be until he specifies more clearly what would mediate between the competitive market economics and psychology of his workers' cooperative society and the self-consciously social arrangements of full communism.

My fourth main criticism of Lawler is that he misuses the idea of logic in Marxism to give the market socialist outcome that he favors a degree of necessity that it does not have. For Marx, "logic" refers to the patterns that emerge from the ongoing interaction of parts inside an organic whole. It is the set of rules this whole seems to follow in reproducing itself. Such rules exert considerable pressure on everything they touch to develop in ways that are compatible with them. From the point of view of its effects, "logic" in Marxism can also be grasped as the way in which a structured whole, a totality, brings about change in its parts.

To demonstrate some kind of necessary connection between the evolution of post-revolutionary society, as an organic whole, and the spread of workers' co-ops would be a strong argument indeed for Lawler's vision of socialism. But, though he claims such a connection, he doesn't show it. Lawler does show that the rise of co-ops is promoted by the logic of capitalism (chiefly through the mediation of technological change that eliminates the need for capitalist overseers and the onset of the credit system), but he doesn't examine how this same logic (expressed in the rule of profit maximization) severely restricts what co-ops can do of a socialist nature, both before and after the revolution. The fact that capitalism in its normal development gives rise to workers' co-ops doesn't relieve co-ops from taking on most of the traits of any enterprise engaged in the production of goods for the market; nor does it indicate that co-ops have a key role to play in the strategy to overturn capitalism; nor that co-ops offer the ideal economic form for the post-revolutionary society. In expressing his preference for the cooperative form in socialism in terms of the unfolding of a social logic—without clearly explaining what that logic is and where it comes from—Lawler is simply borrowing Marx's language to lend credence to his distinctly non-Marxist conception of the future.

Here as elsewhere, Lawler obviously considers it very important to present his views under Marx's banner. Indeed, the most distinctive characteristic of Lawler's entire essay, as indicated by the title, is his effort to win Marx for his cause. This is my fifth main disagreement with Lawler. If Marx was really a market socialist, then a lot of supposedly Marxist criticism of this position, including my own, would have to be rethought. Lawler is not the first to make this surprising claim. Stanley Moore, who Lawler cites, said as much, at least for the "early" Marx, over a dozen years ago, though Lawler's argument is generally more convincing and, therefore, more in need of rebuttal. Having presented my views on this matter in my opening essay, I will restrict myself here to examining what new evidence Lawler introduces in support of his position.

First, Lawler quotes Engels who says that immediately after the revolution big family estates will be turned over to their workers who will organize them as co-ops, adding the qualification, "They are to be assigned to them for their use and benefit *under the control of the community*" (my emphasis). In commenting, Lawler transfers this control to "the workers in the enterprise." Ownership, apparently without control, is left to the community. With this alteration, Engels is made to appear as a supporter of a cooperative-dominated economy and, by extension, of a social market. If the community were to exercise control, on the other hand, one would expect a community plan and, because communities interact, one coordinated with the plans of other communities in some kind of central plan.

Second, Lawler takes Marx's reference to cooperative factories in capitalism as the "first sprouts of the new" as a clear indication of the kind of economic forms he favored for socialism. This interpretation is supported, according to Lawler, by Marx's famous declaration that workers "have no ideals to realize, but to set free elements of the new society with which old collapsing bourgeois society itself is pregnant." The question is, however, just what are these elements, and also what does it mean to set them free? Lawler does not hesitate to answer that it is workers' co-ops that Marx had in mind, and that setting them free means allowing the market dynamic already operating—with a little help from the workers' state—to spread co-ops over the entire economy. But capitalism is full of "elements" that indicate the possibility of socialism, either by resembling a socialist form (as in producer and consumer co-ops, nationalized industry, public education, and even political democracy) or by setting out an important precondition for the development of socialist relations (as in the advanced state of technology, complex economic and social organizations, and a literate, highly trained, and hard working population).

It is largely through his dialectical analysis of these and similar "elements" that Marx is able to catch a glimpse of the future in the present. "To set free elements of the new society," however, involves a radical transformation in what they are and in how they work that goes far beyond replacing a capitalist state with one run by workers, since these elements are all seriously distorted—as Lawler admits—by the capitalist context. In no instance is socialism simply or even mainly a matter of extending what is already in place. A qualitative break has to occur. "Sprouts," after all, are not trees, even young ones, and being "pregnant" is not the same as holding a baby in one's arms. Lawler has misunderstood Marx's metaphors as pointing to a later phase in communism's process of becoming than was Marx's intent. The result is a trivialization of the enormous transformation any "element" would have to undergo in becoming suitable for the "new society," which also makes it easy for Lawler to dismiss the need for a central plan to help bring these changes about.

Third, Lawler takes Marx's acclaim for the Paris Commune as evidence that he also accepted their full economic program. Marx declared the short-lived Commune to be a model of the dictatorship of the proletariat, and the Commune did not abolish the market. Instead, it introduced measures aimed at altering the balance of power between workers and their employers in capitalist enterprises and encouraged the creation of co-ops. Does this show that Marx discounted the role of central planning in socialism? Hardly. Marx's endorsement of the Commune had to do mainly with the political form that it took, with the way it combined democracy and working class rule, which is the aspect of the Commune to which he directed most of his remarks, and not with all the policies it adopted. He certainly disapproved of the military policies, for example, that left it so weak in face of the reactionary forces that eventually destroyed it. In any case, we have already seen that the steps Marx advised workers' governments to take immediately after the revolution left the market largely intact, and this is the situation—rendered even more difficult by the ongoing civil war—for which the Commune's program was intended. As a true dictatorship of the proletariat, the Commune, had it survived, would have moved relatively soon to put into effect the other main elements of the socialist stage, including extensive planning.

Fourth, Lawler misinterprets Marx's comment on "labor vouchers" in socialism to refer to a kind of money, which again allows Lawler to claim that Marx accepts the continued existence of a market. Marx spoke of workers in socialism receiving "labor vouchers," based on the amount of time they worked, which they can exchange for articles of personal consumption. Marx says these vouchers are "no more money than a ticket for a theater." Why isn't such a ticket money? Because it doesn't circulate. Hence, it plays no role in determining what gets produced. That is decided in this period by the plan. Like theater tickets, labor vouchers are also limited in what they can exchange for: unlike money, labor vouchers cannot buy means of production, social means of consumption, status, influence, or friends. Because they are given to people in proportion to their own work, and because no one can acquire them from the work of others, labor vouchers, as Lawler rightly notes, are "personalized." They allow one person, and he or she alone, to take from the common stock (after investment and welfare needs have been met) an amount that is proportional to what they put into it. Rather than being, like money, a way of rationing power, labor vouchers are simply a means of rewarding work. With such restricted functions, it is inaccurate to refer to labor vouchers as money, and equally misleading, therefore, to view the exchanges in which they are used as a market. Lawler also seems to have overlooked the fact that if it is the number of hours people work that determines how many labor vouchers they get, this offers further evidence that workers' co-ops, where income is determined by the success (or failure) of one's enterprise, have ceased to exist by this time.

Fifth, and last, while Lawler admits that Marx sometimes speaks of planning under socialism, he never examines why Marx does so, why he may have believed extensive planning was necessary. Yet Lawler himself, quotes Marx's most important comment on this subject: "if cooperative production . . . is to supersede the capitalist system," Marx says, it must *"regulate national production upon a common plan"* (My emphasis). Why? Because this is the only way to put "an end to the constant anarchy and periodical convulsions which are the fatality of capitalist production." Lawler is only concerned with the reference to "cooperative production" and "cooperative societies" here, but no one is disputing that Marx believed there would be more cooperation in socialism (cooperation not being the same thing as workers' cooperatives). Still, for Marx, the more important economic decisions that are now left to the market would be made relatively soon after the revolution by the plan.

The "anarchy" and "convulsions" referred to above are the result of a lack of alignment between production and consumption. Because production follows the logic of profit maximization while consumption follows the logic of effective demand (individuals buying what they can afford of what they want), there is always too much or too little of everything, never just enough. Waste of some factors of production and some finished goods goes on continually, as do the unsatisfied demands of a major section of the population, and periodically the build-up of this contradiction produces an economic crisis with its widespread destruction and losses of all kinds. As Marx shows, these problems are the result of things being produced in order to be sold in the market, and not just of capitalist ownership of the means of production. Thus, this "anarchy" and these "convulsions," however attenuated (though even this is not certain) would continue under the new conditions favored by market socialists. It is largely "to put an end" to just such horrors, however, that Marx sought to "regulate national production upon a common plan." Such a plan would align production with consumption to insure that full use is made of the available forces of production to satisfy people's wants.

Even Lawler is forced to recognize that when occasionally too much or too little of something is produced, some adjustments are called for, and that this would require "new mechanisms of adjustment." But under market conditions, there is always too much or too little of something, and "mechanisms of adjustment" means planning. Where this is required, as it would be on a national and eventually on a world scale, this means central planning, but this remains an idea that Lawler steadfastly rejects.

In conclusion, I want to express my surprise at Lawler's conclusion. He ends his essay by saying that the "final goal of communist development . . . is the maturation of an ongoing process of humanity struggling to free itself from its own self-alienation, and using that very alienation as a means of its liberation." With this conclusion, one would have expected more discussion of alienation earlier in the essay. How, for example, does self-alienation manifest itself? What forms does it take, and how do they participate in the process of liberation? Marxists have linked the market to various expressions of alienation such as competition, greed, consumerism, fetishism, mystification, etc. How much of this alienation would market socialism inherit from capitalism, and how would a "social market" do away with it? To justify a conclusion that points to the disappearance of alienation, Lawler would have to provide answers to such questions. He doesn't, and he doesn't because he can't. Market socialism is awash in alienation, and anyone who, like Lawler, wishes to help build our communist future will have to discard all markets sooner or later. Sooner is better.

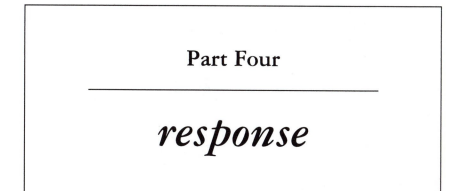

Part Four

response

9

Response to Schweickart

HILLEL TICKTIN

INTRODUCTION

Schweickart's critique of my article is largely summarised in his foot-notes. He has argued that I have not produced the outline of an alternative socialist economy. That is true. I have not done so. I have done so elsewhere, but a total description of the alternative is impossible in the few pages devoted to this subject in my article. I argued in my critique of his article that a socialist society would have two characteristics which would make his demand less important. The first was that a socialist society would be one moving towards abundance, and the second was that the workers in such a society would be more and more involved in non-hierarchical creative social labour, which would cause them to iden-tify with the society and therefore with the planners, because they would themselves be the planners.

Nonetheless, I can produce a reasonable outline of aspects of a social-ist economy, which at least attempts to answer Schweickart. In the first instance, one can assume that there will be elected planning organisations at a whole series of levels within the society. Their task would be one of coordination and the formulation of important decisions to be taken at the particular level which is appropriate to them. They would have to decide between the use of surveys of public opinion and the use of refer-enda in particular cases. As the planners would be regularly elected and recallable, it would be hard for them to act against the public interest.

THE SOCIALIST ECONOMY

There would be three crucial "economic" aspects of such a society. One would be the existence of substantial stocks of all items. This would mean that the planners could always correct their mistakes by drawing on stocks. Mistakes would be assumed to be normal, because there could be no way of determining costs or the intensity of demand other than by regular surveys. Since workers would no longer be abstract labourers there could be no value. Hence, any pricing would be purely artificial. In this respect, in my view, Von Mises was correct against Lange, in their well known debate on calculation in a socialist society. If we translate the Marxist language, this means that individuals would work at different rates determined by their capacities, and hence that there would be no common yardstick to produce a price. There would only be relative quantities of items required to produce the product. As the society moved closer to relative abundance problems would diminish, though there would always be a question of time required to actually produce what was needed.

It should be noted that Schweickart's market socialist society would have to be similar in permitting workers to work at their own rate, unless the workers were to be subjected to control by machines and management. At this point his own society unravels, because, if there is no abstract labour, value calculation becomes impossible, in which case prices become adrift of costs and are purely arbitrary. Competition in this context becomes largely meaningless. If, on the other hand, workers do work at similar rates to workers elsewhere and are subject to the control of the machine, management, competition, etc., then the workers are abstract labourers and so alienated from their labour process and inevitably from their own product. Such workers would have no reason to prefer this society to capitalism.

In the transition towards abundance, the coefficients of the relationships between sectors of production, as shown in an input-output analysis, would become known. This is the second key "economic" aspect of socialism. In the initial phase, moving out of capitalism, growth would be fast and the coefficients would change rapidly, but after that period they would become more predictable. Hence, the planners would be able to work out their requirements for old products based on history, and for new products by referring to these coefficients. When they made a mistake, which would occur regularly, they could draw down their stocks while learning from that mistake. After a period of time of accumulated mistakes, planners would make fewer errors though they would continue to make some.

The third "economic" aspect of the society would be the decentralised form already mentioned. In this context, it would mean that at the lowest level planning would need coefficients less and surveys more. The planners would obtain the nature of consumer demand by asking people directly.

In the initial phase after taking power, money and the market would continue, but as production rose, more and more aspects of the society would drop out of the money economy. Thus, education and the provision of health would be made entirely free very quickly. Pharmaceuticals would follow very shortly thereafter. As public transport was developed, it too could be released from the market. The next step would be to introduce free housing and thereafter free utilities. All these parts of the economy have been partially freed of the market in various Stalinist and social democratic countries over the past fifty to one hundred years. The point, of course, is that these sections of the economy tend to operate poorly under the market. Finance would gradually disappear as money came to be limited in its use. The arms sector would be abolished. As productivity rose much of manufacturing would consist of very few workers operating a few machines which either produced other machines or the necessary consumer goods. In time, they would also cease to be exchange values and so lose their prices. Distribution would be greatly simplified in the absence of money. Clearly most workers would be in new kinds of jobs.

There would be a large number of workers who could be employed in creative labour. Whether it will be in research, education, health or manual labour of different kinds makes little difference since they would all be able to move to new jobs in time. Education itself would change its nature. Modern education ruins the naturally inquiring mind of the child by instilling a deadening discipline. Instead, everyone will learn a method of understanding which will allow them to grasp new concepts and new disciplines much more quickly than they do now permitting an easier shifting of jobs than at present. Labour power will have ceased to be a commodity. The worker will control his own product, he will control his own labour process, and he will be at one with humanity as a whole. That is surely the meaning of socialism.

THE TECHNICAL QUESTIONS

Schweickart, however, asks a series of technical questions. Who will decide which factories will contract, which will expand, where they will go, and what they will produce? How will the decisions be made? Modern economists spend all their time on these questions, which they claim to be of prime importance because human wants are infinite and resources scarce. If we reject both assumptions, of scarcity and of the infinity of human wants, the situation becomes different. Society will work towards a situation of relative abundance, where these questions become relatively unimportant. Very few people will work in factories. With full employment and with everyone engaged in creative labour, no one needs be disadvantaged by change. Society will have the luxury of allowing change to occur gradually, when necessary, and then only by agreement. Hence the decisions mentioned above become far less important. Of course Schweickart is implicitly pouring scorn on the idea that there can be relative abundance and that human needs are not infinite.

This is a debate I used to have with Alec Nove, who taught in my department here at the University of Glasgow, until he refused to have a public discussion of the matter. For it had become evident that once abundance is accepted everything else I have maintained about socialism follows. On the other hand, if scarcity is permanent, socialism is ruled out. Trotsky put this point very graphically when he used the example of the queue to point out what happens when there are shortages: discontent, the police, competition, fighting, etc. As I have already argued in my critique of Schweickart, the labour theory of value assumes the possibility of abundance and must be abandoned if this possibility is rejected. Marxism then falls as well. Of course Marxism may be wrong, but then it is not at all clear why anyone would want socialism, as Marxism is the only theory that provides an explanation of the necessity of socialism.

As for people's wants, finding out what they are would not be too difficult. There are certain basic common needs like the ones detailed above: for housing, health, education, and transport, which are common and would be publicly supplied. Major issues in these spheres would be determined by direct enquiry, whether by survey, referenda or public meetings. Nor does this assume that we are talking of thousands, millions or billions of people all the time. After all, many questions can be discussed locally and dealt with locally. Others will require regional, national or international decisions. But in that case a referendum can be held, if the issue is important, or a survey can be done. If the questions asked are wrong, or the results turn out to be contrary to what people really wanted, it will not be difficult to hold a second referendum or survey upon popular request. For other goods, which are more private, people will have more choice than at the present time when the big corporations basically decide what it is that people want.

The assumption that Schweickart makes that the market can be open to all like a democratic Hilton Hotel if there are no rich or poor is fantastic. He accepts the argument for different levels of decision making, but feels that they ought to be making market-type decisions, as over investment. In fact, provided that the investment was expressed less in price terms and more in total quantities, we would not differ. Where we do differ is in his discussion of the success and failure of enterprises. They will fail, we are told, if consumers do not like their products. Presumably, they will also fail if their costs are too high, if their competitors produce the commodity more cheaply by making false economies which will only show up in later years, if workers demand higher wages, or if the manager is inefficient. How will consumers decide what they want and don't want? At the moment that is decided through advertising, lack of alternatives and through education. A socialist educational system will alter people's wants radically and suggest more social ways in which to satisfy needs. A total restructuring will be required. The point is that the competitive enterprise has little to do with choice. At the same time, the market only has meaning if labour power is sold and the worker loses control over his product. Yet Schweickart wants his workers to elect their managers. What, we may ask, is to stop workers demanding the highest possible wage? The answer given is that the market will restrain them, i.e. competition with other firms. In that case, however, we have state capitalism, where there is no capitalist class, as he insists, but workers still sell their labour power to enterprises that go bankrupt if they do not make an adequate profit. In this process, their workers will be dismissed and forced to join the reserve army of labour. Labour power, here, is still a commodity, and is controlled by the usual capitalist means of unemployment and the fetishism of the commodity. If, however, unemployment is rejected and workers do not lose their jobs, there is nothing to stop workers from demanding their full product, which would destroy any profit. But Schweickart suggests that workers would put the interests of the society before their immediate interest. In which case, we can ask why we need to put up with the waste of competition in order to run such a society in the first place. Where workers have attained this degree of consciousness, surely we can dispense with the market.

THE QUESTION OF MARKET AND PLANNING

Schweickart says that there is no antithesis between market and planning in the real world. Schweickart calls conscious organisation "planning." I do not agree because it implies that any time a number of people decide something on the economy at whatever level they are planning. Of course modern economies are more and more consciously controlled. The problem with this kind of definition, however, is that it does not examine the real process involved. The control over quantities of goods supplied to a particular factory, over the relations between parts of a factory or between different factories within one enterprise, over the quantity of money in the economy, interest rates, totals invested in the arms industry, etc. are all examples of what Schweickart calls planning but what I would call the interface of organisation and the market. In a sense it is proto-planning in that it has elements of planning without actually being planning. He is right to point to the ubiquity of this proto-planning, but we have to describe the essential nature of this process. When we do so, it becomes clear that it is partly conscious and partly unconscious, that it is based on some but not enough information or knowledge, and that the decisions are only sometimes implemented and then often only partially. A simple decision to raise the interest rate is no more planning than a decision to raise the salary of a manager. Planning requires conscious regulation of the activity of the producers, and that is why it is unlikely to succeed unless the direct producers are themselves involved. This seems to me to be the real world. It is one where the direct producers are in conflict with the decisions of those who play crucial roles in the operations of a market, a market that is increasingly "organised," but not planned.

Schweickart objects to the above definition of planning. Any socialist ought to consider that every economic category is a social relation. Orthodox economics avoids this point and tries to make its categories apparently value free by ignoring their human component. Capital appears as a thing and so does planning. Neither are things in themselves. They are social relations. What then is the planning social relation other than what I have described above. It must involve both planners and workers. The problem then is that so-called planners are in the business of controlling workers, but workers do not like being controlled and have to be forced to comply. There are only two forms for compelling obedience: the market and force. If force is used in a modern industrialized economy, it simply malfunctions because workers work badly, which then feeds back into the entire system. As I have consistently argued, this is what took place in the Soviet Union, which is why it failed. Surely, we cannot use a definition so broad that it applies to the Pharaohs planning pyramids and irrigation, to the feudal lords planning their estates, to the capitalist planning his firm, and even to Milton Friedman planning capitalism because he advises the use of monetary statistics to determine the course of the economy.

It is true that organisational forms have been used from the dawn of time, and indeed this was the basis of Bogdanov's introductory textbook on Marxist political economy which was so extensively used by the Bolsheviks. Proto-forms of the market have also existed for a very long time, but it was only when capital came into existence that the market truly functioned. There are always elements of the future in the past, but it is very important not to identify the two. Man is not an ape, even though our DNA is practically the same as that of the ape. Yet we can only understand the ape in terms of what came to be a man.

More specifically, I have argued that conscious decision-making and related organisational forms conflict with the market. Capital prefers to be untrammeled, and when it is regulated it malfunctions. That is a major point on which Schweickart and I differ. This difference was of course rehearsed in the twenties in the debates between Bukharin and Preobrazhensky, even though both believed there would be no market under socialism. Clearly, Hayek, Friedman, Thatcher, Reagan, etc. had a point when they wanted to roll back the state. They were attempting to install a reactionary utopia, one in which capital would be freed of all controls like income tax, environmental restrictions, labour regulations, etc. Capital needs mass unemployment to function properly, because unemployment produces subordinated workers who carry out instructions correctly because they have no choice. The fact that capital has accepted limitations on its activities does not show that it is planning but rather that it has accepted restrictions in order to survive. Even its "planning" inside the firm constitutes a constant irritant, because it means that it must use non-market criteria for success, criteria which are inevitably indeterminate and which permit workers to raise their profile.

CONCLUSION

I began by referring to Schweickart's footnotes and I want to end there, because a rebuttal of his footnotes provides a convenient summary of my arguments.

As regards Schweickart's first footnote. I reject the view that my definition of socialism is normative as opposed to positive, or that a value neutral definition is possible. Socialism stands opposed to the alienation, exploitation and fetishism of capitalism and hence must be defined in terms of its new social relations. They must involve the negation of the features just mentioned. That must mean that abstract labour is abolished and with it alienation and the fetishism of the commodity. The whole point of the market, however, lies in its use of abstract labour, the reduction of the labour-power of the worker to a commodity. If, however, labour is not a commodity, then there is no control over labour and there is no capital either. Nor is there any basis for secure calculation. In other words, there is no market.

Contra Schweickart's second footnote, it is hard to argue that capitalism gives workers some control over the economy because they spend money on goods. It is true that in the post war years workers' in the developed world have become consumers on some scale but this was a consequence of a social-democratic concession made by the capitalist class as a means of avoiding the inevitable. In an earlier period it was less true. In any case, workers' demand is largely determined by the big corporations rather than by the workers themselves. Workers in so-called market socialism, we are told, would get the same income as everyone else. Hence, it is they who would determine consumption. If there is scarcity, however, some people would get more than others unless there was rationing. The history of the limitation of money under the Stalinist system and in wartime elsewhere showed that, in conditions of scarcity, unless there were an extreme variation in prices, rationing was necessary. Assuming that everyone received the basic necessities, there would have to be goods which everyone wanted but which not everyone could get. These goods could either be rationed or given to the relatively better off. The point here is that the market necessarily makes for inequality. You cannot have a fair market or fair salaries in a market. In a truly socialist society such goods would only be produced when most people could be supplied with them, but, since generalised scarcity would be a thing of the past this would not be a source of worry.

The third footnote asks if I have examined any of the models of market socialism. I am tempted to respond that, having Alec Nove as head of my department, I was forced to do so, but that is not really the issue. I speak of capitalists as well as workers under market socialism because, in my view, the function of the capitalist, if not the capitalist we know, continues to exist, and because I regard market socialism as a variety of capitalism. In other words, modern capitalism does have many of the "planning" forms to which Schweickart correctly refers, but in my view, this only leads to a malfunctioning capitalism. Capitalism is undermined by the very same conflict that I perceive in market socialism.

I do not see the relation between market and plan as a contradiction. There is contradiction between labour and capital, but between worker and capitalist and between planning and the market there is a fight to the death. There is supersession from labour and capital into a planned economy, but between plan and market there is only violent, vicious and massive conflict, sometimes hidden and sometimes taking monstrous, temporary, mediating forms but always finally taking the form of a direct conflict. This conflict is a feature of our times and must be understood if we are to understand modern capitalism at all. Capitalism is not an unchanging system. It came into being, matured and declined, and we live in its decline, which is marked by just this conflict. The socialisation of production, of which Marx spoke, must necessarily lead to the elimination of value and its replacement, first by proto-planning or organisational forms and then, ultimately, when capitalism is overthrown, by a form in which humans decide their own future in a direct, conscious way.

Schweickart has very nicely concluded by trying to find some common ground. We are, of course, both socialists, but we see the existing world and the future very differently. His definition of socialism allows him to see Stalinist countries as socialist, whereas I regard them as being as far, or even farther, from socialism than any capitalist society. For me, there is every reason for optimism in their downfall, and I now look to the decline of capitalism, evidenced in the decline of the value-form, as a clear pointer to the ultimate demise of the old social order. Although Schweickart and I disagree on these fundamentals, I would hope that when the chips are down we will be on the same side.

10.

Response to Ticktin

DAVID SCHWEICKART

Too many debates about the merits of market socialism proceed abstractly without reference to specific models. Although both Ticktin and Ollman in their criticisms have tried to be more concrete, it appears that neither has grasped certain distinctive features of Economic Democracy—which is the specific model of market socialism I wish to defend here.[1] For example, Ticktin thinks that in Economic Democracy managers, given competitive pressures, will have to force workers to accept lower wages; otherwise profits will disappear. Ollman, for his part, thinks that capital—as self-expanding value—will continue to exist under Economic Democracy. Neither Ticktin nor Ollman has understood that the terms "wage," "profit" and "capital" mean something very different under Economic Democracy than they do under capitalism.

Strictly speaking, there are no "wages" in a worker-self-managed enterprise. All workers, including managers, receive a share of the "profits," not a contractual wage or salary. These "profits" are calculated differently under Economic Democracy than under capitalism. In both cases profit is the difference between sales revenue and costs, but under Economic Democracy worker income is *not* a cost. It is the residual; it is what is left over after inputs have been purchased, depreciation allowances set aside and taxes paid. So managers cannot force workers to take a lower wage so as to enhance company profits. Those profits are precisely what constitute their "wages." Nor can workers insist on wages so high as to eliminate profits. Again—those wages are the profits.[2] The only way workers can raise their incomes without working more efficiently or using more productive technologies is to have their managers raise the prices of their products—but this they cannot do without endangering their competitive standing.[3]

If there are no "wages" under Economic Democracy, is there "capital"? Ollman, following Marx, characterizes capital as self-expanding value.

This seems right to me. A capitalist system is structured in such as way that powerful incentives, both positive and negative, compel individual capitalists to reinvest much of their profits, so that the value of capital (except in periods of economic crisis) tends to increase. But under Economic Democracy there is no such relentless pressure toward expansion. Hence, there is no "capital"—not in Ollman's or Marx's sense. To be sure there are funds ear-marked for reinvestment. But these funds derive from a tax on the capital assets of enterprises.[4] This rate is set democratically—not by market forces. That is to say, the decision as to the overall rate of reinvestment is under conscious control and subject to democratic debate.

It should be noted that there will always be arguments to be made on both sides. Raising the rate of investment will make more money available to enterprises desiring to expand. But raising the investment rate means raising the tax rate, thus lowering the immediate consumption of everyone. That this tradeoff is made explicit under Economic Democracy is one of the virtues of the model. Under capitalism too there is a trade-off between investment and consumption, since the investment rate can be raised only by lowering wages or raising prices (which in real terms amounts to the same thing), but this tradeoff is disguised, and in no way subject to democratic adjudication.[5]

Rather than continue with specific criticisms of Ollman and Ticktin and specific defenses against their charges, let me conclude by taking a different tack. To see where our differences really lie, let us imagine that there has been a major political upheaval in an advanced capitalist country, and that those now holding the reins of power have a popular mandate to institute radical social change. The people, let us suppose, want socialism. What is to be done?

Interestingly, Ticktin, Ollman, Lawler and I would all give pretty much the same answer. We may disagree as to whether we should call this new society "socialist" just yet, but all of us agree that the market would have to be maintained—at least for a while. So the new economy will be market—something.

Then it has to be asked, who would run the enterprises? I think we would all agree: the workers. Workers in enterprises should elect their managers (or elect a council which appoints the managers). The alternative—since *someone* has to be in charge—would be for the State or the Party to appoint the managers, but I don't think either Ollman or Ticktin would find this option desirable.

What about the investment mechanism? Where would the funds come from to finance new investment, and how would these funds be allocated? Neither Ollman nor Ticktin seems to have given this matter much thought, but both insist that the economy needs to be planned. But economic planning involves, above all, the planning of investment, since any *changes* in the pattern of production must be effected through new investment. So Ollman and Ticktin would probably agree with my general formulation that investment needs to be "socially controlled." Since there aren't any capitalists anymore from whom to entice investment funds, it would seem that these funds would have to be generated through taxation (either explicitly or implicitly). These funds now have to be channeled back into the economy in such a way that urgent problems are addressed. I don't see any reason for Ollman or Ticktin to object to having them distributed via nationalized banks.

In short, I see no reason for Ollman or Ticktin to object to instituting, in the immediate aftermath of the revolution, precisely the sort of model I call Economic Democracy. They may want to argue about various technical features of the model, but they have no grounds to object in principle to a market economy with enterprises run democratically by workers and investment socially controlled. They may not want to call it socialism, but they would have to admit that they have no alternative to propose for the period immediately following the accession to power of a socialist government able and willing to institute radical change that would better fit their definition of socialism. Something like Economic Democracy is what we should aim for.

So, in a sense, the real debate is about what to do next. Let me concentrate on Ticktin's scenario. Ticktin thinks that the massive waste that we have under capitalism—military expenditures, advertising, reduplication of products, unnecessary sales outlets—would be quickly eliminated, leading to a sharp rise in consumption for almost everybody (excepting, of course, the ex-capitalists, who would now, presumably, have to work for a living). At the same time we could begin shifting important sectors out of the money economy. Health care and education could be made free at once, with pharmaceutical and public transportation rapidly following suit. In due time housing and utilities could also be offered as free goods.

While these developments are underway, machinery would be increasingly employed in the manufacturing sector, reducing the need for onerous labor to a minimum, thus allowing people to seek genuinely rewarding and creative jobs. As people increasingly take more pleasure in their work and less in mindless consumption, we will soon enough find ourselves in a state of "abundance," i.e., with enough goods on hand to satisfy everyone's now rational desires. So we will no longer need to charge for anything. Planners, using surveys and referenda, can ascertain what people want. These goods will be duly produced and sent to retail outlets. People will come and help themselves. No more market, no more money, no more scarcity.

As a Marxist I do not find this scenario as preposterous as most non-Marxists likely would. I do not think that desires are so infinitely insatiable that scarcity can never be overcome, nor do I believe it impossible that we could one day live in a society where most people actually enjoy their work. However, I do have serious reservations about this particular scenario—which, I must confess, is quite similar to one that I myself proposed some years ago, when trying to describe how society might make the transition from a worker-self-managed market socialism to full communism.[6]

I no longer find this scenario plausible—or even desirable. First of all, it vastly underestimates the difficulty of getting rid of the waste we will inherit from capitalism. For example, it is easy enough to say, abolish arms production, but even if that were feasible (i.e. the whole world has suddenly become pacifist-socialist), there is the problem of what to do with the tens of thousands of workers employed in those industries. They can't simply be laid off. Not only would this be a betrayal of the socialist commitment to full employment, but such a move would also cut drastically into domestic demand, and so all the industries dependent on selling to these workers would find themselves in a slump. But relocating these workers is not easy, nor is it so easy to find alternative uses for the productive facilities designed to build weapons of mass destruction. It will be necessary to channel large amounts of "capital" into those areas to aid them in the transition, funds that will not appear miraculously from the elimination of "waste," but must be generated via taxation, i.e., from other workers' consumption. Ticktin appears not to grasp a paradoxical fact about a modern economy. It costs money—or, if you prefer, labor and resources—to eliminate waste. In the long run the economy and everyone in it can be made better off, but in the short run people must pay.

Even more serious than Ticktin's underestimation of the difficulties and costs of reducing waste is his underestimation of the difficulties involved in eliminating onerous labor. I suspect that academics are particularly prone to this mistake, since our own work situation is exceptionally privileged. If one is a tenured professor, one has job security, a decent income, long vacations and even sabbaticals, usually considerable freedom over the content of the courses one teaches, often significant input into the governance of one's department, etc. One wants to believe that the conditions under which we labor could be extended *readily,* i.e., in a few years, to most of the rest of the workforce. (Actually, most of us complain about our work, so we want conditions even better than our own made quickly available to almost everyone.) But this is wishful thinking bordering on delusion. I do not deny that most jobs would be better than they are now if workers had some control over their design, nor do I deny that *eventually* the most onerous jobs can be mechanized or redesigned or rotated, so that people doing them can feel genuinely fulfilled at their work. But this will take a long, long time and moreover—and here we come to a major disagreement I have with the other contributors, certainly with Ticktin and Ollman and perhaps even with Lawler—I do not think we will *ever* reach the point where economic incentives can be eliminated altogether. I could be wrong. None of us now living will ever know, since it isn't going to happen in any of our lifetimes. In any event I think it foolish to count on such an eventuality—or even to consider it terribly important. I will return to this point below.

A third problem I have with Ticktin's scenario is his eagerness to have as many items as possible removed as rapidly as possible from the money economy. I think this desire is ideologically driven. Because one opposes the market, even if one is compelled to accept its temporary necessity, one wants items removed from the market even when there is no good reason for doing so. For example, Ticktin wants housing to be provided free. This strikes me as an exceedingly bad idea. It is one thing to guarantee everyone a place to live, and, until jobs can be created that pay decent incomes, to subsidize the housing of the poor (who will still be with us after the revolution). It is quite another thing to say that housing for everyone should be free. Such a policy rests on the assumption that housing will all be of more or less the same quality, and that people's desires in this regard will be pretty much uniform. If not, then desirable housing will still have to rationed, but by some other mechanism than by price. If housing is rationed by price, then individuals or families can set their own priorities, determine how important certain features are to them, how much *extra* they are willing to pay for more space, a yard, a garage, a better view, a more convenient location, higher quality workmanship, a more aesthetic appearance, etc., etc. Notice, it is not possible to determine housing needs by surveys or referenda *in the absence of prices,* for how would one know how to answer the survey? Everyone could be asked to specify his or her dream house, but what good would that do? The planners would need to know *how important* the various features are and what tradeoffs individuals would be willing to make—unless there is *such* abundance that everyone can have whatever house one desires, since there are *no* real differential costs nor any locational constraints. (Can anyone who wants one have a house on the beach? Do we prohibit anyone from having such a house, since not everyone can? Do we institute a housing lottery?)

It is possible that with sufficient ingenuity, Ticktin could come up with an alternative allocational mechanism. But the important question to ask is this: *what's wrong* with allowing housing to be rationed by price? If everyone has sufficient income to afford *decent* housing and no one can get exorbitantly rich via real estate speculation—and these are conditions our new society can insure—why would we want to take housing out of the market? Apart, that is from an ideological aversion to the market itself.

Let me suggest a scenario different from Ticktin's for a transition from capitalism to a post-capitalist society. Let us begin again with Economic Democracy, which, I've argued, is the first stage for both of us. As Ticktin maintains, we can certainly move rapidly to a system of free health care and free education. Of course by "free" we don't mean costless to society, but universal coverage financed from tax revenues. We would probably want to do the same for pensions. Everyone should be guaranteed a decent life after retirement.

This may be as far as we want to go with free goods in a post-capitalist society, certainly in the short run, perhaps even in the long term. There might be a few other items that should be offered to everyone free of charge, but these would have to be decided on a case by case basis—without any presumption that just because they *could* be offered free of charge that they *should* be. Urban mass transit is a case in point. Buses and subways could be made free. There is no danger of excessive, wasteful use. But whether they should be free would depend on housing patterns and citizen preferences. "Free" transportation means requiring non-users to subsidize users. If a community wants to opt for such a system, on the grounds that this would provide incentives for people to shift away from excessive reliance on private automobiles, so be it. But the case should be made based on the deleterious effects of having too many cars, *not* on the inherent desirability of removing sectors from the market whenever possible.

A first priority after the revolution would have to be a channeling of significant new investment to those areas of terrible urban and rural poverty so as to rebuild the housing, educational facilities and infrastructure there and to set up as many new enterprises as is feasible. The aim would be to provide a decent, productive job for everyone. Until profitable, self-managed enterprises can be established, the government itself will have to serve as a major employer.

We should not pretend that this undertaking will be simple, easily financed out of the savings brought about through the elimination of capitalist "waste." As I have already argued, eliminating this waste will *also* be costly. It is not true that the vast majority of the citizenry will experience an immediate improvement in their consumption levels. It might well be that consumption will go down, not up, for many people, since the financing of these necessary endeavors must come from taxation.

What will go up immediately for almost everyone is job security and the opportunity to participate in the governance of one's enterprise. This reform is costless. It should also lead in most instances to greater internal efficiency.

What will also increase immediately is the opportunity to participate meaningfully in community affairs. This opportunity already exists, formally, in capitalist democracies, but now, for the first time, the citizenry would have a guaranteed flow of investment funds coming into their communities, the disposition of which is up to them. This new opportunity can be expected to energize local governance.

Let us now fast-forward into the future, some fifty years or so hence. Suppose our inner cities have been rebuilt, the health and educational opportunities of our citizens equalized and enhanced, and our communities stabilized. More and more we can expect that the new investments our enterprises make will be for the purpose of reducing work time (shorter workweek, longer vacations, employee sabbaticals) and for making jobs more creative and interesting, rather than enhancing income. Suppose we reach the point—and fifty years after the revolution we may be close to it—where almost everyone feels that their incomes are sufficient to free them from financial anxieties and to allow them to lead what on their own terms they would regard as a good life. Not many would say that they have *everything* they want. Tradeoffs would still have to be made. Some people would save to buy a bigger house; others would want to travel extensively; some would want to indulge in expensive hobbies; others would be content just to "save for a rainy day"; some would like to throw big parties; others would like to give extensively to international relief efforts or help fund projects in areas of the world still struggling to overcome the legacy of neocolonial capitalism.

Let us suppose that not only do the vast majority feel financially secure, but most also feel that their main motivation for working is the satisfaction the job provides. It's not that work is play or that they wouldn't prefer even longer vacations, but all things considered they feel good about their jobs—and would want to work at these jobs even if they paid less than they do. That is to say, the size of the paycheck is not the principal motivation.

My question now is this: If we reached such a state, why would we want to reorganize the economy any further? Granted, it is still a market economy. Enterprises still sell their goods, and workers still receive incomes. There is still money, and even competition—though not of a cut-throat variety. The economy is solid and stable. It is not driven by capitalism's grow or die imperative. People can spend their lives without worrying much about economic matters.

I submit that such a society deserves to be called "the higher stage of communism." The society has left "the realm of necessity" and has entered "the realm of freedom." People really do, for the most part, work "according to ability," and consume "according to need." We have here the rational core of Marx's dream. The details may not be precisely what he had envisaged, but I don't think he would be terribly disappointed. In any event, were such a society to come to pass—and indeed become the attainable model for the rest of the world—I for one would argue that Marx's hopeful vision has been vindicated.

NOTES

1. In my opening piece I also sketched John Roemer's model, but since neither Ticktin nor Ollman address that model directly, I will focus my remarks here on Economic Democracy.
2. It should be noted that in the model I propose enterprises are not permitted to reinvest their own "profits." All "profits" are returned to the workers. All funds for new investment come from the tax-generated investment pool.
3. Might not enterprises compete by *lowering* their prices, thus, in effect, lowering their wages. In theory yes—such a "beggar-thy-neighbor" strategy is not ruled out. However, just as capitalist firms rarely compete by lowering their profit margins (as opposed to lowering their costs—one of which is labor), it seems unlikely that such practices would become widespread among workers. The self-destructive nature of such behavior is too obvious.
4. There are "capital assets" under Economic Democracy, namely the material means of production controlled by the workers of an enterprise, but no "capital" as an abstract entity with an inherent expansionary tendency.
5. It is not true that there is *always* a trade-off under capitalism between investment and consumption, although usually there is. If there are both idle resources and unemployed people, it is sometimes possible to increase investment and consumption simultaneously. (This is an essential insight of Keynesian economics.) This would also be true under Economic Democracy.
6. See my *Capitalism or Worker Control? An Ethical and Economic Appraisal* (New York: Praeger, 1980), 219–20.

11.

Response to Lawler

BERTELL OLLMAN

It is a pleasure to participate in a serious debate over the future of social-ism, really the future of capitalism if capitalism is to have any future. The participants in this debate share a profound antipathy to capitalism and an equally strong attraction for communism, but disagree over the kind of society that is needed to bring about the transformation of the one into the other. Unlike anarcho-communists, none of us believe that communism will emerge full blown from a socialist revolution. Some kind of transition and a period of indeterminate length for it to occur are required. It should also be clear that none of us thinks it possible to con-struct a detailed blueprint of the post-capitalist future or that those of our descendants who are lucky enough to live then must heed all of our pronouncements. Still, the first foundations for that day-after-tomorrow will be constructed in large part out of what we do today, and to begin work on these foundations the people who suffer most under the status quo have to recognize that there is an alternative, which is to say they have to acquire a better understanding of how the present, the past and the future are linked together. While our debate focuses on the future, the chief aim is always to affect the present so as to make a communist future possible.

Jim Lawler's main criticisms of my essay are that I have an overly neg-ative view of workers' co-ops and that I underestimate the degree to which a "social market," one dominated by co-ops, could solve the prob-lems associated with markets in capitalism. (Some of the other "weak-nesses" he mentions receive their response in my criticism of his essay). As for my criticisms of workers' co-ops, they were directed almost entirely at the view that co-ops are the ideal economic form with which to build a future socialist society. My attitude toward co-ops in capital-ism, on the other hand, is very mixed. In my essay, I gladly admitted that co-ops can increase, albeit modestly, workers' empowerment as well as their sense of dignity. Co-ops also give a powerful boost to such crucial socialist arguments that production can go on without capitalists and that workers have what it takes to run their own enterprises. Since co-ops often get started when a capitalist owner goes bankrupt or is about to move out of the community, co-ops also play an important role in providing workers, who would otherwise not have them, with jobs.

Admitting all these progressive effects, however, should not keep us from recognizing that co-ops participate in the capitalist economy like any privately owned enterprise, which means that they treat their consumers, their competitors, people seeking employment, the environment, and—yes—their own owner-workers in their function as workers in whatever ways are necessary to maximize their profit. Yes, co-ops have difficulty—as Lawler rightly points out—picking up their factory and moving it to Mexico, but this is a relatively minor difference when compared to all the ways in which they are similar to capitalist-owned firms. Undoubtedly, there are exceptions, but they are few, because the rewards and punishments established by the market are simply too great to be ignored and—I might add—too easy to rationalize. Promising wealth and threatening lower living standards and even bankruptcy, the market compels workers' co-ops to behave in a capitalist manner, while socializing their new collective owners into whatever it takes for them to become effective competitors. The increase in class consciousness that would ordinarily accompany any growth in workers' power falls victim to the more urgent dynamic that arises out of market relations. Thus, to the surprise of some, workers in workers' co-ops are no more radical socially and politically than other members of their class. If the very existence of workers' co-ops bolsters some arguments for socialism, to wit that capitalists are not indispensable, their practise and most of the attitudes they generate in their members allow those who defend capitalism to claim, erroneously, that a worker run society would not be very different from the present one. Despite this mixed record, I am usually very pleased when new co-ops get started in our society. It's quite another thing, however, to envision a socialist economy composed primarily of co-ops even when, as in the Schweickart model, the only market operating is in finished goods.

Here, I must register my surprise and disappointment that Lawler does not confront my main criticism of market socialism, which is that people's experience in exchange will produce the same mystified consciousness that it does in capitalism, and that without a clear and accurate understanding of their conditions it is impossible to build a socialist society. More than anything else, it is because of the role of workers' co-ops in helping to reproduce this mystification that I cannot see them operating under socialism. Capitalists can ignore this problem—indeed, they have to. Market socialists cannot. Complete transparence of social relations can only be obtained by production based on a rational, democratic, centralized plan, which will also foster cooperation not only in but—unlike the case with co-ops—between the worker managed enterprises of this new era.

As regards the market, Lawler criticizes my position as too inflexible. After all, markets have undergone considerable reform and regulation since Marx's day. This shows it can be done. Replacing capitalist owners with workers' co-ops, a process that has already begun, would be the biggest reform of all, since it does away with the market in labor power. Lawler equates this change with the abolition of capitalism itself, which he understands as a system dominated by a class of capitalists who extract surplus value from workers. With the capitalist class removed, Lawler believes, there is nothing to keep the market from being reshaped to serve the interests of the new ruling class, the workers. But if it is not the capitalist class but capital that is the essence of capitalism, then what?

Marx, as we all know, entitled his main work not *Capitalism* but *Capital*. Unfortunately for the English-speaking reader, the distinction he was trying to make was watered down by Engels' mistranslation of the subtitle of volume I, which is *Critique of Political Economy—The Production Process of Capital*, as *The Capitalist Process of Production*.[1] In any case, it is clear from the body of this work that Marx's concern is with capital and not with the capitalist class, which he refers to time and again as the "embodiment" and "personification" of capital. Though I touched on it in my original essay, this point deserves to be expanded. Capital is self-expanding value, not simply wealth or whatever it is that produces it, but wealth used for the purpose of creating more wealth. The contrast is with wealth used to satisfy need, or serve God, or expand political or military power, or attain glory or status. With capital, wealth becomes self-centered, interested only in its own growth. As a particular function of wealth, capital is expressed in whatever social relation is required for it to work and embodied in agents—like the capitalists—who incorporate this function in their practise.

The market, before all else, is a moment in capital's process of self-expansion. It is internal to capital itself, part of what it is and how it functions, and conveyed in the full meaning of its concept. It is the moment of circulation by which the value produced by capital moves in a series of exchanges through the economy only to return as a larger mass of wealth than what it was when it began. Buying and selling is its mode of movement, while money serves as the mediation between each act of exchange and the system of value expansion as a whole. Marx's *Capital* tries to characterize this entire process in a way that brings out its overwhelming impact on all that comes into its path. It is like a whirlpool, which nothing and no one completely escapes. As a moment in capital's accumulation, the market (and its con-stituent parts—value, commodities, money) partakes fully in capital's power to embrace and to transform what it embraces.

In his attempt to preserve some kind of market for socialism, Lawler asks us to recall that capitalism did not invent the market. To be sure, there were goods exchanged before capitalism and some of the places where this took place were called "markets," but not every soci-ety that produces a surplus and engages in some exchange can be said to have a market. Barter, for example, whether between individuals or whole societies, does not constitute a market, because the act of exchange in this case is not organically related to the process by which the goods that are exchanged come into being. It has no influence on production; nor does production have any influence on it. To have a market that plays a role in the economy, it is not enough for a society to produce a surplus some of which gets exchanged. Only when a por-tion of goods are produced with the aim of selling them is it worth speaking of a market, at which point we can also see the first signs of capital emerging in the crevises of this pre-capitalist social formation. For the age of capital is far older than capitalism, the name we give to the civilization in which capital has become the dominant form of productive wealth. Once the full power of capital and with it of the market is released, however, humanity's only respite from all the suf-fering brought on by capital can come from abolishing it altogether by replacing self-expanding value operating through a market with a rational plan to produce what people need. Anything less, that is par-tial reforms of all sorts, runs the risk of being pulled back into the whirlpool, as the logic of capital, now grown to gargantuan propor-tions, reasserts itself, destroying all measures intended to control it (various economic regulations and the welfare state today) and trans-forming even radical attempts to redirect it into new embodiments of its essential function (market socialism tomorrow).

Lawler says little about capital. Yet, it is the power of capital that is at stake here, and its ability to expand no matter whose hand is on the rudder, whether it is that of the capitalist class, the state, or workers' co-ops. Once goods are produced to sell and to make money, which will enable those in control of the means of production to make more goods to sell and to make more money, once this rhythm has been established, it is the rhythm itself that is responsible for the host of ills associated with capitalism and not the capitalist class that currently enjoys its benefits. That's why capitalists can be rehabilitated, whereas capital cannot. And this is why my opposition to the market is so inflexible.[2]

My disagreement with Lawler over workers' co-ops and the market, then, reveals an even more fundamental difference over the nature of capitalism and socialism. Whereas Lawler understands capitalism primarily as a society ruled by the capitalist class, I understand it first and foremost as a society dominated by capital. Marxists have generally stood out from other kinds of radicals in opposing not just our rulers but the system in which, by which, and for which they rule. As that which gives capitalists their power as well as their purpose and helps to reproduce both, capital stands at the core of capitalism and is the most essential part of what is meant by the "capitalist system." And while socialism for Lawler is—again, primarily—a society ruled by the working class; for me, it is chiefly a time when the logic of capital has been replaced by a production logic that has as its overriding purpose to serve social needs. Before this new logic is fully operative and part of common sense and everyday practise, it must be planned and new rules and regulations put into place. Hence, the need for a democratic dictatorship of the proletariat and democratic central planning in the first stage of the post-revolutionary society.

At the start of this response to Lawler, I said that though the focus of our debate is on the future, our main aim was to effect the present so as to make a communist future possible. The kind of world we both desire, however, will not be created by the people of today but by those who are formed in the struggle to fashion a better tomorrow. Politically, then, my chief complaint against market socialism is that it takes workers as they now are—and leaves them that way. As far as human beings are concerned, the socialist sprouts Marx saw in capitalism are not helped to grow to their full stature but simply rearranged on the same landscape. Teaching workers how to become their own capitalists has replaced socialist consciousness raising.

It is not surprising that workers today react more favorably to co-ops than they do to the idea of a rational economic plan. Too mystified by their experiences in the market to suspect that there may be an alternative to it, most workers would favor any reform that improves their competitive position. But rather than an argument for market socialism, as Lawler believes, this is another reason to increase still further the amount of critical fire directed at the market. This is not a plea, as Lawler suggests, for letting corporations off the hook, but for criticizing them in a way that links their humanly destructive behavior to both private ownership and market logic. For only when the majority of workers understand that most of the problems from which they suffer come from the domination of capital and the operations of the market, and not just from the rule of the capitalist class, will socialism move to the top of the political agenda. At a time when the internal ties between our worst social problems and the market—just as the elements of a rational, democratic, socialist alternative—are easier to see than probably ever before, both in the U.S. and around the world, the school of market socialism has arisen to redirect workers' attention elsewhere. Offering a solution that is itself a version of the problem, market socialism hides its real solution. We can do better. History will not forgive us, nor should it, if we fail.

NOTES

1. Meszaros, Istvan, *Beyond Capital* (Monthly Review Press, 1996), 980.
2. For an excellent discussion of the distinctions between capitalism, capitalists, and capital, and their fuller implications for this debate, see Meszaros.

12.

Response to Ollman

JAMES LAWLER

To make the point he has Marx on his side, Bertell Ollman extracts from a larger passage from Marx, cited in my essay "Marx as Market Socialist," the assertion that "cooperative production," to overcome capitalism, must "regulate national production upon a common plan." In the hindsight of the Soviet experience, it is natural to interpret this passage as meaning something similar to Soviet central planning, with planners elaborating the requirements of a vast system of production without any determination by markets. But closer inspection of Marx's passage reveals significant differences from Ollman's interpretation. Marx recognizes that between the time when the proletarian government takes power and the time when communist regulation of production according to a common plan can be established, the working people "will have to pass through long struggles, through a series of historic processes, transforming circumstances and men." The establishment of consciously regulated production is not, Marx stresses, some kind of utopia to be introduced "by the people's decree." This passage is completely consistent with the detailed analysis given by me of "The Principles of Communism" and the *Manifesto*. Production according to a common plan, Engels stressed, is not possible in the aftermath of a proletarian revolution because the working people themselves do not yet have the capacity for it, not because there are not enough educated planners.

So, in the larger citation Marx does not say, as Ollman's excerpt has it, that "cooperative production" must be regulated according to a common plan. He says that "the cooperative societies" themselves will regulate production according to a common plan. Such language is the basis of my argument that communism is not a system in which central planners, however democratically informed, determine the nature of production, but one in which the direct producers themselves do so. Only after a long period of transformations will there be the material and psychological transformations that make such direct self-regulation by the producers themselves of their own interdependent social production possible. Establishing a central planning board or boards to do this in relatively short order short-circuits the complicated process of development involving markets which leads to the direct producers themselves cooperatively planning their own production.

Marx clearly emphasizes the notion that a "long" period of transformations is needed before production according to a common plan will be possible—as though he in fact worried that "utopians" would want to do such a thing in short order, "by decree of the people." I have argued that it is in this intervening period that socialist market production will be necessary. In my essay I distinguished two stages of this transition period, one in which capitalist production persists, and a "pure market socialism," in which worker-owned cooperatives are predominant. The communist society, discussed by Marx in his "Critique of the Gotha Program," comes *after* this period. The dictatorship of the proletariat does not create a system of central planning. It is the political form of the transition period. It is not the establishment of the central planning of communism but the political rule of the proletariat during the time when capitalist firms continue to compete with "socialist" ones and—here I project the outcome of this first stage of transition—when cooperatives operate without capitalist firms though still in something like a capitalist mode. When "a common plan" becomes possible in the communist society the state has essentially withered away.

What is Ollman's response to this position? On the one hand he appears to accept the necessity for continued market production after a socialist government comes to power. On the other hand he views this period in a purely negative fashion. It is "awash with alienation." He asks me how such market production could possibly prepare for communism. But don't I have the right to ask him the same question, as he too says there should be markets after capitalism?

To help clarify Marx's conception of production according to a common plan, I want to return, for the third time, to Marx's analysis of the Factory Acts. The Ten Hours Bill, we recall, was the first time the "political economy of the middle class" (i.e., the law of capital, the law of the capitalists) succumbed in broad daylight to the political economy of the working class. How does Marx define the latter? It consists in "social production controlled by social foresight." The law enacted by the British parliament, with little or no direct representation by the working class, nonetheless rose above the political economy of the middle class consciously to control production for the sake of the wider interests of society. This law, this "rule of the game," was regarded by Marx as an instantiation of social control. We don't have to wait for the distant future of communism for some degree of conscious social control to make its appearance. Such social control is emerging, haltingly and with reverses, within bourgeois society itself, promoted by the logic of capital itself which tends to generate its own negation.

Already in the mid nineteenth century, the "whirlpool" of capital (to cite Ollman's "Response to Lawler") was producing a counter-current a whirlpool of a polar opposite tendency. What might be called a logic of Society for the first time prevailed over the logic of capital. Consequently, it is not necessary to have a wholly market-less society for there to be some significant degree of control by society over its productive life, some important degree of reappropriation by society of its alienated powers. Ollman says that I neglect to point to "elements" of capitalism that pre-pare for the common planning of communism. But the significance of such recognition is not what Ollman would have it. It is not a matter of *either* market production *or* central planning, but a dynamic mixture in which social control—the logic of society—grows up in the context of continued market production.

A major practical issue facing socialists today is whether to propose market-less "central planning" as the immediate objective of a socialist government, or whether a socialist government will continue to permit market production while advocating fundamental changes in the forms of ownership (e.g., job-creating public works, facilitation of cooperative and various forms of public ownership) and new "rules of the game" (such as a reduced workweek, extended unemployment benefits and other forms of social security, etc.) Ollman has, unfortunately, not taken up my offer of a compromise which I thought was based on our common position. Let us settle for fifty or so years of market socialism, and make the best of it. Instead he argues, perhaps even more strongly, that market socialism is hardly any improvement over capitalism. In fact, I suspect, he thinks it may be worse. As long as workers continue to produce goods for sale there will still be, he believes, the same blindness to the social nature of production, the same worship of the thing as in a traditional capitalist society. One might also say, contrary to Marx, that the Ten Hours Bill was only a rule of capital, since this was a rule of market production.

The main idea that needs to be defended in this connection is the idea of "dialectical socialism," that within capitalist society there is a new society coming into existence. Capitalists generally take credit for the humanistic elements of this new society. But not only capitalists. Instead of saying that the rules imposed on the blind march of capital are manifestations of the counter-current of the logic of society, what I call "nihilistic socialists" see nothing in progressive reforms but the deviousness of capital. While on the one hand, Ollman defers to the dialectical approach of Marx, his conception of a whirlpool logic of capital appears to undermine this acceptance. While on the one hand, he admits that there should continue to be market production after a socialist government takes power, as a necessity of transition, he provides no dialectically progressive understanding for this stage of market socialism and wants to get rid of it as soon as possible.

Ollman says that I do not show how the market can be tamed so as to constitute a real transition from capitalism to communism. Perhaps I have not been sufficiently explicit. I begin by saying, with the Ten Hours Bill: limit the length of the working day, limit or ban child labor, etc. I go on by saying, with the welfare state: provide health, education and welfare for working people irrespective of income. If we can do these things, we are taming the market, turning its operation from a blind process to one that is increasingly controlled by society. These achievements have occurred under capitalism. Why should not market socialism represent a further development of that process?

I do not, according to Ollman, offer any help to the unemployed, who must continue to exist under market socialism, together with economic crises. I should defer here to David Schweickart, who has written in detail of these matters. A society consisting of cooperatives will not have the same crises, or at least the same depth of crisis, as in capitalism where workers' wages are reduced to maximize profits going to capitalists and as a result there is a systemic divergence between production and effective demand. But in a market socialist society, profits are essentially returned to the workers themselves, i.e., to the vast bulk of the consumers. As for the unemployed, a working-class state in a market socialist society will have to establish "rules of the game" for this eventuality. Democratic politics will determine what those rules will be. They should be considerably less harsh than under current United States capitalism, but not so lenient as to make workers indifferent to success or failure in producing to meet consumer needs. As long as labor is not life's prime want, as long as a substantial amount of work is done for the sake of money, even in the attenuated form of "labor tickets," some penalty for failing to meet consumer demand will be required. Unemployment, however temporary, will eventually be too harsh or clumsy a punishment, as I suggest in connection with communist society proper, when more conscious means of adjusting production will have evolved.

Ollman asks how I foresee the transition to full communism. I do not in fact argue, as Ollman interprets me, that "pure market socialism" is the transition to "full communism." I follow Marx's position in the "Critique of the Gotha Program," according to which the transition period, whose program was first delineated in the *Manifesto*, is followed by communist society in its first phase. So the question might be, how do I see the transition from "cooperative socialism"—i.e., the society dominated by cooperatives—to the first phase of communism? The transition I suggested in my essay may be connected in some degree to the problem of unfair market rewards for capital-intensive operations. Under capitalism, giant corporations earn profits on the basis of their total capital, though the "dead labor" embodied in machinery and other forms of "constant capital" generates no surplus. Only the living labor of actual workers, Marx has argued, generates surplus value. Market mechanisms enable the capitalists of such enterprises nevertheless to garner a rate of profit proportional to their total capital, rather than to the variable capital invested in living labor. Under capitalism the fetishization of capital makes this return in proportion to total capital seem not only necessary (who would invest in capital intensive industry if the returns were based on surplus labor alone?) but also fair and just.

However, under market socialism, where the profits of capital intensive industries would be divided among a relatively small number of workers, the unfairness of such a method of reward would quickly come to light. Why should workers make exceptionally high incomes for the simple reason that they work in capital intensive industries? A democratically elected working-class government could not tolerate large inequalities of this kind. This is a good example of the way in which market socialism creates advances on the way to overcoming capitalist fetishization of the commodity. A "natural" way for this situation to be handled, I suggested in my essay, was for the state to reestablish a greater degree of fairness via income taxes. After a general period of adjustment to this regime of mediated or indirect state redistribution of income, the transition to a more direct method of payment "according to work" would seem both justified and practical. Premature imposition of such socialization of labor payments runs the risk of depriving the worker of an immediate or concrete sense of ownership of work and interest in the outcome of work.

The members of a cooperative are vitally concerned with whether or not their products satisfy consumer demand, since their livelihood depends on it. In the "socialist" scheme (Marx's first phase of communism), however, the worker is paid for work whether or not it results in something valuable to society as determined by demand. A higher or more general level of identification with the interests of society is required of workers to maintain interest in the results of labor if payment is largely independent of this. However, the successful evolution of the

cooperative system should produce a series of fine tunings, including perhaps compensatory taxing policies for differences in the organic composition of capital or, as Schweickart argues, socialization of the investment
funds. The effects of these fine tunings and compensatory social inter-
ventions will gradually, I suggest, approximate to the "socialist" distribution of wealth "according to labor." At some point this socialist method
of distribution will seem to be a more efficient or simpler way of achieving essentially the same results that have come to operate *de facto.* A
higher level of "socialist" consciousness, encouraged in part by nationwide democratic politics, will by this time have emerged. But to force
the method of payment according to labor prematurely would likely produce the famous stalemate reflected in the Soviet workers' motto, we pretend to work and they pretend to pay us.

Under the first phase of communism, I argued, there will still be
attenuated market production, though not deserving to be called market
production in the full sense of the term. Worker's incomes will not
depend directly on the profits of their firms, but on the quality and quantity of their labor. They will still, however, be working for something
like money, rather than for the sake of the work itself. However restricted
and personalized, a labor ticket or voucher still has the primary motivat-
ing force that qualifies this stage of production as alienated, if less so than
before. But such alienated production is a necessary means for overcoming alienation. Workers must work for money before it is possible for
them to work creatively, for the sake of the work itself.

The strongest argument against the idea that under communism there
will be Soviet-style "central planning" is connected to the inherent
nature of communist society, in its mature development, as the society of
"free labor." No doubt there must eventually be the kind of technocratic
(or "elitist") planning by specialists of the essentially automated production machine that society will create to satisfy many basic needs in "the
realm of necessity." But such largely automated production will be only
the precondition of the creative labor of individuals that automated production will liberate, Such creative labor, constitutive of the "realm of
freedom," will not follow the plans of anyone but the workers themselves, who will cooperate with one another consciously and without the
mediation of buying and selling. The sphere of market production will
progressively become narrower with the growth of a sector of interdependent complexes of essentially automated production, on the one
hand, and an economy of freely cooperating, creative labor, on the other.
David Schweickart plausibly suggests an intermediate form of "communist market production" in which workers engage in creative labor, but
continue to receive money, not as the motive of work, but as its reward—

much as Kant sees the relation between duty and happiness in his *"summum bonum."* The rationing of certain goods by money continues for a long time to be necessary. But certainly by the twenty-fourth century, in accord with Gene Roddenberry projection in *Star Trek*, the money economy will have completely withered away.

Criticizing the accuracy of my interpretation of the positions of Marx and Engels, Ollman refers to a passage, cited in my article, in which Engels writes of Marx's strategy of "buying out the capitalists." Ollman primarily notes that Engels calls for turning certain agricultural property over to farmers "under the control of the community." Does this mean Soviet-style "extensive" central planning? But we have seen already that for Marx's "social production controlled by social foresight" does not mean planning on this level of detail. It means setting the ground rules of the game, such as whether the land can be sold or whether there can be hired labor, rather than how many pigs should be raised. The basic point for my argument is that the strategy of buying out the capitalists presupposes the continuation of market production.

In 1847, in his "Principles of Communism," Engels posed the question clearly: "Will it be possible to abolish private property all at once?" The answer is unambiguous: "No, such a thing would be just as impossible as at *one* stroke to increase the existing productive forces to the degree necessary for instituting community of property."[1] Engels is consistent over the years. In his comments on the draft program of the German Social Democratic Party, for its congress in Erfut in 1891, he approves of the following passage: "The Social Democratic Party had nothing in common with so-called state socialism: a system of fiscal nationalisation which places the state in place of the private entrepreneur and imposes the double yoke of economic exploitation and political oppression upon the worker."[2] Engels merely asks whether it is possible to adhere to other points of the program, calling for free legal and medical service, without *some* state-run operations.

Let us now return to the issue of the "whirlpool" logic of capital (developed most fully in Ollman's "Response to Lawler"). Capital, Marx argued, has an inherent tendency to expand. But that doesn't mean it necessarily expands at all times and under all circumstances. When workers win higher wages, this doesn't expand capital. When workers achieve a reduction of the work week, this doesn't expand capital. Capitalists have an interest in lengthening the work week and reducing wages, so as to expand their capital. But in an economic system in which workers own their own enterprises, it might be supposed that such owners will have a strong incentive to increase their "wages" and reduce their working time.

Certain critics of market socialism argue that such a system will be highly inefficient, because of the natural tendency of workers to be easy on themselves. But Ollman argues that as long as a system of competitive production persists, the logic of capital will operate, even where there are no longer "capitalists" in the traditional sense. Where workers become capitalists to themselves, Ollman seems to suggest that the competitive struggle for survival will force workers to work longer hours for less money in pocket, while reinvesting their earnings in technological advances, so as to produce more cheaply than their competitors. Under capitalism, workers resist these tendencies of owners to accumulate capital as rapidly as possible. But under a cooperative socialist system, in which the workers stand as capitalists to themselves, Ollman may be suggesting that the "whirlpool" of capital could suck the entire system down into a nightmare of self-inflicted abstinence and workaholism, with no countervailing force, no opposite "logic of society" to counteract this descent into a hell of the unmitigated logic of capital.

But to state the problem in this way is already to solve it. Ollman wonders how market socialism surmounts the fetishism of commodity production. The scenario just supposed provides an excellent example of how cooperative market socialism discloses the irrationality of the intrinsic logic of capital more effectively than is possible under capitalism proper. While workers and capitalists battle it out over wages and working hours, settling for some sort of middle course between the extremes, the apologists for capitalism, making a virtue of necessity, claim that this middle course is evidence for the humanity and reasonableness of capitalism. But when capitalists no longer exist, and workers stand to themselves as capitalists, the inhumane absurdity of the pure logic of capital is patent.

The problem of how workers are to regulate their own labor when they become owners of it themselves, in a competitive market economy, should not be answered once and for all, in the abstract. Following my outline of stages of the development of communist society, we should look at the issue (1) in a capitalist society, where cooperatives struggle to come into existence in a predominantly capitalist economic and political environment; (2) in the first stage of a cooperative socialist society in which a socialist government actively facilitates the emergence of cooperative production, side-by-side with capitalist enterprises; and (3) in the higher stage of the transition in which cooperatives predominate.

(1) Worker-owned cooperatives arise out of the logic of society, even if they remain affected, as an emerging form of social development must be, with the old logic of capital. The objective of the workers in taking control of their own means of production is optimally to reappropriate their product, or minimally to avoid the social death of unemployment. The fact that, other things being equal, they can produce more efficiently

than their capitalist competitors, stems from the higher motivation that comes from working for themselves, the more intelligent character of the pooled resources of their cooperative labor, the diminished need for purely disciplinary supervision, etc. Hence, cooperatives can compete often effectively in a capitalist market and so demonstrate, as Ollman admits, that production does not require a distinct class of capitalists.

But what if cooperative workers decide to work for even less than the prevailing wages of the workers in competitive capitalist industries? Perhaps the capitalist mania of accumulation will seize hold of them, and they will set a bad example for workers in the capitalist sector. Labor unions may be suspicious of cooperatives for this reason. To gain crucial political and financial support from unions (and municipalities, progressive state governments, etc.) for cooperatives in the capitalist context, there may be agreements setting minimum wage levels, and other socially necessary rules, for cooperatives.

(2) A socialist government comes to power through democratic elections, because it proposes a realistic alternative to capitalism. The socialist political party or parties will be successful in part because they are able to point to existing cooperatives as examples of an alternative and practical form of ownership that counteracts the whirlpool in which international corporations pick up and move on elsewhere, or else blackmail communities as a condition of remaining in place. The revolutionary program may call for turning such corporations over to their workers for breech of the public trust, paying a fair price in accord with the requirements of the fifth amendment, but only after social subsidies and social costs over the years have been deducted. In addition, the socialist government can offer a transitional program with minimal disruption of the existing economy. Marx's understanding here, as I have interpreted it, is more gradualist than that proposed by Schweickart, who advocates Economic Democracy as a complete system to be established immediately after a socialist revolution. Instead, a socialist program would be more attractive were it to propose an experiment in which a cooperative sector, structured along lines such as those indicated by Schweickart, is established gradually and tested against capitalist industries.

Ollman suggests that under market socialism workers will be forced by the logic of capital to work more cheaply to compete with one another as capital demonically builds up over them, giving nothing and taking all. The success of cooperatives up to this point may have been connected to labor solidarity between workers in cooperatives and those in capitalist industries, or citizens in a municipality fighting to maintain local industry. Certainly a worker's government must cement such solidarity with laws regulating the terms on which cooperatives operate, just as governments have previously done under capitalism, thanks to the pressure of society for conscious control of social production. In the scenario proposed by Engels in "The Principles of Communism," the downward spiral of the whirlpool of capital is counteracted by a state sector that pays higher than average wages while soaking up unemployment. Market relations of relative labor scarcity help workers in the private sector to raise their wages to that of the state sector. But if we assume, in accord with the "cooperative market socialism" of the later Marx and Engels, that the state industrial sector is relatively small, other means of regulating the accumulation of capital must operate in a supplementary way. Perhaps above all else, progressive limitations of the length of the working day as a function of productivity gains will be a key means of insuring that the returns of labor in fact return to the laborers. Taxes no doubt constitute another means, necessary to the build-up of a social and cultural infrastructure based on the principle of distribution according to need. Moreover, the problem suggested by Ollman of the unmitigated logic of capital will not arise in pure form as long as there is a competitive capitalist sector. For workers in that sector will fight, as they always have done, for higher wages, shorter working hours, etc.

(3) It is only when all or nearly all workers engage in cooperative production that the nightmare scenario according to which market socialism may appear to be even worse than capitalism becomes conceivable. For the whirlpool of capital to suck society into its spiraling maw, one would have to suppose that when workers finally gain ownership of their means of production (though in the still mixed context of market production) and all the capitalists have been buried, that they will then decide to bury themselves. Market socialism would then represent the pinnacle of alienation. In place of this Dantesque scenario, it is reasonable to suppose that the evolving logic of society will continue its course, and find under full-fledged cooperative socialism an even more propitious terrain for making advances. Schweickart proposes regulating the percentage of profit available for reinvesting in technological expansion, forcing workers to take so much of their earning in wages. Of course the issue of limits to the working time will still be central to the advancing communist society. Thank goodness for such rules, the workers, in control of their government, will no doubt say. Let's have more of them.

NOTES

1. Karl Marx. Frederick Engels, *Collected Works* (Moscow, Progress Publishers, 1976), Vol. 6, 350 (Referred to below as MECW.)
2. *MECW*, vol. 27, 596.

Select Bibliography on Market Socialism

Adaman, F., and Devine, P., "On the Economic Theory of Socialism" *New Left Review*, no. 221 (Jan.–Feb., 1997).

Albert, M., and R. Hahnel, *Looking Forward: Participatory Economics for the 21st Century* (South End Press, Boston, 1991).

Albert M., and R. Hahnel, *The Political Economy of Participatory Economics* (Princeton University Press, 1991).

Arnold, N. S., "Marx and Disequilibrium in Market Socialism's Relations of Production," *Economy and Society* no. 3 (April 1987).

Arnold, N. S., *The Philosophy and Economics of Market Socialism* (Oxford University Press, 1994).

Bayat, A., *Work Politics and Power: An International Perspective on Workers Control and Self-Management*, (New York: Monthly Review Press, 1990).

Bettelheim, C., *The Transition to Socialist Economy* (Harvester Press, Sussex, 1978).

Bidet, J., "Marx et le marché," *Théorie de la modernité* (Press Universitaires de France, 1990).

Brus, W., *The Market in a Socialist Economy*, (Routledge, London, 1972).

Cockshott, W. and Cottrill, A., *Toward a New Socialism* (Nottingham, 1993).

Devine, P., *Democracy and Economic Planning* (Cambridge University Press, 1988).

Draper, H., *Karl Marx's Theory of Revolution, vol. IV, Criticisms of Other Socialisms*, (Monthly Review Press, N.Y., 1990).

Elson, D., "Market Socialism or Socialization of the Market," *New Left Review*, no. 172 (Nov.–Dec., 1988).

Forrester, V., *L'horreur economique* (Fayard, Paris, 1996).

Horvat, B., *The Political Economy of Socialism* (M. E. Sharpe, Armonk, N.Y., 1982).

Horvat, B., M. Markovic and R. Supec, eds., *Self-Governing Socialism: A Reader*, 2 vols. (International Arts and Science Press, White Plains, N.Y., 1975).

Kasmir, S. *The Myth of Mondragon: Cooperatives, Politics, and Working Class Life in a Basque Town* (State University of New York Press, Albany, 1996).

Kornai, J., *The Socialist System: The Political Economy of Communism* (Princeton University Press, 1992).

Laibman, D., ed., *Science and Society*, vol. 56, no. 1 (Spring, 1992). Special issue on Market Socialism.

Lane, R., *The Market Experience*, (Cambridge University Press, 1991).

Lawler, J., "Marx's Theory of Socialisms: Nihilistic and Dialectical," in L. Pastouoras, ed., *Debating Marx* (Edward Mellon Press, Lewiston, N.Y., 1994).

Lawler, J., "Lenin and the Dialectical Conception of Socialism," *Socialist Future*, London (April, 1995).

Le Grand, J., and Estrin, S., eds., *Market Socialism* (Oxford University Press, 1989).

Lindblom, C., *Politics and Markets* (Basic Books, 1977).

Lindblom, C., "The Market as Prison," *Journal of Politics*, no. 44, 1982.

Macpherson, C. B., *The Political Theory of Possessive Individualism* (Oxford University Press).

Magdoff, H., "A Note on 'Market Socialism'," *Monthly Review* (May, 1995).

Mandel, E., "In Defense of Socialist Planning," *New Left Review*, no. 159 (May–June, 1986).

Marx, K., Introduction to *A Contribution to a Critique of Political Economy* (Foreign Languages Press, Peking, 1976).

Marx, K., Engels, F., and Lenin, V. I., *On Communist Society* (Progress Pub., Moscow, 1981).

McMurtry, J. *The Invisible Prison: Breaking the Global Market Code* (forthcoming).

McNally, D., *Against the Market* (Verso, London, 1993).

Meszaros, I., *Beyond Capital* (Monthly Review Press, 1996).

Miller, D., *Market, State, and Community* (Clarendon Press, Oxford, 1990).

Moore, S. *Marx Versus Markets* (Pennsylvania State University Press, 1993).

Nove, A., *The Economics of Feasible Socialism* (Allen and Unwin, London, 1983).

Nove, A., and I. Thatcher, eds., *Markets and Socialism* (Edward Elgar, Aldershot, 1994).

Ollman, B., "Marx's Vision of Communism," *Social and Sexual Revolution* (South End Press, Boston, 1978).

Pierson, C., *Socialism After Communism: The New Market Socialism* (Pennsylvania State University Press, 1995).

Polyani, K., *The Great Transformation: The Political and Economic Origins of Our Time* (Beacon Press, 1970).

Roemer, J., *A Future for Socialism* (Harvard University Press, 1994).

Roemer, J., and P. Bardan, eds., *Market Socialism: The Current Debate* (Oxford University Press, 1993).

Roosevelt, F., and D. Belkin, eds. *Why Market Socialism? Voices from DISSENT* (M. E. Sharpe, Armonk, 1994).

Rowling, N. *Commodities* (Free Association Books, London, 1987).

Rubel, M., and J. Crump, eds., *Non-Market Socialism in the Nineteenth and Twentieth Centuries* (Macmillan, London, 1987).

Schweickart, D., *Capitalism or Worker Control? An Ethical and Economic Appraisal* (Praeger, 1980).

Schweickart, D., *Against Capitalism* (Cambridge University Press, 1993).

Sohn-Rethel, A. *Intellectual and Manual Labor* (Macmillan, London, 1978).

Stauber, L., *A New Program for Democratic Socialism: Lessons from the Market-Planning Experiences in Austria* (Four Willows Press, Carbondale, Ill., 1987).

Stone, R., "Why Marxism Isn't Dead (Because Capitalism Isn't Dead)," *Ventures in Research: Lectures by the Faculty of Long Island University*, Series 19, ed., B. Horowitz.

Ticktin, H. H., *Origins of the Crisis in the USSR: Essays on the Political Economy of a Disintegrating System* (M. E. Sharpe, Armonk, 1992).

Ticktin, H. H., "What Will a Socialist Society Be Like?" *Critique*, no. 25, 1993.

Yunker, J., *Socialism Revised and Modernized: The Case for Market Socialism* (Praeger, 1992).

Index